LEGACY

REFLECTIONS OF A HOMESCHOOLED, HOMESCHOOLING MAMA

RUTH ADAMS

Edited by Sony Elise

ISBN-10: 1973737825
ISBN-13: 978-1973737827

Dedication

I would not be able to speak from experience about the pioneer days of the modern homeschooling movement had my parents not been brave trailblazers during my childhood. I am thankful that, not only did they choose to courageously embark on home education when many did not even know what a homeschool was, but they also discipled me as we walked along the way morning, noon and night. Their loving discipleship imprinted my life, shaping me into who I am today. Thank you, Dad and Mom, for all your sacrifices. I am forever grateful.

The idea for this book was birthed one evening when my husband was listening to me share with him what was on my heart concerning spiritual discipleship within the context of homeschooling. In particular I was expressing a desire that those who are new to homeschooling would understand the history of homeschooling and what it was that motivated the pioneers in the movement to be trailblazers, paving the way for all of us today. The reason I feel this history is important to understand is because many of these original families began homeschooling with a vision towards the spiritual discipleship of their children. With the explosion of homeschooling, many today are homeschooling for numerous reasons, and it is important to me that the original vision that started the movement not be lost. I think we can learn a lot by looking back at these mothers and fathers who, in some cases, had to battle court cases for the freedom to homeschool. Many of them had great tenacity and determination, deep conviction of heart, and great spiritual vision for future generations. As always, there is something to be gained by looking back at history and applying lessons learned to our lives today. As my husband was listening to me share my heart, he told me that he thought I should write a book telling about my experiences being homeschooled and my conviction that homeschooling should be primarily about discipleship. Honey, thank you for believing in me and encouraging me along the way, especially when I thought about giving up on this project. You believed that I could and should embark on this crazy endeavor of writing a book, and you carved out time for me to work on it. Thank you for the nights you put me up in a hotel, giving me time to process my thoughts, seek the Lord, and communicate my heart through the written word. I cannot imagine my life without you and all the sacrificial leadership you give to our family.

To my children Lauren, Gabriel, Annagrace, Abbie Joy, Lilly Faith, Nathaniel, and Ella Ruth, you have been on my heart so much as I have scripted this book. At times I have stopped typing to pray that these things I

i

am sharing will be true in our family and in your lives. May you always know without a doubt how much your parents love you and are looking out for your best interest. I pray that the trajectory of your lives will always be moving closer toward knowing, loving, obeying and serving the Lord Jesus. This will bring the most blessing and the most joy to your lives. You are the fulfillment of my life dream of being a mama, and I feel incredibly blessed because of you. My greatest goal is that you will love Christ and make Him known. I love you with all of my heart.

"I have no greater joy than to hear that my children are walking in the truth" (3 John 4).

Table of Contents

Introduction

Legacy. I think it is a beautiful word when referring to something of eternal value passed down from one generation to another. Gratefully I can say that I am living the legacy of faithful, purposeful, first-generation Christian homeschooling parents. My parents came to know the Lord a few years before my birth and determined by God's grace to raise me in His ways. With the Lord's help they did their best to establish a Christian home and to teach me about being a follower of Christ. Neither of my parents entered parenting knowing how to disciple children as neither of them grew up in strong Christian homes. When I was born they were young, new believers setting up a first-generation Christian home without having had an example of how to do so. The Lord was their faithful guide and, by His grace, He led them, and I reaped the blessing of their efforts to walk in obedience to Him. Now I am raising my family and am privileged to be able to stand on their shoulders as a second-generation Christian homeschooling mama. Not only did my parents establish a Christian home, but they also followed the Lord in embarking on the journey of homeschooling my brother and me. This homeschooling journey began when I was a little girl growing up in the late seventies. This was back in the day when if you told someone you were homeschooled a common response would be, "What's that?" We could definitely be classified as a vintage homeschool family. These were the days where there was a risk involved in homeschooling and parents knew that there was the potential of being thrown into jail for their decision to homeschool. With this kind of risk there had to be a motivating factor causing these pioneering parents to go against the flow to educate their children at home. For my parents, and many of these grass roots homeschooling parents, that reason was a desire to disciple their children and a vision that their children would follow Christ. It was their desire that their sons and daughters would take higher ground than the declining cultural trends.

To share a little more about my upbringing, I grew up in a pastor's home. My dad has been in the ministry ever since I can remember, and the ebb and flow of our family life as I was growing up wrapped itself around the ministry. My dad moved our family to Houston, Texas when I was eight and a half. He then proceeded to knock on doors and personally invite people to be a part of a church he was starting up in our living room. My dad's office was in a back room of our house, so he was at home with us throughout my homeschool experience. This journey of birthing a church out of nothing was a long road with many hardships, but I was able to see my parents live out commitment and steadfastness to God's call upon their lives. It was not until I was grown and married that the church was finally established enough to purchase land and build a building. This is the environment I grew up in. In many ways, I was gingerly sheltered from the corruption in the world as the culture of our family was one of seeking to honor Christ and serving Him at home and in ministry. This path of ministry came with many hardships for our family, but the Lord was ever faithful year by year. Through it all, I know the Lord had me in His divine training ground that He had ordained even before I was born. He used the struggles, the hardships, the blessings, the opportunities, and everything that is a part of my story to shape me and make me who He wanted me to be. There have been many blessings to being so sheltered and growing up in a ministry-focused home, but there have also been some rude awakenings as I have grown older.

One of the hardest things for me has been grappling with the decline of culture, yes even Christian culture, all around us. I grew up with wholesome, conservative values and a heart to please the Lord. My mother taught me to choose not the good but the best. She used to tell me that the good is the enemy of the best. Over the years, it has been my dismay to see many ministry leaders, pastors, homeschool speakers, and other evangelical leaders fall into sin and disillusion those who followed them. Also, it has grieved my heart to see scores of young people from Christian homes walk away from the faith. Statistics tell us that up to eighty percent of young people raised in Christian homes are rejecting the Biblical truths they were taught. I have personally seen this happen with families far too often. It has been my sad observation that homeschooling is no guarantee that our children will love Christ. Growing up in Christian and homeschool circles I was not prepared for this falling out that I have witnessed in my adult years. Sadly, these apostasies are happening in increasing measure and at an alarming rate. It has left me searching for answers, seeking God's wisdom, and praying for the Lord's mercies as I raise my own children.

It is abundantly clear to me that we live in an increasingly pagan culture. It is only by the grace of God that any child in this narcissistic, humanistic, existentialistic society would die to self and live for Christ. The good news is that, "He who is in you is greater than he who is in the world" (1 John 4:4).

Even though our best efforts as parents are no guarantee that our children will embrace our faith, we can be encouraged that our Lord is greater than all the evil pervading the apostate times we live in. Though we cannot save our children, the Lord is able to draw them unto Himself and use us to teach them His ways. As parents, we dare not put our trust in a formula or in

2

homeschooling to guarantee that our children will love and serve Christ. Homeschooling is no panacea guaranteeing our children will know and love the Lord. I believe parenting with Biblical wisdom, strategic discipleship, tons of love, and homeschooling are tools God can use towards this end, but I also believe that my children will not cling to Christ and live for Him unless He does a regenerating work in their hearts. As much as I would like to change their sinful hearts, only Christ can do that. I am learning that this is the most important of all things for me to pray for. Unless their sinful hearts are regenerated and captured for Christ, no amount of behavior modification, character training, high standards, catechizing, drilling Scripture, etc. will produce godly children. That is why I find myself praying often that the Lord will give my children a love for Himself. As Ken Ham says, "We can lead our children to the ark, but only God can draw them in." [1] Let me be very clear here that, in this book, I am going to be talking extensively about all of the above as I think we should be vigilant in doing all of those things with our children. At the same time, I want to stress that the most important thing is that our children know and love Christ and bow the knee to His Lordship. For the Christian parent this should be the supreme goal.

I think today's Christian parents are facing monumental challenges due to the rapidly declining culture we live in. We do not live in a primarily Christian nation anymore. Sadly, we live in an increasingly postmodern Christian culture where kids are apostatizing from the faith in droves. Our children are exposed to immorality at every turn: to humanism, feminism, evolution, pluralism, materialism, existentialism, atheism, deism, and views that are overtly opposed to Scripture. The tides of evil in our day are strong, but we can take heart in knowing all things are possible through Christ. We must cling to Christ, pray continually, walk in faith, do everything we can to disciple, encourage, and direct our children. We know that we are not without hope in this generation even though the statistics are discouraging. The landscape and reality of what Christian parents are up against is sobering, but we must keep our eyes fixed upon Christ and be faithful in what He has called us to do. We can also take encouragement from Biblical examples such as Daniel who stood for God in the midst of the pressures of the king of Babylon. Also, Noah was considered the only righteous man in his time. Because God accredited righteousness to him, he and his family were spared on the ark. These stories make it crystal clear that it is possible to stand alone even when the tides of evil are strong!

This book has been written in our family living room, in airports, in our van, in coffee shops, in restaurants, and in hotel rooms over the course of a little over two and a half years. I have prayed through this writing process, and tears have fallen, as I have pleaded with the Lord to give me wisdom and to do what only He can do in the lives of my children. As I was getting closer to sending this book off to the editor I went away for a weekend to clean up the manuscript and make revisions. Before leaving the house I asked my children to get down on the floor with me and pray with me and for me that the Lord would be glorified through the book. My oldest daughter prayed aloud and melted my heart with her words. She asked the Lord to please let "God be the author and Mama be the pen." I couldn't have said it better myself! In this book I want to share with you what I have observed as I have lived most of my life in evangelical and homeschool circles. Through these decades I have witnessed much of what has transpired in evangelical and homeschool culture, and I would like to share what is on my heart about what I have observed and what the Lord is still in the process of teaching me. Since I am still very much in the thick of raising my own children, I am not coming to you as the expert who has successfully raised a house full of exceptionally brilliant and perfectly behaved children. No, I am the parent desperately pleading with Jesus, my Lord and Savior, to make the salvation of all of my children sure and to give them a love for Him and a passion for His Kingdom. I am the mother calling out to the Lord morning by morning saying, "Lord, please give me vision for this day. Please help me to remember that all my mundane work today has eternal significance." "Jesus, please help me to make the gospel believable to my children by the way I live and interact with them today." "Father, please help me to set a godly example before these lambs looking up to me today." "Lord, I cannot change their hearts. Please help them to love you …. please help them to love one another … please help them to not be self-centered but others-centered." Can you hear in my prayers how desperately needy I am before the Lord on a daily basis? Being desperately needy is not a comfortable place to be, but you know what? Being desperately needy at the Father's feet is exactly where we need to be! It keeps us humble before Him. Remember this verse?

"Therefore it says, 'God opposes the proud, but gives grace to the humble'" (James 4:6).

By God's grace I have wanted to serve Him and please Him all my life. In His faithfulness, the Lord has preserved my faith, even through the valleys of disillusionment that could have sent me for a tail spin and derailed me on many accounts. I have seen the good, the bad, and the ugly in many ministries and could have lost all hope, but when Christ takes hold of a person, He has that person in His grasp and nothing can take them from His hand. Think about the significance of the following verse:

"My Father, who has given them to me, is greater than all, and no one is able to snatch them out of the Father's hand" (John 10:29).

While I have been around ministry and Christian circles my whole life, I am writing this book out of obscurity. Yes, I have been involved in Kingdom work but church was always small growing up, and I have never had a big name or been a public figure in any way. So why am I, a crazy busy mama living in obscurity on a fourteen-acre farm, taking time to write this book? Well, as I have said, I have witnessed some sad stories in Christian and homeschooling families and in many ministries through the years. I have watched some very sad atrocities unfold within the homeschooling movement and have seen young people jump ship and reject what their parents invested years trying to teach them. I have agonized over these things and have tried to make heads and tails of it. Praise God there are some really great outcomes from some homeschooling families. I have known and met homeschool graduates who love God, honor their parents, and have become very successful in business and in Kingdom work. What really excites me is when I see second-generation homeschool graduates now homeschooling their own children and becoming serious about family discipleship. These stories give me hope, but, unfortunately, there are also some very disappointing stories where things did not turn out well for very well-meaning homeschooling families. One reason I am writing this book is because I want to be a voice saying that I still believe in homeschooling and in family discipleship. In fact, you will see that my personal belief is that, if the reason for homeschooling is not to raise our children in the nurture and admonition of the Lord, then what's the point? Other people can teach my children academics as well as, or better than, I can, but I feel that the Lord has entrusted me with their spiritual discipleship. That is a responsibility I do not want to abdicate. I want to live with my babies, who are growing up way too fast, teaching them as we get up and as we lie down and as we walk along the way. I want to point them to the goodness of the Lord all throughout the day.

"And these words that I command you today shall be on your heart. You shall teach them diligently to your children, and shall talk of them when you sit in your house, and when you walk by the way, and when you lie down, and when you rise. You shall bind them as a sign on your hand, and they shall be as frontlets between your eyes. You shall write them on the doorposts of your house and on your gates" (Deuteronomy 6:6-9).

While there are some loud voices on the internet screaming, "I hate homeschool," "Homeschool ruined my life," "Homeschooling is a cult," etc., I desire to be a voice saying that I am grateful that I was homeschooled and that I have the privilege of homeschooling my children. When reading the voices of disgruntled homeschool graduates, it has been evident to me that these people are not showing Biblical wisdom in what they are saying. Many claim to be angry post-evangelical millennials. Some avow some kind of relationship with Christ while hurling profanity and blaming God, the church and their parents. I think the lack of character in these grumblers alone should make the reader think twice before swallowing the message they are shouting. They would have the world believe that homeschooling is a prison that cripples children and leaves them barely able to make it in the real world. Some claim they have had to spend time with counselors just to recover from their upbringing. I know that there are those unfortunate cases where there was abuse, as is also the case with some families who send their children to government schools. What I am addressing here is those homeschool graduates who are just angry for no good reason. Some of these graduates just did not want to surrender to their parents or to Christ and are angry due to rebellious hearts. In reading their stories I have noticed they are often rooted in personal emotions rather than in Biblical truth. My home was not perfect, but the Lord used the faithful efforts of my parents to shape me into who I am today. I am grateful for the sacrifices they made and the legacy they gave me. I know that I am not the only one who is grateful for a Christian, homeschool experience. Statistics from the recent Gen2 survey, which I elaborate on later in the book, indicate that many homeschool graduates plan to homeschool their own future children. That is exciting! I want to share things I have observed over the course of thirty-five plus years and what the Lord is in the process of teaching me now.

What I am NOT wanting to do in this book is give a formula that says copy my family and check off a list of boxes and you will produce the perfect model of godly young people. You see, it would be really risky for me to write this book to be a "how-to-raise-godly-children" manual, as our family is very much in process. With nine sinners living in our home, we have daily struggles like every other family, and we are humbly looking to Christ to shine the light of His truth so that we may see clearly the paths we should walk in. We do not have everything figured out. We struggle with obedience, bad attitudes, and sibling rivalry just like other families, but we are endeavoring to handle those struggles in a Biblical way. The vulnerable part of writing this book is that we do not have a finished product and do not know the course our children will take. Hopefully, I will not come across as giving rules or formulas here but rather as sharing principles I have learned and encouragement for the journey. In areas where God's Word speaks clearly, I will share absolutes. In contrast, where God's Word does not speak clearly, I hope to share

6

principles which will help us think Biblically. When we are thinking Biblically, we will be able to make wise decisions.

Another reason I write this book is to encourage fellow mamas to understand the importance of their calling in faithfully raising the children God has lent to them. Homeschooling is not for the faint of heart and should not be done in our own strength. Over the years, the Lord has given me a clearer vision as to which things are truly important and of eternal value and also some strategies for keeping the many plates of life spinning. In this book, I will be exhorting tired mamas to remember how important the mission of motherhood is, while trying to share some practical ideas that can be implemented to help manage the home and schedule. I am concerned for tired, exhausted homeschooling mamas who are trying so hard to make sure their kids know all their Latin and are prepared for scholarships to prestigious universities, yet they are missing the enjoyment of their children. I want to encourage frazzled mamas to go back to the main things which are mothering, nurturing, and training our children to love Christ, and equipping them for His plan and purposes for their lives. If He has gifted them to earn Ivy League scholarships they will probably find a way in spite of us, but I don't think we need to put that kind of pressure on ourselves while trading in the more important aspects of our calling as Christian mamas.

In increasing measure, the Lord is giving me a growing compassion for younger mamas who are a little behind me in their own journey of motherhood. Sometimes I see a frazzled, younger mama out in public, or one who has a toddler and a growing belly, and I have this desire to sit down and exhort and encourage her to embrace Biblical priorities in the rearing of her children. While I usually do not get that opportunity, the Lord often prompts my heart to pray for these mamas, that they will raise their children to know and love Christ. Scripture says that, "When He (Jesus) saw the multitudes, He was moved with compassion for them, because they were WEARY and scattered, like sheep having no shepherd" (Matthew 9:36, NKJV). I believe there are many weary moms today who are screaming out for someone to have compassion. There is a lack of Titus 2 mentors in our culture, and I know many young mamas really need this kind of exhortation from more seasoned mamas. Sometimes I see groups of mamas in little playgroups, and I wish I could tell them to let go of the comparison games and look to God alone and His Word for answers to their parenting questions. So often I feel like young parents look to other young parents for advice, and, sadly, in this culture it is more often than not based upon human reasoning rather than Biblical principles. In our modern society, young mamas often get caught up in "Mommy Wars" and comparison games about whose children are doing what, and the pressures can feel overwhelming. The truth is that so many of these competitive pressures, such as whose kids slept through the night, who potty-trained their toddler the earliest, who has the cutest clothes, etc. are of fleeting earthly value. When I reflect back to the days when my oldest were toddlers and the Mama groups' conversations that were typical in my circles, I remember how much of it revolved around temporal matters, such as cute clothing brands, Gymboree classes, preschools, elaborate birthday shindigs, vacations, home renovations projects, etc. Very rarely were these Mama conversations centered around our calling to raise our children to be Kingdom-minded arrows that we would launch into a dark world. In hindsight, I see that our time in raising our children is quickly fleeting. We have no time to waste on meaningless fluff. No, it is absolutely not wrong to enjoy chatting about cute toddler clothes or redecorating a room, but I would submit that the bulk of our focus should have much greater intentionality and vision. In writing this book I want to encourage mamas to seek first the Kingdom of God in their families, as time is quickly ticking away. The time is now to put distractions and lesser things aside and become intentional mamas who carefully choose those things which are above in the training of our children.

"If then you have been raised with Christ, seek the things that are above, where Christ is, seated at the right hand of God. Set your minds on things that are above, not on things that are on earth" (Colossians 3:1-2).

May the Lord be glorified in what I write. My heart and prayer for this book is that it will offer encouragement to people in all walks and seasons of life. Perhaps some readers will identify with a lot of what I share because they too have been on the homeschooling journey for many years. Others may find the stories in this book helpful in understanding the roots of the homeschooling movement and some of the ups and downs of the history of homeschooling over the past few decades. I pray that what I say will resonate with homeschool graduates like myself, as well as people who are brand new on the horizon. I pray that this book will minister to the ultra-conservative all the way to those who have a terrifying fear of what they perceive as legalism. That is a very scary word for some, and we will talk more about my views on that as the book progresses. Overall I pray that this book will encourage any parent, whether homeschooling or not, to take seriously their God-given responsibility to disciple the hearts of their children. What a privilege it is to be entrusted by God to help shape and mold the lives of little children, that they may grow up to be sharp arrows which will pierce the darkness. We need very sharp arrows now more than ever! Let's pray that by God's grace we may raise warriors for the Kingdom of God. May our sons and daughters advance the Kingdom of God. May they stand upon our shoulders and go on to do bigger and greater things for the Lord as they carry the light of truth into the next generation. Please, Lord Jesus, let it be. For your glory we pray. Amen!

Chapter 1
My History in Homeschooling

The Early Years

I remember when I started kindergarten. It was a short-lived experience in a Christian school. It was a long commute and my parents decided it made better sense to just teach me at home. Since kindergarten was not even required by law, my parents thought it would be better to take my ABEKA kinder books home and let me learn the basics there.

For first grade, I headed back to the Christian school environment. I remember a few things about my only full year of attending an institutionalized school. I stayed there for all of first grade and only part of second grade. During my second grade year my dad felt a call from the Lord to be like Moses in the Bible and go to a foreign land. That foreign land, for our family, living in a small town in East Texas, meant relocating from the country to the city. My parents took me out of the Christian school, packed our belongings, and moved us to Houston where my dad began knocking on doors and inviting people to a get-to-know-you meeting in preparation of starting a new church. Some of my memories of my short time in Christian school include the smell of the pencil sharpener on the wall, the smell of erasers, my partiality to the sky blue Crayola crayon, my Holly Hobby book satchel, the taste of tea in my lunch thermos, time on the playground, the citrus smell of the soap in the bathroom, and the yummy Twinkies my mother would sometimes put in my lunchbox. I also remember that one of my teachers read *Charlotte's Web* out loud to my class. I am partial to that sweet story to this day. Since we arrived in Houston during the school year, my mother homeschooled a little boy and me for the remainder of second grade and called it a church school.

The following year I started third grade in a Christian school in Houston. That was a short-lived experience. I remember my teacher and the portable buildings we met in, but this arrangement was not working for our family. My third-grade teacher sent home lots of homework to be done in the evenings. In fact, I remember the teacher requesting that we read our at-home reading assignment not once but three times. With the busyness of starting a church it was difficult for my parents to do homework with me all evening, and it left very little quality family time. Another thing that I remember about that school experience is the day my teacher verbally praised something that my parents had a conviction against. It was a personal family conviction, but I think it hit my parents hard that, by sending me away all day every day, they were allowing someone else to have a strong influence in my life and shape my thinking. I still remember when they told me they were going to remove me from the school and homeschool me. There was no turning back after that. I finished out my school years in our homeschool which my parents named Faith Christian Academy.

In those days, there was a price to be paid for homeschooling, and that price for some families proved to be legal court battles. By God's protecting hand our family was never taken to court, but there were families who did face that reality. Parental freedoms to homeschool were being challenged. Because the climate was so shaky, my parents drilled my brother and me on how to answer the typical questions people ask children. If someone asked us where we went to school, we were to give the name of our Christian school. "I attend Faith Christian Academy." The wrong answer would be, "My mommy homeschools me." Also, we did not want the neighbors noticing that we were home in the day. If we left to go somewhere during school hours we were asked to duck down in the backseat of the car. We took every precaution we could to avoid any unwanted attention and the possibility of unwanted visitors (i.e., a truant officer or CPS) at our front door. Back in these early days of the homeschool movement, there were very few parents homeschooling. These were the prehistoric days of homeschooling, before James Dobson had Dr. Raymond Moore on his broadcast in the early eighties and the homeschooling movement really took off. My parents were in that group of "pioneer parents" who showed great courage and sacrifice to homeschool. These parents had such tenacious conviction about homeschooling and such sharp vision for raising a godly family that they were willing to go to jail if necessary. My parents and others like them paved the way for the birthing of the modern homeschooling movement in the early eighties. I say modern homeschooling movement because you can see examples of homeschooling throughout the continuum of history going all the way back to ancient times. My mother was involved in coordinating one of the first, if not the very first, homeschooling conferences for Houston. I am grateful for the sacrifices my parents made and how the Lord used the early pioneering parents to pave the way for the explosion of homeschooling about to take place in the coming years.

I know that the core reason my parents taught me at home was so that they could raise me in the ways of the Lord and challenge me to grow into a godly young lady. Discipleship was at the heart of their motivations. From the time I was born my parents taught me the importance of obeying, being respectful, and not following the tide of cultural worldliness. The vision I was taught at home was to not follow the crowd but, rather, to be a leader in righteousness.

My dad was twenty-one when he came to know the Lord, and my mom was seventeen. They were discipled as new believers in a group of very conservative Christians. When I was a baby my dad was attending school at a highly conservative Bible college. Due to much of the teaching my parents received as new believers, they established some very countercultural standards for our family. Some of those standards were that I was not to wear pants, play with Barbie dolls, listen to music with a syncopated beat, dance, and television was carefully monitored. For most of my upbringing I did not have many like-minded friends who shared the more conservative values my family had so I learned to stand alone. Through the years, the style of my dad's ministry changed and some of these standards were relaxed as well. Even so, the Lord used the teaching of my parents and a conservative upbringing to be a safeguard in my youth. During high school there was a period of a few years where we were involved in a very conservative sect of the homeschool community. I loved the wholesomeness of the friends I was making and, overall, I felt very encouraged. During the historic days of homeschooling there were many families who got on the homeschooling bandwagon and then suddenly adopted an ultra-countercultural way of life. For our family I believe some of the more countercultural ideas I was raised with were more a result of the teaching my parents were under as new believers than the influence of the early homeschooling movement.

Graduation

My homeschool graduation ceremony is a funny story. Back when I graduated, Houston did not offer the massive graduation ceremonies to the homeschool community that we have today. One of my sweet homeschool friends told me about a graduation ceremony in Pasadena, Texas that we could join in on. It was kind of weird because I did not know this homeschool group that I was graduating with, but my friend and I signed up, bought the cap and gowns, and enjoyed the celebration!

The year I graduated, 1992, I was able to travel to Russia with a large group of homeschool students. We stayed on a boat and would go out and minister in Moscow in the day and enjoy fellowship on the boat at night. I remember when I first arrived after the flight to Russia. When the bus drove us to the boat, there was a large group of students standing on the deck welcoming the newly arriving students by singing hymns. At night, groups of students would chamber together and play violins. The atmosphere was edifying and encouraging.   That was pretty much the end of my homeschooling experience until I had my own children and began homeschooling again several years later.

After Graduation

After homeschooling I took some local junior college classes and some online classes, as well as a year of music at Houston Baptist University. My life was also busy with various areas of ministry in the church my dad pastored, but I went through a bit of a wilderness season in my spiritual walk. I was still trying to serve the Lord but I was not thriving.   Through the many years since my dad started the church, our family had walked through much trial and struggle in the ministry, with my mom's health and with finances. After graduation my social life did not revolve around homeschool friends, as many of them had married in their late teens or early twenties and had started families. I found myself in an uncomfortable situation where I was an adult still living at home, trying to go to school, teaching piano, and attending a small church where I had few friends and seemingly no prospects for marriage.   Overall I felt like I was lacking strength to be the strong, very conservative girl I had tried to be in this place of loneliness. This was probably the beginning of some wandering and searching years for me. By God's grace they were not what most people would call rebellious years.   I was still actively serving the Lord in church ministries and seeking to walk in what I knew was right, but I did begin making small compromises in an attempt to feel a little more normal in the environments I was in and to make friends and fit in somewhere. Most of my life, I had felt "different" from most people I knew, whether friends, family, church members, etc. I had been raised with such high standards that I had always felt different. So during what I think of as my wandering years, I still was trying to live for the Lord while lowering some standards and convictions I had previously had. Some of what I am saying might even be laughable to many people because I'm not talking about going out and committing any big sins. I'm talking about things like beginning to listen to some music that was not edifying to me, watching some movies that were fueling discontent in me, and a few things along those lines. It is interesting that, when I began ignoring my conscience and compromising what I knew to be best, my mind and heart became more dulled and I became less sensitive and less obedient to the Lord in these areas.

"Finally, brothers, whatever is true, whatever is honorable, whatever is just, whatever is pure, whatever is lovely, whatever is commendable, if there is any excellence, if there is anything worthy of praise, think about these things" (Philippians 4:8).

I remember my thought processes when I first started making compromises in my movie choices. I felt like my Christian friends were going to see these movies and seemed okay with them. I felt like, if I was going to have a close group of friends to spend time with and have fun, then I was going to have to bend some and loosen up just a bit. This compromise led me to begin going more often to movies, even on my own just for fun. Even though these movie choices were acceptable with most Christians, I knew they did not turn my heart towards things above, and I basically had to ignore my conscience to watch them since I had been taught differently. I think of the verse that says, "Everyone to whom much was given, of him much will be required" (Luke 12:48). I had been given better training and discernment and, thus, I felt guilty because I knew this was not best. I rationalized it because I was trying to fill the void of loneliness I felt. These choices and compromises did not bring me closer to my Lord.

"So whoever knows the right thing to do and fails to do it, for him it is sin" (James 4:17).

During these wandering years of my early twenties, I think I became weaker and weaker. Thankfully, by God's grace, I still walked a pretty straight and narrow path. In many ways I still held to very conservative standards in comparison to both the Christian and non-Christian culture. I was also teaching piano lessons in my parents' home during this time and became a discussion group leader at a Bible Study Fellowship group for singles. Outwardly I probably looked much the same to a lot of people, but inwardly I was not thriving spiritually due to "small" compromises. My focus was becoming increasingly fixed upon myself. Michael W. Smith's popular song "Place in This World" describes how I was feeling.

> The wind is moving But I am standing still
> A life of pages waiting to be filled
> A heart that's hopeful
> A head that's full of dreams
> But this becoming
> Is harder than it seems
> Feels like I'm
>
> Looking for a reason
> Roamin' through the night to find
> My place in this world
> My place in this world
> Not a lot to lean on
> I need your light to help me find

My place in this world
My place in this world

If there are millions
Down on their knees
Among the many
Can you still hear me
Hear me asking
Where do I belong?
Is there a vision
That I can call my own?
Show me, I'm

Looking for a reason
Roamin' through the night to find
My place in this world
My place in this world
Not a lot to lean on
I need your light to help me find
My place in this world
My place in this world [2]

As I write this I realize that there was a real lack of understanding of who I was in Christ. There was insecurity, feeling I needed to fit in with people, and there was also fear of my future. If I had stayed rooted strongly in the blessings of my identity in Christ I could have stayed focused on His purposes for me and not have derailed like I did. Also, I got off-track in trying to "fit in." As believers we are not called to fit in with the world. The Scripture tells us that we are pilgrims, sojourners, of another Kingdom, etc. This world is not our home and trying to fit in here should not be our aim.

One huge area of discontentment was in my singleness. I felt that, since I was in my twenties and had never had any marriage prospects, I was probably headed towards being an old maid. I remember having a real fear that the Lord might not want me to get married. He had put me in a place of ministry all of my life. What if He felt I could serve Him better being single FOREVER??? Satan is a master at messing with our minds and emotions, and he can get a real footing with fear. I think we women can be especially prone to this kind of thinking. I was so concerned about getting married, and I was losing heart that I had never had a boyfriend. Pretty much all of my homeschooled friends were married years before me. I remember how much I struggled when I would attend yet another wedding. It was so easy to feel sorry for myself. I would plead with the Lord, "Lord, I have always tried to serve you, I have tried to be a good Christian girl, I have tried to wait on your best for marriage, and here I am, Lord. PLEASE! Hear my cry and send me a godly, Christian husband and allow me to have the family I have always dreamed of having." Here I was at the time just floundering about, not knowing what to do but to keep living with my parents and doing what I had done my whole life. I desired a change but, by my mid-twenties, I felt like things might never change.

My grandmother had given a certain amount of college money that eventually ran out. I was in a music program at Houston Baptist, and people were telling me that music and medicine were the most demanding degree programs and that I would need to move on campus in order to spend mega doses of time in the library listening to music recordings. I knew college money was gone, so I decided to just quit and focus on teaching piano lessons. I remember discouragement and loneliness leading me to search out some kind of Christian singles' group that I could get involved with. I found one in a large church in the Houston Metroplex. They had a Saturday night service which worked well since I served in my dad's church on Sundays. I went and was warmly welcomed and invited to join the after-class fellowship time. I quickly found out this singles' group had something going on almost every day of the week. I could be involved in this group as much as I wanted. I suddenly felt I could have all the companionship I desired. I got very involved and was spending a lot of time being involved with Bible studies, serving, and group fellowships. At first it was highly exciting, as I finally had a large group that I could be a part of. Of course, my hope was that I would meet Mr. Right. It seemed everywhere I went I was focused on meeting Mr. Right. At church on Sunday I would *hope* he would walk in the doors of our tiny church. At BSF I would look around for any potential Mr. Rights. At this very sizable singles' group I was certainly keeping my eyes open as well. A problem began to surface quickly, however. The more time I spent with this group, the more I saw how much I really did not fit. Some of what was going on was not good for me. Most of these singles were independent, career-minded. Although they were older than I was, most had not been nurtured in the faith to the extent I had been, and many lacked conviction about being set apart from the world. I remember one particular small group Bible study I attended where a group of girls was discussing whether it would be wrong to have your boyfriend spend the night at your apartment as long as he slept on the couch! This was a different Christian culture than I had been raised in. That kind of compromise would be out of the question in the more conservative Christian world I had known. Thankfully, God in His grace saw fit to answer my prayers for a husband at

17

this time, but it was NOT in the huge singles' group I had taken myself to. No, it was back at the teeny tiny church my dad pastored.

There was a young man there that I had gotten to know very well through the years. Without going into the whole long story, he was my younger brother's friend. My family had spent a lot of time with his family and he had showed previous interest in me. I think the Lord blinded my eyes to him being my Mr. Right until the timing was right. We had been kind of thrown together through various circumstances and had been serving the Lord together in the music ministry at our church. Well, in 1998, he graduated from college, and I began to see him with a new set of eyes. As the old *Charlotte's Web* movie says, "Fay is seeing Henry Fussy with new eyes." Indeed, I began to see Matthew Adams with new eyes, and the Lord was definitely at work drawing our hearts together. I saw how much he had grown from a fresh-out-of-high-school boy into a fine young man. The Lord took the blinders off of my eyes, and, for the first time, he and I both mutually felt the Lord might have a plan for our future together. Once this became evident to me I never returned to the singles' group. I had only been involved in that for a couple of months. The Lord showed me through that experience that He does not need me to take matters into my own hands and try to make things happen. Here, I was thinking I would go out and get involved and strategically place myself where I might have ample opportunity to meet a charming young man. As soon as I did that, the Lord basically turned me on my heels and brought me right back to my daddy's little church and to the husband He had for me.

Here I was, twenty-five years old, and I had never been on a date before. Matt asked me if we could go out and discuss things. I remember he picked me up and took me to a park where we took a walk around a pretty pond. We sat on a large rock that evening and prayed, committing this relationship to the Lord and asking Him to help us to honor Him through it. Having never dated before, this was a huge step for me, and we both entered into this relationship with a serious mindset. We were not playing childish games. Matt and I made a real effort to seek the Lord together during our months of dating. From our first date and all through the months leading to our marriage, prayer was an important element of our relationship. That helped set a habit so that we already felt comfortable praying together once we were married.

After several months of meeting with a mentor couple who shared with us life lessons from their own marriage, we both spent individual time seeking the Lord's will concerning entering the next step of engagement. Our mentor couple was taking us through a study book called *Preparing for*

Engagement by Family Life, and there was a final assignment of getting alone with the Lord to make this monumental life decision.

One day I took a drive to Galveston Island and spent the day seeking the Lord and preparing to accept Matt's proposal when he asked. Soon after that, Matt asked me out on a date and suggested I wear a pretty dress. That was a pretty big hint. ☺ I remember going to get my nails done and thinking, *I'm going to get engaged tonight.*

Matt borrowed a red Mazda Miata for the evening from our mentor couple. When he opened the door, there was a rose waiting for me on the passenger's seat. He proceeded to take me to a quaint little Italian restaurant, after which he drove me to Crystal Beach. Matt parked that little red car on the sand and then suggested I go look at the waves. At that point, he promptly pulled out his guitar from the trunk of the car and asked me to turn around. When I did, he serenaded me with the song, "Will You Be Mine?" This is a song he wrote for me to ask me to marry him. At the end it says, "Will you take my name?" I responded, "Yes" to which he said, "I didn't ask you yet." He placed a diamond ring on my finger that night, and excitement was in the air for the next few months as we prepared for our wedding.

We did much to prepare for marriage during our engagement. We watched a video series on having a healthy marriage relationship. We also read a few books together. Between the pre-engagement counseling, the Christian books we read on marriage, and the videos we watched, I think we went into marriage more prepared than most. I have always been grateful we spent so much of our dating months preparing for the marriage God brought us to. We knew from the start that we were not just playing around, but we were both looking at this as a path leading, Lord willing, to marriage. We took it seriously and prepared diligently for it. We also took this habit of studying together into our marriage. One special thing we did on our wedding night is we began our very first marriage devotional book together. Then we continued on in those early days reading through that daily devotional as a newly married couple. Although we have to purpose to find the time to read together these days, we still enjoy reading , watching documentaries, listening to podcasts, etc. We've always had this culture in our marriage where we enjoy growing closer to each other by growing together in God's wisdom. One way we try to keep our marriage from growing stale is to keep learning together.

Even though I can look back to my early twenties and recognize some years of barren land in my own soul, if you fast forward several years you will see a much more intentional, spiritually thriving, and discerning woman. The Lord in His providence has ways of bringing His children back on track when they wander off. As a young mother I began looking at things with more discerning eyes and became more intentional in many areas. I remember as a young mama with a couple of little people demanding so much of me, that I cried out to the Lord asking Him to bring an older Titus 2 mentor into my life who would help me in my journey. No such lady appeared in my church or on my doorstep, but the Lord continually brought me back to the teaching ministry of Nancy Leigh DeMoss (now Nancy DeMoss Wolgemuth). I began listening to her radio program, *Revive Our Hearts*, more and more faithfully and began feeling convicted and challenged in some areas of my life. Over time I came to clearly see that the Lord had answered that prayer for a Titus 2 mentor in the form of a radio teacher. I saw her speak at Houston's First Baptist Church back around 2008, and I remember sitting there crying and feeling so broken as the Lord stirred my heart. There was also a day at home around this time when the Lord specifically was convicting me of things that I needed to surrender to Him. I remember crying out in repentance, and somewhere in the midst of this time, He changed my heart and turned me back towards a more wholehearted desire to walk in obedience and holiness before Him. Since then, I have attended several Revive Our Hearts conferences and also visited the ministry headquarters. I am grateful for the way the Lord has strengthened me and discipled me through Nancy's teaching. It is as if so much of what I had known to be true and had suppressed for a season was brought back to light by the teaching of Nancy. Through her teachings I was reminded of things I had known but had grown weak in. The Lord used Nancy and other circumstances to bring me out of some measure of lukewarmness and to ignite within me a passion to live more wholeheartedly for the Lord's glory and honor.

Failed Ministries

Around the same time, I was also highly motivated and encouraged by a homeschool ministry that encouraged the building up of strong Christian families. It helped to strengthen the vision that my husband and I had for our family and to give us greater intentionality. While we did not take everything this ministry taught as gospel truth, we were propelled forward by the charge to raise up mighty young men and women for the glory of the Lord. That message resonated with me, reminding me of my roots and the way I was reared to raise the bar high in having godly standards to honor the Lord. Sadly, that ministry crumbled a few years back due to the leader of the ministry living a private life of sin.

To my dismay this homeschool ministry is only one of many ministries that I have witnessed the obliteration of due to sin and hypocrisy. There have been ministries I have been around since I was a baby that have been decimated by sin. As I look back throughout my life I can share a timeline of various ministries wrecked and ruined by moral failures in the lives of its leaders. Growing up I wanted to do what was right and was very trusting of various ministry leaders. In my adult years I have walked through times of disillusionment, as so many leaders in the evangelical world and the homeschool arena have fallen hard. One pitfall in Christian circles, and definitely in homeschool circles, is that of placing sinful men on a pedestal that they should never be on. We must beware of doing this. We must never forget that the men we most respect, and under whose teaching we have grown immensely, are still just sinners saved by grace. The problem is that when we elevate men to a status of hero worship, when they fall, it can shipwreck the faith of their followers. Sadly, sometimes when this happens their followers run very far in the opposite direction. In this case the rippling effects really hurt the cause of Christ. This is why I would caution believers and homeschoolers alike to always elevate Christ and be careful not to look more to a charismatic teacher than to Christ Himself. The Lord uses men, but He never intends for us to look to those men instead of to Christ. Also, in listening to advice from a conference speaker, a preacher, a radio personality, an author in a book, etc., we would be wise to be Bereans and to test what is being said by the plumb line of Scripture.

"Now these Jews were more noble than those in Thessalonica; they received the word with all eagerness, examining the Scriptures daily to see if these things were so" (Acts 17:11).

"But test everything; hold fast what is good. Abstain from every form of evil" (1 Thessalonians 5:21-22).

When I look at the culture at large, the many downfalls of various ministries, how many kids from Christian homes are statistically walking away from the faith, and then some of the heartbreaking stories of spiritual apostasy, even amongst homeschool graduates, I can grow very dismayed. However, this is NOT where God wants me to stay. Isaiah 41:10 says, "Fear not, for I am with you; be not dismayed, for I am your God; I will strengthen you, I will help you, I will uphold you with my righteous right hand."

My lifelong journey through evangelical circles, different churches, and the homeschool community has taught me that Christ has to be center to all. My hope is not in a pastor, in a conference speaker, in a homeschool guru, or in anyone else. My hope is in Christ alone. As Edward Mote wrote in his hymn, "On Christ the Solid Rock I stand. All other ground is sinking sand."

If my hope is in anyone or anything other than Christ, then I am standing on sinking sand. I have watched several huge movements within Christian circles scatter in devastation as their beloved spiritual leader is found to be in secret sin. Often, the followers of such ministries are left reeling and trying to find some kind of stable footing to catch their balance. What these situations have taught me is that our footing should always be firmly planted in Christ. We need to remember that any ministry leader is still a fallen human being and capable of great sin. We need to pray for our leaders to be faithful and finish their race well. When we are rooted in Christ, we will be able to withstand these falling outs when they tragically occur. Because all of our hope was not in a person, we will be able to stand.

Another thing that I have had to grapple with is that, just because someone who I have previously learned a great many truths from has fallen, this does not mean that everything they ever taught is wrong. Many people throw out and discount any teaching from a leader who has fallen. I believe that is an overreaction that is unfortunate. It is normal to question what has been taught by someone who proves unfaithful, but we need to examine the teachings in light of Scripture. It would behoove us not to throw away that which has been in accordance with the Word of God just because it came from someone who has fallen. At the same time if something is extra Biblical or just an application but not a correct interpretation, then we can re-examine to see if we have been misled at any point.

I have also learned to be very discerning and cautious in listening to others. Just because something is said at a homeschool conference or from the pulpit does not mean it is Biblical. We need to compare all that we hear with the Scriptures. Because Satan is a sly enemy he will often hide false teaching in a lot of truth. Even today I am very sensitive to a strand of false teaching that I call hyper-grace teaching. In many ways, this teaching sounds almost right and, yet, I believe it has some dangerous pitfalls. Hyper-grace teaching often comes packaged in a lot of truth and yet there are some erroneous errors within it that one might not catch if they are not familiar with it or keenly discerning. Specifically, it cheapens the grace of God by making light of the believer's need to walk in obedience to the commands of Scripture. These teachers love to quote the verse which says, "There is therefore now no condemnation for those who are in Christ Jesus" (Romans 8:1) while leaving out verses that follow which talk about walking in the Spirit and setting one's mind on the things of the Spirit.

22

"Who walk not according to the flesh but according to the Spirit. For those who live according to the flesh set their minds on the things of the flesh, but those who live according to the Spirit set their minds on the things of the Spirit" (Romans 8:4-5).

Hyper-grace teachers tend to confuse positional sanctification with practical ongoing sanctification. These teachers will say a lot of things that are true, all the while leading people to some very unbiblical conclusions about their Christian walk. In contrast to hyper-grace teaching I believe that, because of God's amazing grace, we are given the desire and the power to do what God commands.

"What shall we say then? Are we to continue in sin that grace may abound? By no means! How can we who died to sin still live in it?" (Romans 6:1-2).

I recently took my two oldest daughters to a Christian young ladies' conference geared towards homeschooled daughters and their mothers. One of the speakers gave an analogy that we have often referred to. She held up a wheel and showed the hub of the wheel and the spokes around the hub. She explained that Christ should always be our center or our hub. As Christian families we may share many common values such as homeschooling, teaching apologetics, dressing modestly, valuing children, teaching godly character, etc. Those values are considered the spokes, but Christ must always be the hub. Without the hub the spokes all come crashing down. If we focus too much on any one spoke and ignore the main hub, our lives will be out of balance and off kilter. I thought that was a powerful analogy, because sometimes in Christian (and especially homeschool) settings, there can be a tendency to focus too much on a particular spoke while ignoring the hub. The spokes are very important to the wheel and need not be ignored but the hub, or Christ in this analogy, is the supporting core that holds all the spokes or secondary issues in place.

Be Discerning

Through my personal journey with so many different ministries and the disappointments that have shaken my world, I think I have emerged with greater discernment and spiritual backbone. I know what I believe and why. My convictions are not because some leader gave me a list of dos and don'ts. I know a conviction is not worth holding to if it is not solidly based in Biblical principles. I understand the difference between clear black-and-white commands of Scripture and gray areas where I must be personally led by the Spirit of God. I know that, in some of these less clear areas, there is freedom in Christ for believers to come to different convictions. Even though I need to give my fellow Christian friends grace to be led by the Spirit and Biblical principles, I have come to a place that I am secure in holding fast to my own convictions. If I feel the Lord has laid something on my heart for myself or my family I am confident in living out that conviction, even if I am the only one. Maybe that conviction is not for my fellow Christian friend, but it is where the Lord has led my family and me. As my children grow into adults I will have to give them room to live out their own convictions, even if that may look a little different from my own. Of course, I would hope that they would fall closely in line with me and with our family, yet in areas where Scripture is not abundantly clear, it is important to remember Christian liberty and grace. I am growing in this confidence and ability to listen to the Lord and stand firm in what He leads us to do as a family. My convictions will not be shattered if another Christian leader bites the dust, because my convictions are formed upon principles from God's Word and by the guidance of His Spirit in my heart. I also see the need for humility to realize that I can still learn from others who may not hold to every conviction I have. I am also open to change should His Spirit direct in different ways in different seasons. However, where the Scripture is clear on a given issue, there is no room for change. There are things in Scripture that are mandates and commands that must be obeyed at all times and in all places. One such example is the command to marital fidelity. That is not a matter of your conviction versus my conviction. That is a clear Scriptural command to be fully obeyed. On the other hand, I may have come to a certain personal preference or conviction based upon Biblical principles that may be the way the Lord is leading me individually in this season of my life. In that case I should not judge others who may not share that conviction or preference. That would fall more into the category of Christian liberty versus clearly defined Biblical commands.

Chapter 2
Blessings Gained Through Being Homeschooled

Being homeschooled, along with parental discipleship, greatly shaped who I am today. One of the things I am grateful for is that being homeschooled made it easier for me to avoid plunging into youth culture. I was able to walk through my teen years with increasing maturity and I knew how to relate to people of all ages. Because I was not submerged into an environment where everyone was the same age I learned how to have friends of all ages. Sometimes homeschoolers are accused of not allowing their children to live in the "real world," but I would argue with that reasoning. On the contrary I do not see putting a classroom of thirty sixth graders together as being anything like the real world. In non-school settings people have to know how to relate to people from different age groups. Some of my best friends growing up were women in my church whom I would babysit for and also get to know as friends. Some of these ladies became mentors to me as I observed how they walked with Christ, how they served their husbands, how they loved their children, etc. This was Titus 2 in action as I had the blessing of spending time with these ladies who loved the Lord and served Him by lovingly serving their families.

Youth Culture Has Not Always Been a Cultural Norm

When you look back through history, youth culture is a fairly new thing. For thousands of years young people matured in their teens and took on great responsibility at young ages. As an example the prince of preachers, Charles Spurgeon, gave his first public speech when he was fifteen years old. At age nineteen, he was teaching other students. Then he became London's famed pastor of New Park Street Church at the age of twenty. His testimony is that he "put on Christ" a few weeks before his sixteenth birthday. The day was May 3,1850, and happened to be his mother's birthday. [3]

In fact, when we look at the age groups in the Bible, we see babies, children, young men and young women, older men and older women. It is significant that there is no mention of teenagers in Scripture. Instead of youth culture, you had maturing young adults. It used to be that young men and young ladies married very early, somewhere between their mid-teens and their early twenties. They grew up, began families, and took responsibilities seriously. Sadly, our culture today tells kids it is normal to have a season of life called the teen years when you are known for laziness, bad attitudes, irresponsibility, peer dependency, immoral behavior, craziness, and rebellion to authority. Isn't that sad? What also grieves me is that this season is constantly being pushed back to younger and younger ages. In addition to youth culture invading the childhood years, it is also tragic that many young people today are not ready for adult responsibility until their late thirties or into their forties. We have an epidemic in our culture of young men who refuse to grow up and be men. Instead of getting a responsible job and taking on the high calling of being husbands and fathers, these young men are often still living off of their parents and addicted to video games and pornography. Many young men want to have a perpetual life of adolescent behavior and of rampant immorality without the responsibility of marriage and family. Is it any wonder our culture is crumbling?

Robbed of Childhood

Children are often being robbed of their childhood these days. It is not uncommon for people to tease little preschool or kindergarten girls about who their boyfriend is instead of encouraging these little girls to play Mommy with their baby dolls. The culture encourages little girls to act like sassy teeny boppers and then tweens, and then they are quickly pushed into their teen years. It is quite common for young parents to stand around and laughingly comment about the sassy attitudes their little girls are displaying as they try to dress and act like miniature divas. It is my impression that this youth culture is stealing the sweet, innocent, formative years from our children to their detriment. Have you noticed how so many children look spaced out or hopeless and sad? Tragically, because of the powerful influence of youth culture screaming at our children through media and environmental influences, many little ones never even enjoy a sweet, innocent childhood. The other day I was shopping for diapers and was saddened to see a particular brand had put out a diaper design of skulls and bones. I am accustomed to diapers having cute little things like fuzzy animals or hearts. Why do we want to put skull bones on our precious babies? Take a look at some of the sayings on baby clothes these days—things like "chick magnet," "rock star," "stud," "diva," "I'm the boss," etc.

Recently, while perusing a rack of baby onesies, I found several sayings that bothered me. One was black with a baby bottle on the front. The slogan was, "I'll drink to that." Really??? Do we want to take a precious new baby and dress him in a shirt laughing about alcohol consumption? Is it a laughing matter? How about this one? "Mom … my first tattoo." Here are some other ones: "Mama's little bad boy" and "Lil' Miss Sassy Pants." Are parents to celebrate their babies being bad and having wrong attitudes? Then there was the cute onesie with flowers on it that said, "Does this make my butt look big?" Another one said, "Little dude, big trouble" and then the slogan "Rock Star" is on all kinds of baby paraphernalia. The thing is that we set our children on a trajectory for wisdom or for folly from their earliest moments, and my heart is to encourage parents to be intentional that their children's trajectory is on the narrow path that leads to life. Proverbs has so much to say about embracing wisdom rather than folly, and children so often live up to the expectations we have of them. If we raise them to be bad boys, rock stars, absorbed with themselves, tough and tattooed drunkards, what do we expect their outcome to look like? My plea to parents is to seek Godly wisdom and to be purposeful in passing on a legacy of righteousness to the next generation. Paul, after condemning the love of money, charged his spiritual son Timothy to:

"But as for you, O man of God, flee these things. Pursue righteousness, godliness, faith, love, steadfastness, gentleness" (1 Timothy 6:11).

We have enough of the systems of this world to combat without encouraging it in our little ones. As I think about these slogans parents often laugh at and put on their children, these verses come to mind.

"Woe to those who call evil good and good evil, who put darkness for light and light for darkness, who put bitter for sweet and sweet for bitter!" (Isaiah 5:20).

I am not a fan of youth culture. Instead of pushing this youth-crazed, media-driven culture on our children, why not encourage them to be young men and young ladies of God? Why not encourage them to do great things for God in their youth? Paul told Timothy:

"Let no one despise you for your youth, but set the believers an example in speech, in conduct, in love, in faith, in purity" (1 Timothy 4:12).

As I stated above I matured early. I was taught that with greater responsibility comes greater privilege. Basically, my parents let out the rope and gave me freedoms as they saw I was mature enough to make wise decisions. If I wanted freedoms I had to prove worthy of them giving me those freedoms. I was encouraged to not go the path of youth culture in many ways. Even as a young teenager I was quickly maturing into a young lady.

As a young girl, I was challenged to stand strong and to be a leader in righteousness. My parents taught me that I should always stand for what is right even if I was the only one. Instead of following the crowd, I should be a leader and seek to encourage others down paths of wisdom.

I also remember my Sunday school teacher teaching from the book of Daniel. She talked to us girls about how Daniel purposed in his heart not to defile himself with the king's meat or wine. It was a predetermined decision before the temptation occurred. I remember my teacher challenging our class to determine ahead of time that we would not compromise our standards but would be obedient to God. I was shaped by this principle that I should determine ahead of time to obey God's Word, and now I find myself challenging my own children with that same vision. Just the other day I was sharing with my children over breakfast that they should stand for what is right even if they are the only ones.

Learning to Serve

Young single people typically have a lot more free time on their hands than their adult, married counterparts. Because peer groups were not my whole world during my youth, I was able to take on my parents' vision for ministry within the small church my dad had started. I started as a very young girl, watching the nursery and bringing in some stories to teach the little ones. I remember my excitement over having the opportunity to teach a flannel graph series of lessons on the life of Amy Carmichael. This is a series one of my children's church teachers taught to me as a little girl. I enjoyed it so much that she made me my own little flannel graph board and gave me the flannel graph series. Years later, I was able to put it to good use teaching the children in our church. As the years progressed I began teaching classes, leading children's choir, teaching youth, playing piano for our church, and eventually leading some women's events. It started very small in a tiny little nursery room and grew into bigger responsibilities through the years. I really loved the children I worked with and considered some of them to be almost like little siblings to me. Having purpose in ministry helped me through my teen years. I had somewhere to channel my energies and time and something to be motivated and excited about. Serving the Lord is exciting, Kingdom work is rewarding, and it is good for young people to have vision as to how they can be busy serving Christ in their youth. Many young people are getting into trouble because they are bored and enslaved by youth culture and peer pressure. I think many Millennials are actually tired of materialism and entertainment and are living in a state of hopelessness. I think giving our young people something bigger, grander, and more rewarding than pop culture and self-gratification will help them navigate their teen years with purpose.

Mega Doses of Time with Family

I did not realize it when I was growing up, but life goes by incredibly fast. Looking back, I am glad that, because of homeschooling, I had all day every day at home with my family. My home was a refuge and a safe environment for me to grow up in. We had Christian radio playing all the time, and my parents were constantly telling us about the ways the Lord was moving in our church and in our family. It was a 24/7 lifestyle of discipleship. Also, looking at the present I am incredibly grateful that I have the privilege of spending my days with my children who are growing up way too quickly right before my eyes. When you think about it we are usually shaped by those we are around the most. Let's look at what Luke tells us.

"A disciple is not above his teacher; but everyone when he has been fully trained, will be like his teacher" (Luke 6:40).

I am grateful that I was discipled by parents who wanted me to know, love, and serve Jesus. They did not want me to be "conformed to the pattern of this world."

"Do not conform to the pattern of this world, but be transformed by the renewing of your mind. Then you will be able to test and approve what God's will is—his good, pleasing and perfect will" (Romans 12:2, NIV).

It was a blessing for me to grow up in the classroom of my home where I learned that a personal walk with Christ is most important, that serving Christ is our mission, and that we are here to glorify and reflect the Lord Jesus. When I think about what a contrast this model of parental teaching and discipleship is with the state of education in public schools I am so grateful for the way I was educated. Instead of atheism, I was taught Biblical creationism; instead of feminism, I was taught Biblical roles for men and women; instead of humanism, I was taught to do all things to the glory of God; instead of being taught moral relativism, I was taught that absolute truth is found in Scripture. This was my foundation, and I am grateful for it. You may notice that I have not really said anything about the education I received from being homeschooled. That is because I think I could have received a good education in another setting. Had I attended public or private school, I could have graduated with great knowledge and, yet, it would have been much more challenging for my parents to disciple me. They would have had much less time to teach me about life and model the ways of the Lord in front of me. Had I been in any school setting I would have had much less time for ministry and probably less of an interest in ministry as well. Truly, homeschooling was a tool the Lord used to teach me and train me to be who He wanted me to be.

Carrying the Legacy into the Next Generation

I am furthermore grateful that I have the freedom to educate my own children at home where we are learning that history is His Story, that science proclaims the works of a wonderful Creator, that music is a way we can glorify our Lord, that reading enables us to read the very words of God, and so forth. In all of our studies, we are trying to paint a picture of divine providence and the sovereignty of God. We are trying to instill a Biblical worldview so that our children can see all of life through the lens of God, His Word, and His ways.

I also do not take these freedoms lightly. My family lived through the years in the eighties when there was a huge battle raging in Texas to try to stop families from homeschooling. At one point our family traveled to Austin to stand with thousands of others being a visual witness to the Governor of Texas to let him know just how serious our homeschool families were about protecting the freedom to homeschool. Recently, Governor Greg Abbott recognized June ninth as "Leeper Day," a special day celebrating the 1994 Texas Supreme Court decision that unanimously voted in favor of freedom to homeschool in Texas. I understand that the homeschool freedoms we enjoy today were fought for by persistent, committed, brave dads and moms a few decades ago. I know they fought for a reason; they had a vision that they would train their children at home to know and love the living God. They saw their homes as discipleship centers and did not want the government interfering with the vision God had given them. This propels me to want to share the message that our freedoms today are not just a given. Brave, courageous men and women fought hard to secure our freedoms to homeschool, and they did it because they had vision. The least we can do is to understand the history of homeschooling and be intentional in protecting our freedoms from heavy-handed government while passing the torch of faith to the next generation.

Chapter 3
Second-Generation Homeschooling

Can I do this?

It was March of 2001 when Matt and I welcomed our first baby into our lives. She was long anticipated, and we were thrilled to be parents. Being a mommy is something I had dreamed of my whole life. When I learned that we were having a little girl I was beyond ecstatic. I went to work sewing beautiful rose bud bedding for her nursery and decorating with a Precious Moments theme. Everything was going to be as sweet and girlie as I could make it. When Lauren Elizabeth joined us it did not take long to realize that this mothering thing was not as intuitive or easy as I would have dreamed. Part of that was her personality and part was our inexperience. She did not sleep well at night, and she did not take to my nursing schedule. It did not help that I lacked experience as a new mama and did not know what I was doing in many ways. As she grew into a toddler and then into a little girl I knew I did not have an easygoing, firstborn daughter like many of my mama friends. No, our precious Lauren was more of a creative, independent thinker whom we had to watch closely. I remember getting together with other mamas watching all the little babies sitting contentedly on the floor playing with toys, but my Lauren was looking for adventure. She was not content to blend into the group.

When Lauren was a toddler I went with some mamas to a pool that was created to be much like a sandy beach environment. The group was having a nice time together when I suddenly realized Lauren had wandered off. Where was she? This time her adventurous spirit had led her to join another group nearby, helping herself to their potato chips. This happened so quickly, and my thought was, *Why can't she just be happy staying in our group like my friends' toddlers*?

As I watched her grow I began to have doubts about whether I could homeschool this daughter of mine. How would I get her to focus? Since she was a social butterfly wouldn't she be happier being in the midst of a lot of children? She was not shy but adjusted well anywhere. At the same time, many of my Christian friends had already put their little ones in preschool and were planning on public education for their children. Thankfully, my husband was a voice of wisdom to me when I was facing doubts. Having been public schooled all his school years, my husband told me that he did not want his children being brought up in the public school environment. Since we did not have the funds for private school that pretty much settled the matter, and we began reading about and preparing to homeschool. From time to time, however, I would have new doubts arise based upon the challenging preschooler Lauren was, and I would ask the Lord again if He really wanted me to homeschool her. It amazed me how often I would pray that prayer and, within a day or two, something would happen or I would hear or read something that would be a huge confirmation. His answer every time was a resounding, "yes!" In fact, right before Lauren's kindergarten year, we learned about a local classical academy where she could attend class a couple days a week and be homeschooled the rest of the time. We decided this would be a great option for her and enrolled her in the class. The Lord, however, will have His way, and He swiftly brought down this plan of ours. Something happened with the leadership of the school, and they were no longer able to offer the kindergarten class that we had planned on. I remember feeling like this was an overwhelming blow. This was Lauren's first year of school and here we were with our plans falling through! Now I look back on that experience and just laugh. What was the big deal? I now know that kindergarten is a great year to play, snuggle, read lots of good books, explore the great outdoors, and learn through nature, etc. It absolutely does not have to be a serious academic atmosphere. With fear and trepidation we kept Lauren home, and I did my best to work with her, even though she was wiggly and hard to teach. Lauren's younger brother Gabriel was at home too, and I was pregnant with another baby. Lauren did not have good focusing skills, and she seemed to think anything was a reason to be distracted from her work. I remember sitting at a child-sized school table with her while we tried to do her phonics workbook. She was the little girl who would be tapping her fingers, kicking her legs, noticing something on the wall, or a zillion other things like that. A few months into her kindergarten year I also gave birth to Annagrace, a very colicky baby who would scream for hours upon end.

Trying Preschool

Well, at some point I broke and decided the answer was to put Gabriel in a nearby preschool program. When I look back at our short stint in preschool the only things that I have fond memories of are that his teachers really liked him and were sweet to us and that he made super cute crafts. In many ways my strategy of simplifying our lives by putting Gabriel in preschool backfired. It was not fun to get up on preschool mornings and have to dress three children and get out the door early with a newborn. Then, when we arrived, I had to take them all into the building and then drive Lauren and

Annagrace back home and get them out of the van. Then we tried to do some school, but Lauren was still fidgety, and Annagrace was still fussy. Before we knew it, it was time to load them into the van again and pick up Gabriel. Then, of course, we had to unload everyone and all of our things upon arriving back home. Also, when you put a lot of youngsters in a room together, they will share plenty of germs, increasing the chances of sickness in the family. I also did not think that the preschool environment was good for Gabriel's character development. Again, when you put a lot of preschoolers together with their selfish, sinful natures, there can be many attitudes and behaviors that are not a helpful influence. As I reflect upon that time I really feel it was all unnecessary and it complicated our lives in many ways. Overall, I don't think it helped sending him away and I wish that we had not. If I had just realized my day didn't have to look so schoolish with my kindergartener then we could have embraced a gentler form of reading books, going over phonics, and focusing on Scripture memory and character training for all. I think that would have been much more effective for Lauren's learning style and for our family as a whole. Gabriel only went to a preschool program for a little more than a school year, and none of our other children have ever attended preschool. My purpose here is not to judge anyone who does appreciate a Christian preschool program. I feel that sending your child to a God-honoring preschool program definitely falls within the realm of Christian liberties. I am just saying that, in hindsight, I did not feel that it was worth it for our family.

Our Classical Experience

A few years into homeschooling we entered into the world of a once-a-week classical, community group where there was a big focus on rote memory drill. I still remember my frustration sitting in front of the white board in our homeschool room with four children, trying to teach memory work. We were drilling things like Latin conjugations, the periodic table, history timelines, etc. I personally know many wonderful families who love this form of education, but it was draining the life out of our homeschool experience. It was not fun for us having a couple young elementary-aged children, a toddler and a baby all sitting in a circle trying to memorize so much content. It felt impossible with my oldest who was still a distracted learner, my second who was just starting school and needed more of the basics, and fussy little ones. I felt like I was going insane. Also, we would go to this group on Fridays and be gone all day. My nappers were in the nursery class at the classical community and missed their naps. I was also having a painful pregnancy, and trying to teach a preschool class during part of that time. We would all get home mid to late afternoon and be exhausted. After a couple of years and with the news of our fifth baby on the way, we decided to pull out of the community. I was asked to go up front and share our plans, and I remember saying that we appreciated the group very much, but with the new baby on the way, we would have more preschoolers and babies than school-aged children. I told everyone that we needed to be home, and that our nappers needed their naps. This was hard as we had close friends in the group and had received much loving support there as well. I remember it was as if that were a time of drawing a line in the sand and saying for this season we are going to be home. It was also a time where the Lord was showing me that His main purpose for our homeschool was that our children would be taught His ways. It would not matter if they knew a lot of academic facts, Latin words, historical dates, etc. if we did not have the time we needed to really focus on the Word of God and grow in His ways. Over the previous years the Lord had been wooing my heart towards staying home more. As a new mother I had allowed church activities, library days, and play groups to take us out of our home almost daily. As I had more children the Lord was drawing my heart to stay home and be more intentional in keeping my home. This last step of pulling out of the classical community, and even publicly stating why, was a pivotal moment in our family. It was a good move for us, and I have never looked back. I knew we were doing what the Lord was calling us to. Not long after that, we moved to a house on 3.5 acres and brought home our fifth child from the hospital. I was in over my head with busyness and Matt entered into a season of more international travel. Home was where I needed to be. Then a few years later we moved to our current farm and had our sixth child. At that time, the Lord provided for us to be able to stay home and not even go out for piano lessons anymore. When we moved to our farm I had just had Nathaniel and it was going to be an hour drive to piano lessons. At this point our dear teacher said she wanted to drive to us and spare me that drive. It is amazing how, when we do what we can do to honor the Lord with our priorities, He provides what is needed. Now we have seven children and our teacher is still driving to us once a week. God is faithful!

Our journey has continued in and out of varying seasons, different curriculums, ups and downs, and various challenges. Through the years I feel like the Lord has been showing us more and more that this homeschooling journey is more about discipleship than academics. Yes, we aim at preparing our children for life and equipping them for whatever God calls them to, but the reason we homeschool is to teach them to know, love, and fear the Lord, and to walk according to His Word.

"But seek first the kingdom of God and his righteousness, and all these things will be added to you" (Matthew 6:33).

Matthew 6:33 has become the verse I go back to over and over again in thinking about our homeschool. I know the Lord is calling me to "seek first His Kingdom and His righteousness," and all these other things (whatever our kids need to know academically) will be added as well.

"He has told you, O man, what is good; and what does the LORD require of you but to do justice, and to love kindness, and to walk humbly with your God?" (Micah 6:8).

Chapter 4

Observations from Over Three Decades of Involvement in Homeschooling

The Early Days

My parents started homeschooling me around 1979. This means that I have been around and observing the trends of the homeschooling movement for close to forty years. Over time I have seen some serious cultural and philosophical shifting in the homeschooling movement. When I look back over thirty-five years of involvement with homeschooling, I see that some changes have been for the better while other changes leave me with concerns. Let me just share with you that homeschooling has come a very long ways from the primitive days when I was being schooled at home. The options and opportunities for homeschool families today are astounding. Back when our family was embarking on the unknown waters of homeschooling, there were only a few curriculum companies to choose from. There was not a plethora of huge homeschool conventions; the worldwide web did not exist with all the free homeschooling resources that can now be accessed online; there were no podcasts to tune into for encouragement and inspiration. I know my mom went to a few small conferences and probably came home with some notes and a few cassette tapes, but, back in the day, homeschooling resources were hard to obtain. Homeschooling has since exploded, opening up doors and opportunities that would have been unfathomable to the minds of homeschool families several decades ago.

Curriculums Abound

In contrast, now there are so many various curriculums and styles of educating, such as Classical, Charlotte Mason, Literature approach, Unit Studies, and the list goes on. There are all kinds of video schools, internet classes, co-ops, and more. Back when I was being homeschooled, we were fortunate to get our hands on some ABeka textbooks and try to recreate traditional school at home. I well remember my mother transforming our family living room into a traditional school room with old-fashioned school desks, flags, a bulletin board, etc. She would sit up front and conduct school from an ABeka teacher's manual just as a teacher in a Christian school would do. When the manual said it was time to stand and say the Pledge of Allegiance we stood, and when the manual said to sing a song we sang. That can still be an effective way to educate at home, but homeschool families now have many other options available. Fortunately, this generation of homeschoolers has no problem accessing curriculums, a plethora of good resources, and many wonderful learning opportunities in their homeschools. Our own family is currently using some online classes with several of our children as well as DVD math courses. In the past, our oldest daughter has taken some writing courses through email where she writes, sends off her papers, and has an instructor grade them and give feedback. Homeschool options have evolved far beyond a boxed curriculum. Sometimes the boxed curriculum is just the right fit, and other times some of these newer educational options are a lifesaver. I would say our family is very eclectic, using many different things across the board.

Conventions and Vendor Halls!

Today's homeschoolers also have wonderful conferences all over the nation where they can become better equipped through listening to many experienced speakers and meandering around huge vendor halls where they can peruse and choose from a vast number of curriculum and resource suppliers. In many cases we can personally talk to the authors of the curriculums and books right there at the conventions. There is a whole world of blogs about homeschooling where parents can take advantage of free resources, reading book lists, and lesson plans for free! Some homeschoolers choose to educate their children for free using online book lists, a library card, and a Bible. It can be done!

Usually at least once a year I have opportunity to enter the world of a homeschool convention hall. When I walk through those doors, there is a mixture of emotions contending inside of me. On one hand I am excited to see what great new resources I may find to bless my family; on the other hand there are so many choices that it can still overwhelm me. My heart goes out to newbies in the homeschool movement who are seeing all the curriculums for the first time and trying to make decisions for their first year of homeschooling. When choices abound confusion can reign. Sometimes it is easier to have fewer choices. Not only are there so many choices, but we are not comparing apples to apples when looking at curriculums. Many of the curriculums have vastly different philosophies in styles and methods of education, and the parent has to assess what will be the best fit for them and their children. Even after having been homeschooled and homeschooling for so many years I still pray for discernment and the leading of the Lord as I enter the sea of choices within a convention's vendor hall.

Homeschool Activities

While I value the progress that has been made on the homeschooling landscape, I also have some concerns. As the number of families embarking on the journey of homeschooling has exploded, I am concerned that some of the newer homeschooling families may be losing some of the original vision and purpose that motivated many of the early pioneers to embark on such unchartered and choppy waters. I have seen many newer homeschooling families get wrapped up in academic competition and extracurricular social activities. Sometimes these families do not look that much different from their public school neighbors whose families are running in all directions and seldom having the whole family home together for an evening meal. It can be tempting for homeschool families to get involved in too many out of the house activities and homeschool opportunities, but we need to be cautious that all these activities do not rob us of the real reason we are homeschooling to begin with. As with anything, we need to be prayerful in setting clearly defined priorities. For our family, a close family unit and spiritual discipleship are at the top of our list. If we are splintered in all directions and running away from home too frequently we will neglect our most important objectives. I think academic and extracurricular activities and competitiveness can become areas of idolatry if we are not careful. While some of these things may be good things in and of themselves, they can really distract us from our main purpose of knowing Christ while glorifying Him and loving Him forever. I do think it is important that our children are educated well and have opportunities that help prepare them for the calling the Lord has on their lives, yet my number one goal is still that they know and love the Lord Jesus and obey Him. I want the focus in our home to be on learning and growing to the glory of God and not on trying to compete with others, which can easily lead to pride. Scripture is clear that the Lord opposes the proud.

"Likewise, you who are younger, be subject to the elders. Clothe yourselves, all of you, with humility toward one another, for 'God opposes the proud but gives grace to the humble'" (1 Peter 5:5).

I want to be careful not to foster this spirit of pride in our children by putting such a focus on academic competition, sports, or any other endeavor, such as music or other electives. While physical training, academic knowledge, and developing skills has its proper place and value, it pales in comparison to walking in humble obedience to our Lord.

"For while bodily training is of some value, godliness is of value in every way, as it holds promise for the present life and also for the life to come" (I Timothy 4:8).

In fact, I usually have a little chat with our musicians before their recitals, reminding them that their focus needs to be on doing their best to the glory of God. We don't want them focusing on performance to promote themselves but rather to do their best to the glory of the One who gave them the ability to play their instrument.

Many years ago I met a lady who told me she was homeschooling her daughter because homeschooling allowed them to build their lives around her daughter's ice skating training. It was a convenient way of allowing her daughter to pursue ice skating with great vigor. I would agree that homeschooling opens up great flexibility to the family schedule; however, I would have loved to have heard that mama say that she was homeschooling to train her daughter in the fear and wisdom of the Lord and then to develop whatever talents she had to His glory. Again this goes back to, what is the main vision for our homeschool?

Homeschool Culture

I have seen the growth of the homeschooling movement over the decades and can definitely see the benefits of the increased opportunities for families to tap into. At the same time, I can also see the dangers of forgetting the original homeschool discipleship vision that many of the pioneer families took very seriously. Back in the early days there was kind of a conservative homeschool culture built within many homeschooling families. In many ways these families took seriously the Scriptural command to not love the world but to be set apart from it. Many of the pioneering families chose homeschooling because they did not want their children to look and act like their public school counterparts. Instead, these parents had a vision that their sons and daughters would mature quickly into young men and women who loved the Lord and were Kingdom minded. Unfortunately, some of these families did not get the outcome they had hoped for, as some of these well-intentioned parents lost their children to the world. In some cases, this could have been caused by parents who failed to develop a heartfelt relationship with their children by focusing too much on scrubbing up the outside of the cup while missing the needs in their children's hearts, or by a harsh, dictatorial style of parental leadership. In other cases, parents put unreasonable standards upon their young people and failed to let them grow and make some mistakes. Part of the purpose of this book is to talk about this tragedy and to seek to form a well-balanced view of Biblical discipleship within our homes. We want to have a Biblical vision and God-honoring standards without harsh legalism. Now let me make it clear that there are many like myself who emerged out of a conservative family and are still loving the Lord and carrying on their parents' original vision towards godliness into

40

the second generation. I think homeschool rebels have gotten a lot of attention, as they are generally the ones making an online scene and writing liberal blog posts about how "oppressive" their conservative upbringing was. I will not argue that some of them had unfortunate upbringings, but I would say it is not conservative values that is the problem. It may be the way their parents handled leadership in the home or just the fact that the rebel does not want to surrender to Christ, but well-balanced godly values are not the problem. Thankfully, there are many great outcomes from a large number of homeschool graduates; they just may not be the ones who are screaming for attention. Conversely, today I see a different paradigm in the homeschooling movement. I see floods of people exiting public schools and entering the world of homeschooling, and I am encouraged that these families are being saved from the humanistic worldviews taught in public schools. While I am thankful for the increase of families choosing home education, what concerns me is that I feel like a vision for godly families that goes beyond the mediocrity of this culture is at an all-time low. So many churches have brought down any standard for mature, godly young people and have chosen to entertain the youth instead of disciple them. I see a youth group mentality in many homeschooling families today as well. Many of these parents are, in fact, very afraid of the ditch of legalism and are running far in the opposite direction, which leads them right into the pitfall of liberty or cheap grace (also called hyper grace). It seems to be a knee jerk reaction to the masses of kids from Christian homes (homeschool, private school, and public school) who have rebelled and apostatized from the faith. In fact, I see many of these newbies to the movement coming in with the mindset that they want every opportunity for their kids that they would get in public school (i.e., dances, proms, social events, dating, etc.). That is the polar opposite of the mindset many of the pioneering families had who wanted something totally different from the public school experiences for their young people. I feel compelled to be a voice saying: Let's not forget our roots. Let's not forget the founding parents who had a vision to raise a generation of godly young people. Let's not get so focused on curriculum, academic achievement, social activities, sports, etc. that we fail to train our children in godly character and disciple them in the ways of the Lord. Let's keep our priorities in order and raise the bar for our families to reflect the light of the Lord Jesus in a dark culture. Let's not be satisfied to have our sons and daughters acting and living no better than the public schooled kids of a generation or two ago. Let's see homeschooling with visionary eyes, with the goal of raising Christ-centered young people who do not love the things of this world. Most importantly, let's go back to Scripture and ask, what saith the Lord about what our families should be? And, yet, let's be careful not to just polish up the outside and

41

ignore the more important aspect of the hearts of our young people. Let's be prayerful to avoid the ditches of legalism and cheap grace. My heart is to see young people who love Christ, who have truly been regenerated, and whose Facebook accounts reflect something different than the status quo of this generation. The goal is not social misfits or frumpy looking children. The goal is winsome, godly, salty, lights shining in a very dark world. Our families can be very different and very attractive at the same time!

"You are the salt of the earth, but if salt has lost its taste, how shall its saltiness be restored? It is no longer good for anything except to be thrown out and trampled under people's feet. You are the light of the world. A city set on a hill cannot be hidden. Nor do people light a lamp and put it under a basket, but on a stand, and it gives light to all in the house. In the same way, let your light shine before others, so that they may see your good works and give glory to your Father who is in heaven" (Matthew 5:13-16).

I think, considering the massive shift of much of today's homeschool culture, it would be healthy for homeschool families to just go back to Scripture as the standard for their families. Forget what you think "homeschool culture" is supposed to look like and ask yourself, what does the Bible say? Forget your fears, whichever side of the ditch they might be on (i.e., legalism or cheap grace), and ask yourself, what is Biblical? How can your family grow in righteousness and godliness? In my generation, there were some families who took conservative values too far and exasperated their children; in the current generation, I believe many families are lacking in a Biblical vision of holiness. There are extremes on both sides of the issue. Our goal is not to fit into a homeschool sub culture, whatever that may look like. Our goal is to reflect the Lord Jesus and glorify Him in all things.

Strong Outward Character Does Not Guarantee a Godly Heart

Having been around homeschooling families for decades, one thing that has greatly alarmed me are the stories of children who grew up in homes where their parents tried very hard to lead them in the ways of the Lord, but they chose to reject what they were taught. I have heard stories of seemingly perfect homeschooled children who looked stellar on the outside only to go absolutely crazy once they reached an age of independence. In some cases, these kids were the ones who looked perfectly groomed, spoke Christianese really well, seemed responsible, and just looked like the child every Christian homeschooling parent would want to produce. It leaves you scratching your head and asking lots of questions.

I think there are many different reasons and explanations for why some Christian and homeschooled children have not walked in faithfulness to what they were taught. We are living in an age where the statistics are alarming as to the number of young people walking away from the faith by their second year in college.

The book *Already Gone: Why Your Kids Will Quit Church and What You Can Do to Stop It* quotes Barna research as saying that "61% of today's young adults who were regular church attendees are now 'Spiritually disengaged.' They are not actively attending church, praying, or reading their Bibles." [4]

The Scripture tells us that the last days will be times where people will be lovers of themselves and disobedient to their parents (2 Timothy 3:2). We need to be aware of the times that we are living in and plead for the Lord's mercies, that our children will not be the fruit of a rebellious generation. Only God's great mercy can produce a different kind of fruit in the midst of such strong tides of apostasy.

"But understand this, that in the last days there will come times of difficulty. For people will be lovers of self, lovers of money, proud, arrogant, abusive, disobedient to their parents, ungrateful, unholy, heartless, unappeasable, slanderous, without self-control, brutal, not loving good, treacherous, reckless, swollen with conceit, lovers of pleasure rather than lovers of God, having the appearance of godliness, but denying its power. Avoid such people" (2 Timothy 3:1-5).

As I have already stated, there is danger in focusing all of our energies on scrubbing up our kids on the outside if we ignore attending to their hearts.

"Woe to you, scribes and Pharisees, hypocrites! For you clean the outside of the cup and the plate, but inside they are full of greed and self-indulgence" (Matthew 23:25).

While I am a strong advocate of teaching our children godly character and right behavior, I also see that we must not stop there. We do our children a strong disservice if we shine them up outwardly but fail to show them how sinful their hearts are before the Lord. The Bible teaches that our behavior flows from our hearts.

"The good person out of the good treasure of his heart produces good, and the evil person out of his evil treasure produces evil, for out of the abundance of the heart his mouth speaks" (Luke 6:45).

So what we dwell on and love in our hearts will impact what comes out in our lives. We must be careful to teach our children that they were born sinners in need of a Savior. Charles Spurgeon left us with a great quote about the nature of our sinful hearts:

"Sin is not a splash of mud on man's exterior; it is a filth generated from within himself." [5]

It is vitally important that our children understand that they are not justified because they were born into a strong, Christian homeschool family that takes spiritual matters, character training, Scripture memorization, and other spiritual disciplines seriously. That does not make them righteous in God's sight. Neither the faith of the parents nor supreme moral training can save the child. Each individual must realize their own sinful heart and utter inability to appease the wrath of Almighty God apart from the glorious working of the Gospel in their own individual life.

It is important that our children understand that there are sins of omission and sins of commission. When they lash out in anger and hurt a sibling, that is a sin of commission. On the other hand, when they fail to love Christ and see their great need for Him, that is a sin of omission. They are omitting something from their lives that they need to be doing. They need to be seeking Christ and loving Him. None of us are born seeking Christ and loving Him, so we are all born automatically committing the sin of omission. When we fail to see our sin and our need for Christ, it is the sin of pride that causes us to feel confident in our own selves.

Here is where I think it is especially easy for a large homeschooling family to unintentionally derail in this most critical area. It is easy for a large family to start functioning as a team or unit out of necessity. If we are not careful, it is easy to start seeing all of the children as a group rather than as individual souls. If we have the group looking spiritually shiny and impressive on the outside, it could be easy to delude ourselves into believing that all of our children have the same hearts for the Lord. Maybe some of them do and some of them do not. It is possible to unify a family group, clean them up, teach them good manners, teach them to be respectful, sing in parts, quote Scripture, etc. and assume that they are all on the same plane spiritually. The problem is that some of these children could possibly just be going along with the unit they were born into and adopting the family group norm. Now this is wonderful that they have learned character, cooperation skills, a good work ethic, how to serve and minister, etc. However, when it comes to salvation and sanctification, it is a case by case, individual matter with each child. As parents we must assess each child's spiritual condition individually. Just

44

because the firstborn may be doing all of these things out of true love for Christ does not mean that child five, six, or seven is doing these things out of the same purity of heart. We must not apply the faith and heart of one child to another child. When it comes to attending to the spiritual heart matters of each child, there are no short cuts. We need to study our children, talk with them, pray with them, and draw them out on these matters. We need to pray fervently that the Lord will make their salvation sure and give each child a heart commitment to His ways. As a parent all I can do is be a faithful steward of the children the Lord gives me. Ultimately, only the Lord can woo their hearts to His. Only He can convict them of their sin and show them their need of salvation. Only He can give them a surrendered heart. At the same time, I cannot sit back and be lackadaisical as I wait for the Holy Spirit to do His work. By no means! I am committed to training my children, to taking them by the hand and leading them to understand the ways of the Lord, to training their character, to teaching them to discern right from wrong, to teaching them respect for authority, to teaching them God's Word and His commands, etc. I have been lent these children, and I must be a faithful steward. The flip side of this is that I have no guarantees. I have to rest in the sovereignty of the Lord to do what I cannot do for them. I am committed to doing everything I can do, yet I know that, ultimately, their salvation rests in the hands of the Lord.

"For this I toil, struggling with all his energy that he powerfully works within me" (Colossians 1:29).

Aim for a Consistent Trajectory

Families will often undergo changes as they walk through the process of growth and sanctification which can be good and healthy as long as the process is overall going in a consistent direction, leading the family forward in spiritual growth. However, I have seen some homeschool families fall into a pattern of shifting their family standards, beliefs and practices quite suddenly and frequently. Perhaps the parents hear a new homeschool speaker who teaches something new to the family and all of a sudden the parents expect their children to immediately adapt to this new teaching. Then maybe a year or two later the parents change their minds and adopt the philosophies of a different speaker. These massive shifts have sometimes been in areas such as courtship, head coverings for women, media choices, church denominations, styles of worship, styles of dress, educational philosophies, etc. Some of these sudden changes can be hard for the children especially if they are older and do not understand or embrace the convictions for themselves. I believe it is vitally important that if/when parents come to a new belief or conviction that they explain from God's Word the reasons why to their children. Young people will be confused if their parents teach them to apply God's Word in a particular way at one junction and then in a different way at another. Without careful explanation for the why of the change, our children can falsely assume that God's Word changes or that it cannot be trusted. If the parents are constantly jumping from one ditch to another, practicing ever-changing ideas, the children may not be able to keep up with all the fluctuating and may become exasperated. Matt and I have grown and changed in some areas, but overall our journey has been consistently moving further down a path towards greater sanctification. We have not done a lot of throwing major surprises at our children thus shaking their foundation. Our processes have been more gradual over time moving day by day, year by year listening to the voice of the Lord and growing in the process. Our children have understood the overall direction our family has been headed, and small adaptations along the way have not taken them by surprise. Parents need to start out with as Biblical of a vision as they can and seek the Lord to help them continue to work out the process of sanctification through the years. I am not saying that we should not make changes as the Lord points out areas that need change but rather that we should be consciously moving in a consistent direction of seeking holiness instead of flip flopping back and forth between opposing philosophies, cultural trends, and worldviews. There is an underlying consistency of direction needed in order to provide a strong, stable foundation for our young people.

Know Their Hearts

Another area that is vitally important is having a strong heart connection with our children. Do we tell them why we believe what we believe? Are we a safe place for them to come and ask questions? Do they know we will not flip out when they ask us hard questions or admit that their faith is struggling? It has often been said that rules without relationship leads to rebellion. We cannot program our children to follow our rules for godliness like we would program a computer. From my observations, I believe that harsh rules-based parenting without relationship is a recipe for disaster. Is it wrong then to have high standards of godliness for our children? No, we are called to shepherd them, to train them, and to disciple them, but there is a right way and a wrong way of working out that objective. The approach of "Do what I say because I said it" without talking through the reasons for our rules and standards leaves young people angry. Furthermore, when we are explaining our reasons for our standards, we need to back them up with Scripture. Our children need to know that our standards and convictions are not just something their parents came up with to make their lives miserable. In addition, our standards and convictions are not because we are homeschoolers! We are Christians first and then homeschoolers. In adopting standards for our family, we are looking to God's Word as our plumb line and prayerfully seeking Him as to the convictions we hold to as a family. Our standards have nothing to do with homeschooling but everything to do with obedience to God's Word. When our children ask us about a particular family standard, we need to know why we hold to that standard and take them straight to the Word of God for the answer.

Model Humble Repentance

Something that breeds anger in young people is the, "Do what I say, not what I do" approach to parenting. Young people have a keen ability to sniff out hypocrisy. This is scary, because we all fall short of the high standards God calls His people to. He calls us to love, to be patient, to be kind, and on and on the list goes from 1 Corinthians chapter thirteen. Though we may try very hard, none of us lives out all of God's commands perfectly. That is why we need a Savior. This is where the beauty of the gospel comes in. A huge dose of humility is needed in Christian parenting. We need to be willing to go before our children and say something along the lines of, "I was wrong when I was impatient with you guys a minute ago. God's Word tells me I need to be patient, so I just disobeyed God's Word by my impatience. This is why Jesus died for me. I am sorry that I just snapped at you. Will you please forgive me? I love you guys, and I know I just disobeyed the Lord. Will you pray with me now that the Lord will help me to grow in patience?" Then you could pray with your children and end by affirming your love for them and thank them for forgiving you.

As a parent this can be humiliating, but isn't it worth it if it keeps our children's hearts tender towards us and towards the Word of God. We also have the opportunity in these times to model for them what Biblical repentance looks like. As parents we may likely feel that humbling ourselves before our children will make us look weak. The opposite is true, however, in that this kind of humility displays a great strength of character and integrity of heart. This kind of humbling ourselves before our children shows them that we take our sin seriously and shows them how to properly deal with sin. It is such a powerful example for our children. I also believe it increases their trust in us in that they know we care enough for them to humble ourselves in order to obey God and keep relationships healthy with them.

Pray Diligently for Their Repentance

The further I go in this parenting journey, the more I find myself calling out to the Lord to do what I cannot do for my children. I am asking

Him to give them a love for Him, to give them faith, and to give them repentance. I can lead them to the Savior, but I cannot make them love the Savior. Parenting is way too heavy a responsibility for parents to not be prayer warriors for their children. As I think about the coming years, I realize that I will have less and less control over my children. My oldest is a few years away from adulthood, and the day is coming when I will not have a say in every decision she makes. As my children are growing older I sense all the more the important part prayer should play in the parenting journey. We parents must be faithful and diligent to do all that we can, while praying for the Spirit of God to lead and guide our young people to love Him with all their hearts, souls, and minds.

Pray in Faith

"And without faith it is impossible to please him, for whoever would draw near to God must believe that he exists and that he rewards those who seek him" (Hebrews 11:6).

This is a verse my mother used to remind me of when I was a young lady. This verse tells us that we cannot please God if we are faithless. Since we know that God is pleased with our faith, we need to be intentional about practicing faith in our parenting. It is also true that we cannot obtain faith on our own; even faith itself is a gift of God. "For by grace you have been saved through faith. And this is not your own doing; it is the gift of God" (Ephesians 2:8). We can be encouraged that God often works generationally. In the Abrahamic covenant He told Abraham, "And I will establish my covenant between me and you and your offspring after you throughout their generations for an everlasting covenant, to be God to you and to your offspring after you" (Genesis 1:7). We should pray that the Lord will help us to be faithful parents, trusting in Him for the salvation and sanctification of our children. It is true that we cannot save our children and that there are no guarantees in parenting, but when we think about the goodness of the Lord, how faithful He is, and how He often works generationally in Christian families, we can put our trust and hope in Christ alone. Let us pray for increased faith, because "without faith it is impossible to please Him."

Chapter 5
Homeschooling is a Powerful Tool
but Not the Savior

As I have already mentioned I have witnessed some tragic outcomes with some kids growing up in well-meaning homeschooling families. I have been exposed to some unfortunate situations where homeschool graduates have rebelled, some cases where they have lost relationship with their parents, and some situations where there isn't full rebellion but great bitterness. Unfortunately, there are also homeschooled graduates who have fully apostatized from the Christian faith they were brought up in. Sometimes the parents are greatly to blame for provoking their young people to wrath, but in other cases the fault lies with the sons and daughters who have chosen to break the fifth commandment to honor their parents.

"Honor your father and your mother, that your days may be long in the land that the Lord your God is giving you" (Exodus 20:12).

When God gave Moses the Ten Commandments, the fifth commandment was to honor father and mother, that your days may be long. Ephesians 6:2 tells us that it is actually "the first commandment with a promise."

I have been grieved to read so many stories from homeschooled graduates who are railing about how their parents brought them up, about how homeschooling ruined their lives, and about how they find Biblical principles to be destructive. There is definitely a spectrum to some of these stories. Some of these graduates appreciate some things about their upbringing and still honor God to some degree. Others are full-blown apostates, embracing all manner of sin the Bible calls wickedness.

I am not taking lightly the fact that there have been some cases of abuse within some homeschool families. Some parents have been too harsh and enforced rules in anger. Some families have gone to crazy, unbalanced extremes and embittered their children, and some parents have employed abusive measures in discipline. In many of these stories I have seen a common thread of parents being dictatorial rather than lovingly discipling the hearts of their young people. These are ugly realities, and I feel for anyone who grew up in such a situation.

What I am really referring to here, however, are those homes where fathers and mothers tried with all of their hearts to raise a family that would love and honor God. No parent is perfect, and I think it takes becoming a parent yourself to realize how hard it is to even know what to do sometimes. I am grieved by those homeschool graduates I see who have apostatized from the Christian faith they were raised in and condone their sin by blaming their parents for the way they were raised. I truly believe that most parents who made the sacrifice to homeschool their children did it out of a desire to bless and not hurt their children.

It is always easy to shift blame, and it concerns me to see the homeschool graduates today who choose to blame their parents for all the things they think went wrong in their lives. They fail to realize that, had they grown up in a public school, there might be a whole different set of problems that they would also be tempted to blame someone for. Sometimes this discontent stems from young people not realizing that we really do not deserve anything good in life. We are born sinners, and any good that comes to us is by the grace of God and is undeserved. Our current culture has an entitlement mentality and, often, even Christian, homeschooled young people grow up thinking they are owed everything they want in life. If this is their mentality, is there any wonder that there are a lot of disgruntled feelings, malcontent, and bitterness? I have also heard adults who grew up in public school state that their parents were not involved in their lives and that they wished their parents had discipled them. It would be helpful for us all to realize that the Lord desires to use whatever our growing up experience was to shape and mold us to be and do what He has ordained for our lives. He chooses to use both good and bad to work His plan in and through our lives. The Bible tells us that we are born to trouble (Job 5:7) and that we will face many trials.

"Strengthening the souls of the disciples, encouraging them to continue in the faith, and saying that through many tribulations we must enter the kingdom of God" (Acts 14:22).

I think it is important that even little children are taught to have grateful hearts and not to expect everything to go their way. Unfortunately, it is man's natural tendency to be selfish and to blame others. This is what we see in the story of Adam and Eve where Adam blamed Eve, and Eve blamed the serpent. Again, it is important to remember the fifth commandment of honoring parents.

As a mama raising seven children, seeing stories of disgruntled young adults who grew up in Christian homeschools has greatly disturbed me and caused me to ask a lot of questions. I have been taking a hard look at what I have known of different kinds of Christian and homeschool families and have tried to observe various outcomes. I have been thinking hard about what the Bible says about the heart of a child and about discipleship, as I try to mentally sort out the confusion. I think, growing up, that I had more of a formula mentality that if you raise your children a certain way and homeschool them, they should turn out right. As I have grown older, I have come to understand that we cannot lean on homeschooling as the Savior or the magic formula that will give us a godly outcome. Ultimately it is the work of the Holy Spirit alone that will bring spiritual life to our children. As parents we must be faithful to employ the tools the Lord has given us, and I firmly believe homeschooling can be a powerful tool, but we must put our faith in the Lord to save our children and not in our methods.

In light of how many young people from Christian upbringings have rejected the faith, we might ask ourselves if it is worth the work and dedication of trying so hard with our families. Is it worth the blood, sweat, and tears I endure to homeschool my children? Honestly, I have asked myself that question a fair number of times. It is disheartening to see young adults from Christian homeschool families reject the truth their parents taught and run as far to the enticements of the world as they can. One thing to remember is that, just because we see a fair amount of this kind of apostasy, this does not indicate that homeschooling is the problem. Rebellion against God and parental authority is wide spread amongst public school, private school, and homeschool families. We are living in an age of rebellion, and this trickles into the homeschool community as well. It is only by God's grace that any of our families can rise above the cultural norms and live lives that reflect the beauty and purity of Christ. Just as it is easy to find homeschool graduates who are bitter about their upbringing and are in process of throwing off every value their parents ever taught them, it is even easier to find those who appreciate the sacrifices their parents made to homeschool them. A recent study called the Gen2 Survey took an analytical look at Millennials who grew up in Christian homes. The principal researcher in this survey was Dr. Brian Ray from The National Home Education Research Institute. Here he explains what the thrust of the survey was about:

> The study focuses on the church life of minors, family relationships growing up, denominational affiliations of the family, cultural and societal influences in children's lives, type of schooling/education children received (whether public schooling/state schooling, private secular schooling, private Christian schooling, or homeschooling) and

the associations of these variables with Christian beliefs, behaviors, and practices in adulthood. [6]

According to www.generationswithvision.com, here is a sampling of some of the survey results.

82% of young people who have been homeschooled plan to use homeschooling for at least part of their children's education.

87% of Millennials who were homeschooled now have strong Christian beliefs.

85% of those surveyed said they were glad they were homeschooled.

This is encouraging! One interesting fact about the survey is that it was not analyzing education alone but other vital factors such as relationship with parents, church affiliation, media exposure, discipline and discipleship within the home, etc. There are many interesting results that can be analyzed online. Overall it is an encouraging survey when you see that most homeschool graduates are quite content with their upbringing and go on to make valuable contributions to society. Statistically, those who are well-adjusted adults today grew up in strong Christian homes with loving parents who disciplined and discipled them. They also attended churches that taught sound doctrine. [7]

Lately I have had the privilege of meeting two happy and content homeschool grads. One was a young lady who checked me into my hotel one night. The hotel staff asked what I was in town for, and when I told them that I was attending a homeschool convention, the young lady told me that she had been homeschooled and thought it had been a good experience for her. Similarly, I recently met a young man who checked me out at an office supply store. When I asked him if the store offered a homeschool teacher's discount, he explained that he had been homeschooled up through middle school. He said that for high school he went to public school, but that it was not a good experience. Since he was so advanced academically, he was able to accelerate his education and graduate early. This was his way of getting out of public high school, which he found to be undesirable after his years of homeschooling. He said that he believes he will homeschool his own children someday. I explained to him that I was encouraged to hear his story in light of some stories of disgruntled homeschool graduates who feel like they missed something in not going to public high school. His words to me were, "They have not missed anything." I was encouraged to talk to both of these young adults who had been homeschooled and to hear them both say that homeschooling had been a positive experience for them.

I have thought through some things I think my parents got right in their approach in raising me. The first thing is that they pointed me to Jesus from my earliest days. I always knew that following the ways of the Lord was the most important thing in life. In fact, I already had a firm foundation in the Lord before my parents ever decided to homeschool me. Homeschooling was just an extension of the discipleship they began with me from my infancy. My parents never had things easy. They struggled and labored in ministry for all of my growing up years. Ministry was never easy and finances were usually tight. I saw that furthering God's Kingdom and faithfully serving Him was what they valued and prioritized above earthly things. They were not caught up in trying to keep up with the Joneses or worldly pursuits.

Also, my parents taught me that the Lord always saw me at all times, even when they were not around. Do you remember the old children's song, "Oh be careful little eyes what you see … Oh be careful little mouth what you say … Oh be careful little feet where you go … for the Father up above is looking down in love so be careful little eyes what you see"? As a child I was made very aware of the fact that Jesus saw everything I did and, ultimately, I was accountable to Him. I think knowing that Jesus always knew and saw my behaviors motivated me to want to make the right decisions, even when my parents were not around. I did not have the mentality of getting away with something. I remember a couple times when I was away from home and had a question about if I should do something or not. In those instances, I called home and asked what my parents thought. I believe it was my understanding that I was ultimately accountable to the Lord that motivated me to want to do right. If I was only accountable to my parents, I could have gotten away with things and avoided consequences. However, when a young person understands that they might get away with something from parents but not with God, that puts the pressure on to walk in obedience.

I was also taught that my actions had consequences. My parents believed in lovingly disciplining me when I disobeyed. They were careful to make sure we talked through what my offense had been and to make sure I understood that I had offended God by my sin. After my consequence was given, they would help me to pray and ask the Lord for forgiveness and they would make sure I was reassured of their love. There was nothing abusive about that kind of loving discipline. On the contrary, that kind of correction and discipleship gives a child security. The child knows his parents are putting safe and loving boundaries around him for his own protection.

Based upon my own homeschool experience, and based upon many others I have observed, I know that homeschooling can turn out very good or very bad. Personally, I feel the Lord really used it in my life to develop character and a heart for His Kingdom purposes. I see it as a powerful tool when used in a Biblical way. I do not, however, put my hope and faith in homeschooling to save my children. I know it is impossible for me to homeschool effectively apart from the grace of God and that it is only His power working in the lives of my children that will produce any godliness in their lives. I am thankful that I have the freedom to homeschool and that this is a tool the Lord has given me to disciple my children by. It is, however, only a tool. The Lord is the Master Builder, and all my faith and trust must be in Him for the salvation and the sanctification of my children. I know that what must transpire for my children to be saved is for the Lord to give them saving faith and repentance of their sins. There is a work of regeneration that only the Lord can work in their hearts. This is my greatest prayer for my children, that they will know and love the Lord Jesus and experience new life in Him.

Chapter 6
Homeschooling Hot Topics

Modesty

Although modesty has often been a hot topic within more conservative sects of homeschool culture, I believe modesty is a Christian virtue, not a homeschool issue. I remember many years back when we were attending a large Southern Baptist church, and I told a lady there that we were homeschooling our children. Her comment to me was, "Just don't start wearing jumpers." If I take a walk down memory lane, I recall that I had many jumpers in my teen years. They were very popular back then and I enjoyed them. There have been many jokes about the homeschool jumper, because many homeschool moms and daughters chose to wear them during the '90's. They were a modest option and looked feminine. Styles have changed, but I would not be surprised if one day jumpers resurface on the fashion scene, as usually what goes around comes around. I know that jumpers have not been the rage for a long time now but jumpers or no jumpers, I believe the virtue of God-honoring modesty is important.

"Likewise also that women should adorn themselves in respectable apparel, with modesty and self-control" (1 Timothy 2:9).

The book *Modesty: More Than a Change of Clothes* by Martha Peace and Kent Keller defines modesty as "an inner attitude of the heart motivated by a love for God that seeks His glory through purity and humility; it often reveals itself in words, actions, expressions, and clothes." [8]

I have sometimes heard the slogan, "Modest is Hottest." I am not a real fan of that statement, because as Christian women we DO NOT need to try to look hot for anyone but our husbands. We need to adorn the gospel with beauty, grace and dignity, but this "Hot Mama" mentality that I have noticed in Christian circles is concerning. I remember being in the bridesmaid's dressing room years ago and hearing one of the bridesmaids talking about how "good" her chest looked in a particular shirt the night before. Here she was in a Christian wedding, in a Christian church, amongst Christian women, talking about things that she should feel shame to be talking about. The sad thing is that no one seemed to flinch at all. What she said was totally received as normal conversation. This reminds me of a verse that states the backwards nature of glorying in our shame. It is a defining mark of our current culture but it is shameful.

"Their end is destruction, their god is their belly, and their glory is in their shame, with minds set on earthly things" (Philippians 3:19).

In contemplating these settings where Christian women are talking crudely, we see how anti-biblical it is when we look at Ephesians 5:3. I like the way the NIV puts it:

"But among you there must *not be even a hint of sexual immorality*, or of any kind of impurity, or of greed, because these are improper for God's holy people" (Ephesians 5:3, emphasis added).

You see, God calls His "holy people" to a different standard than the lost world around us. In Ephesians 4:1 Paul tell us:

"I therefore, a prisoner for the Lord, urge you to walk in a manner worthy of the calling to which you have been called" (Ephesians 4:1).

As daughters of the King of kings it would be fitting for us to ask ourselves if our speech and dress is of a manner worthy of our calling. We are to be the sweet aroma of Christ to those around us. Our purity and modesty should be as a pleasant perfume, drawing people to want to know more about Jesus.

If you have questions about what is appropriate, why not ask your husband whether this makes you look "hot" or "lovely and feminine." Sometimes, in trying to judge the standards we should hold for our own daughters, I will go to my husband and ask, "Does this cause an issue for a man?" He will tell me what he thinks is over the top unacceptable and what could be a distraction. He has shared with me that, when thinking about what our daughters should wear, he will think about what kinds of things he would find himself turning his eyes away from when he is in public. For example, once he was in the room with a teenage girl who was wearing the popular baggy-legged sport shorts. When she sat on the floor you could see straight up her legs. Because he is in the practice of guarding his eyes, he chose to walk out of the room. In conversations about our daughters, he thinks of things like that and, if he knows a certain kind of clothing is something he needs to turn his eyes away from, then he knows he certainly does not want his daughters dressing in like manner. This is a countercultural decision because everywhere you go girls are wearing these short, baggy sport shorts with t-shirts and a messy bun. It is the popular fad, but is it modest? If a girl's whole leg is exposed, is that modest? Another thing that has been so shocking to me is that not only will girls wear these revealing shorts, but I often see them sitting in very immodest positions while wearing them. It befuddles me, because I was trained to sit modestly as far back as I can remember. I am amazed that the things I am talking about here do not seem to even be on the radar of so many girls and women. I believe this is partly due to a culture that has completely thrown issues of modesty, propriety, decency, and lady likeness to the wind. Sadly, most girls are never taught anything about the virtue of modesty.

It is not my desire to create a dress code that all Christian women should follow. My desire goes deeper than that. It is to stir up in all of us a desire to look and care deeply about modesty. Modesty is first a heart issue before it is an external issue.

Matthew 15:18 says, "But what comes out of the mouth proceeds from the heart, and this defiles a person."

This verse could be changed to say, "But the clothing choices a lady makes proceeds from the heart, and this defiles a person."

"For out of the heart come evil thoughts, murder, adultery, sexual immorality, theft, false witness, slander" (Matthew 15:19).

If our external appearance is an indication of our heart motives then we should start with asking the Lord to purify our hearts of any impure or selfish motives. We can ask ourselves, "What are my motives in wanting to wear this outfit?" We can also consider if our clothing choices bring overdue attention to our bodies or if they to draw people to our countenance. The following questions help bring a Biblical perspective.

- Am I seeking to bring glory to my Creator through this outfit or to draw attention to myself?
- Am I showing off skin, curves, or body parts in a way that would incite lust in a man (Matthew 5:28)?
- Are my undergarments appropriately hidden in this garment?
- Am I trying to outdo my friends by my clothing?
- Am I trying to identify with a group of people that are not walking in obedience to Christ?
- Is my outfit exemplifying the order and beauty of my Creator or displaying messiness, confusion, and disarray?

Our Clothes Truly Say a LOT About Our Character

I am not at all advocating that we look frumpy or find clothing from decades past and look as unstylish as possible. No, instead I believe it is fitting, right and good for a lady to honor her Lord and her husband by looking well put together. We can do this by looking attractive, sweet, and distinctly feminine. If I go around looking like a worn out dish rag, I am not reflecting well upon my husband. This can look like he is not taking proper care of me. I am also not making the gospel attractive to a lost world. God's women can look very beautiful, distinctly feminine, and modest without following the dark and sensuous fashions of our day.

Many Forms of Modesty

As stated above I believe modesty begins in the heart and works its way out toward the outward manifestations. There are more issues to consider here than just our clothing. Clothing is just one piece of the puzzle. Here are some other things to think about.

- Body language (Am I flailing my body around in constant motion to be noticed?)
- Tone of voice (Am I purposely sounding seductive, haughty, or overly loud?)
- Hair (Am I sporting outlandish hairstyles to draw attention to myself?)
- Jewelry (Am I being excessively gaudy in my jewelry so that people are distracted by all the jingling and jangling? One caveat here is that my children tell me they know I'm coming when they hear the jingle of my charm bracelet approaching. I am not talking about that so much as a lady who has excessive amounts of jewelry or really outlandish accessories.)
- Makeup (Am I so pasted up that I am drawing undue attention to myself or identifying myself with a group that is not honoring to Christ? For example, am I wearing really dark makeup that has an evil/dark flare, such as people dabbling in the occult might wear? Am I trying to identify with the darkness of the vampire rage? Am I done up in a way that reflects a loose woman?)
- Overly domineering (Am I lording it over everyone else all the time?)
- Overly talkative (Do I know how to be quiet and give others the chance to speak? Do I hog every conversation with my own long-winded stories so that others are left out or do not have a chance to talk? Do I make every conversation about myself?)

"When words are many, transgression is not lacking, but whoever restrains his lips is prudent" (Proverbs 10:19).

We can easily think we are just talkative, but maybe we should ask ourselves if we have a tendency to take over conversations and why. If we are always making ourselves the center of every conversation or have to make comments about everything, then maybe we are actually trying to put the spotlight on ourselves, which does not indicate a modest heart. That might be an area where we should acknowledge this new awareness to the Lord and ask Him to grant us greater humility and a desire to be a better listener to others.

"Know this, my beloved brothers: let every person be quick to hear, slow to speak, slow to anger" (James 1:19).

Am I using any of the above methods or others to draw attention to myself in a crowd? Let's ask the Lord to give us a meek and quiet spirit that honors Him. Instead of trying to make much of ourselves, let's seek to make much of Christ.

"Do not let your adorning be external—the braiding of hair and the putting on of gold jewelry, or the clothing you wear—but let your adorning be the hidden person of the heart with the imperishable beauty of a gentle and quiet spirit, which in God's sight is very precious" (1 Peter 3:3-4).

Sadly, I have noticed an increasing number of internet articles coming out that are written as a case against modesty. One argument used is that men are responsible for their own thoughts so a woman should not be inhibited from wearing whatever she wants to wear. Yes, I agree that ultimately a man is responsible for his thoughts, but because men are wired to be sexually excited by sight, I think it is important for girls and ladies not to tempt them by dressing provocatively. Just as Paul warned the Corinthians to not eat meat if it would make their brother to stumble, I think an appropriate application could certainly be to not wear clothing that is revealing, sexually enticing, overly form fitting, and suggestive.

"Therefore, if food makes my brother stumble, I will never eat meat, lest I make my brother stumble" (I Corinthians 8:13).

Another thing I hear people say is that the Bible does not specify what is modest or give measurements for our clothing coverage. I understand what they are saying, but the Bible does give overarching principles that can be applied in this area of modesty. We know we are not to tempt others or be a stumbling block, we know that we are to have a humble heart that makes much of Christ and less of ourselves, and we know that we are ambassadors for Christ. We are to represent Him well when we go out and about. I believe it is fitting for daughters of the King of kings to dress in a well-ordered way that communicates purpose, radiance, love, and Christ likeness. The current fashion trend is towards messiness, chaos, and purposelessness. Personally

I feel like an overly grungy, messy look does not communicate the hope and life that we have through our Savior Jesus Christ. Our goal should be to draw others close to Him when they see us. This matter is worth praying over and being attentive to. Will we just follow the fashion trends or seek the Lord on how we can most effectively represent Him when we are around others. I believe we can radiantly reflect Him in beautiful, tasteful, stylish, and modest ways. Let us remember that modesty starts in the heart and works its way outward. It is possible to be fully clothed and not be modest because the heart is haughty. Conversely, it is also possible to have some good heart intentions and yet be immodest because of a lack of covering up externally. Modesty is a sticky issue because the Bible does not give us a clearly defined check list. The principles are there, however, for the woman who wants to honor her Lord both in the heart and by covering up the temple in which He dwells. Since modesty is both an inward and outward issue, it is one that God's women will need to continually give attention to and search their hearts while praying for humility and wisdom.

Family Size

I was a baby doll girl all the way. As a girl, I took my baby dolls very seriously. To me it was as if I were a real mommy, and I made them as real as I could in my imagination. I remember one Sunday, dressing up one of my dolls and taking it to church with me. When we got out of our vehicle my dad told me the doll had to stay in the car. I was so upset that I could not take my doll in and mother her through the service. I would carry my very real looking baby doll through the store and get comments from people that they thought I had a real baby in my arms. As I grew older I loved holding babies, babysitting, and working with children. Throughout my growing up and young adult years I had a growing dream of being a wife and mama one day. I had friends who came from large families, and I often thought I would like to have a large family. I had always wanted my parents to have more children, but they only had my brother and me. I looked forward to the day when I could have my own babies and be the happy mother of children. I remember when I was single going to a few young adult get togethers where there would be "get to know you" questions. When I was asked what I wanted to do in life my answer would be that I wanted to be a wife and mother. Looking back now I think that answer probably scared a lot of young men away!

Before Matt and I married we talked of having many children together. The Lord has blessed us with our hearts' desire in giving us the seven blessings we have. Many who have observed us through the years might assume we are in the full quiver camp, as they have watched us have one baby after another. We have indeed been very open to children. We have had a heart for children and have viewed them as blessings from the Lord to be sure. To be honest, though, we have not been fully of the full quiver mindset. The Bible definitely teaches that children are a blessing:

"Behold, children are a heritage from the LORD, the fruit of the womb a reward. Like arrows in the hand of a warrior are the children of one's youth. Blessed is the man who fills his quiver with them! He shall not be put to shame when he speaks with his enemies in the gate" (Psalm 127:3-5).

We believe that children are a blessing with all of our hearts, and yet we have also felt that there are times to prayerfully use wisdom in this area, especially in the area of health issues. Some in the full quiver camp would say that God is sovereign over the womb and that, since He opens and closes the womb, it is wrong to ever try to prevent pregnancy in any way. Although I deeply respect the heart and tremendous faith these people have, Matt and I have been okay with natural family planning at times while always praying for the Lord's will for our family size. We have been completely opposed to any kind of birth control that could be abortive in any way, including pills that could potentially cause a conceived baby to die. In between babies we have prayed about whether the Lord would desire us to have more children. What I mean by this is that we have acknowledged that we want to have the children the Lord wants for us and not decide for ourselves how many we want or think we should have. The posture of our hearts has been for children and not against them, even when we have tried to prevent a pregnancy naturally at times. For us personally, there have been different reasons why at times we tried to put a bit of space between our children. Those things include health issues, Matt traveling a lot while I was left alone with lots of little people, a season when he was working full time and going to school, healing after a miscarriage, etc. Even though we did put some space between some of our pregnancies, there were times when God was sovereign even over our family planning. There have been some pregnancies that we are not quite sure what happened. Our last baby was a complete surprise, because at the time we were really trying not to get pregnant. I was having a lot of physical pain from the previous six pregnancies, and I was in the process of trying to get medical help to figure out what we could do about my chronic pain. The Lord had another plan and gave us Ella Ruth, and we are so glad that He did. As I look back upon our journey I feel okay with how we have handled this. I know our hearts have been to seek the Lord's will for our family and that we have had open hearts and arms to children. I guess that is obvious since we have seven blessings. One thing that has played into our decisions in this area is that my pregnancies have been full of pain that has been almost crippling at times. Between the pregnancies I used to bounce back and be okay, but as I got older I began having lasting chronic pain, even between pregnancies. For years my pregnancies have been times where I had great difficulty taking care of the needs of my family and often had to be off my feet due to pain. Walking has been painful and Matt has had to work overtime to take care of a large family when I could hardly function. The pain has turned into a chronic pain that I still deal with. I am trying to figure it out and praying for complete healing.

Birth Stories

My journey into motherhood began in March of 2001 when I had our first daughter, Lauren, in the middle of the night. She is my only baby who came on her own without an induction. My water broke as we were going to bed one night, and Matt rushed me out the door to the hospital where we met our first of seven children.

Our first son was born in March two years later. When I had an ultrasound and found out our second baby was going to be a boy, I really struggled wondering if I could be a good mama to a boy. I had always been such a girly girl, and I wasn't sure what I would do with trucks, balls, and action figures. One day I was doing my Bible study and I came across this verse:

"Now to him who is able to do far more abundantly than all that we ask or think, according to the power at work within us, to him be glory in the church and in Christ Jesus throughout all generations, forever and ever. Amen" (Ephesians 3:20-21).

When I read the words of those verses the application to my heart was that I could trust the Lord. I was encouraged that the Lord's plans are better than anything I could imagine and that this little boy was going to be more special than I could fathom. Thirteen years later I can testify that this has proven true. My Gabriel has been a sweet delight to my heart, and I figured out how to mother a little boy quickly. Oh, it was so much fun dressing him in little suits, suspenders, and ties that made him look like a grown man. He has always been so sweet to me, and I am thankful to have the blessing of mothering girls and boys. The Lord's plan is perfect.

In 2004 we experienced the loss of a baby due to miscarriage. That was a heart-wrenching experience and left me longing to hold another baby. I grieved for months for the baby that should have been born around Christmas of that year. When Christmas came I was having a rough time with it but something special happened. We had the out-of-the-ordinary experience of having a snowfall on Christmas Eve. Snow is not very common where we live in Texas so when it does snow it is a pretty big deal. That Christmas Eve, as I looked out at the beauty of everything being covered in white snow, I felt like the beautiful snow was a fresh covering over what had been a hard year in many ways. It felt encouraging to my heart like a beautiful gift for our Christmas Eve and a fresh clean start to the year to come.

Annagrace joined our family in October of 2006. I had prayed for her to arrive safely after losing the previous baby. I was concerned about having another miscarriage, but the Lord carried us through that pregnancy and blessed us with our second daughter. Delivering her and holding a baby again was a very sweet time. She was a healing balm to my heart.

Next in line was Abbie Joy in November of 2008. The day of her ultrasound when I found out she was a girl, Matt was out of the country on a business trip. He was also very sick with some kind of a bug. I called him to tell him that we were having another little girl, and he could not talk long. He was too sick to even stay on the phone. After the ultrasound I went by Ross and picked out matching dresses for Lauren, Annagrace, and Abbie Joy to wear after she was born. I was so excited to be able to do matching dresses for three little girls!

Lilly Faith came in July of 2010. She and Abbie Joy are our closest in age and have been a sweet twosome their whole lives. They have had so much fun playing dolls and doing crafts together. Lauren was old enough by this time to really take Lilly Faith under her wing and develop a sweet relationship with her baby sister.

Our second son was born in August of 2003. The interesting thing is that, for all of my pregnancies between Gabriel and Nathaniel, Gabriel always said he wanted another sister. He said he liked the special place of being the only boy. This time, however, the Lord changed his heart. When I was pregnant with Nathaniel, Gabriel started praying that the Lord would send him a brother. The day that we found out that we were expecting a baby boy was very special. We knew how excited Gabriel would be and we were thrilled to tell him that the Lord had answered his prayers. We got a big box and filled it with blue balloons and blue candy. We gathered all the children on the front yard at my parents' house and Matt opened the box and let everyone see the big reveal. Great excitement was in the air!

Lastly, we welcomed Ella Ruth into our home in August of 2015. Her birth was a traumatic experience and my first cesarean, leaving me struggling for my life and hospitalized for eighteen days. The short of it is I developed a severe case of c-diff, a bacterial, intestinal super bug, due to all the antibiotics given during the cesarean. The antibiotics wiped out all my good gut flora, and when I was somehow exposed to the c-diff bacteria, my body could not fight it off. We are so grateful the Lord gave us Ella Ruth, and we cherish this sweet daughter who will most likely be our last.

Ella Ruth's story is explained in greater detail later in this book, but the result of that whole ordeal is that my doctors strongly advised against future pregnancies. Because the cesarean I had was as severe as it was, my OB, who has delivered all my babies, said she could never let me deliver vaginally again and that another pregnancy would be very high risk. She said that if I were to ever have another baby it would have to be by cesarean. That was before I contracted c-diff and came close to death's door. In the middle of that whole ordeal, she said that she was done with my womb. The problem with another cesarean is that I could end up with c-diff all over again due to the antibiotics I would have to be given. The rate of c-diff relapse is very high in patients who survive it. She told my husband after surgery that she had saved my uterus, but that it was far from whole due to the removal of a large fibroid and both horizontal and vertical cuts required to take the baby. The whole thing I went through could easily be repeated if I were on heavy antibiotics and all the good gut bacteria wiped out as it was last time. My GI doctor said that my case of c-diff may be the worst he has ever seen. Due to what I have already been through and my age, another pregnancy and cesarean could be threatening to my life. (Please read my chapter "Homeschooling When Life Gets Hard" for a greater understanding of this story.)

After I returned home from eighteen days in the hospital, Matt and I began having serious conversations about him having a vasectomy in order to protect my life. The doctor that pulled me out of the c-diff crisis said I should never have another baby due to the physical state Ella Ruth's pregnancy left me in. Not only had c-diff decimated my colon, but my immune system was likened to an HIV patient. My GI doctor said that the pregnancy had been like a cancer in my body, completely depleting my body and leaving me very sick. In the midst of the c-diff crisis my body began breaking down on multiple levels, requiring multiple blood transfusions, causing tachycardia, and much more. When I asked my GI doctor in the hospital about having another baby he told me, "I'm telling you, don't do it." That choked me up and was hard to hear. After getting home and slowly recovering, we were faced with the decision about what to do. As we talked I cried and cried and am still crying. I did not want to end this precious season of having babies and growing our family. I tried to think of any way possible we could circumvent the problem and have another baby without risking my life. As I talked to Matt he continued to remind me that he loves me, that a pregnancy would be very dangerous, and that he did not want to be left to raise our family without me. After much talking, praying, and tears I finally agreed to follow his leadership and go forward with the surgery. This was so brutally hard for me on an emotional level, especially on the heels of such a physical battle that I was still working to regain strength from. It all felt so overwhelming to be feeling such suffering and loss both physically and emotionally.

I had a second follow up visit with my GI doctor the day before Matt's surgery. I was hoping he would see that I was doing better and say that there was some chance another pregnancy would be alright. To my surprise he brought the matter up before I even had a chance to ask him about it. Again he confirmed that he felt another pregnancy would be very risky for me at my age based upon the condition he found me in after the last pregnancy. He said he could not guarantee that I would end up with c-diff again, but that he felt it was a strong chance that I would have some kind of major crisis after the strain of another pregnancy. Well, that was the confirmation we needed to follow through with Matt's surgery the next day, but it was a very sad time, and my heart continues to grieve.

The next day Matt, Ella Ruth, and I left for his outpatient surgery. I needed to go with him to drive him back. I cried and wanted to have him turn around and go back home. I did not want to be doing this, and yet we had talked and prayed intensely, and this is the decision we had come to. Ultimately, I felt I needed to follow my husband's leadership in this. I did not want it, but I could rest in knowing this is what Matt felt he needed to do to protect me and to spare his children from losing their mama. Of course, I did not want them to lose their mama either which is one huge reason I agreed to it. As we sat in the waiting room, I held it together until he was called back. Then I quickly pushed the stroller back to the truck where I sat and cried. In an emotional moment I started to text Matt and ask him to run out but I erased it. Our decision had been made and I was following my husband in this. When he came out and said it was done, I had a sense of, "What have we done?" Matt and I had been having babies together for all of our marriage, and I felt like growing our family together had been such a huge part of what the Lord had called us to as a couple. Matt used to tell me I was good at having babies, and he has told me so many times what beautiful babies we have. When you spend fifteen years of your life carrying babies, nursing babies, and raising a growing family, it is an abrupt change when you know this beautiful season has ended. I am still working through this emotionally, and yet I feel so grateful that the Lord spared my life and that He gave us seven wonderful children. We have so very much to praise Him for and to be grateful for. I wish that my pregnancies had not given me so much pain and that I had not had this health crisis after Ella Ruth. I wish I was ten years younger and could have a lot more babies, but this is a reality I cannot change. Here, I must rest in gratefulness for all the Lord has given and trust Him to carry me through the changing seasons. I must say, "Thy will be done." If I could go back to August 27, 2015 and change the outcome of Ella Ruth's birth, I would do it in a heartbeat. If I could have the joy of birthing one more baby and experiencing that precious joy all over again I would. Oh, I would run back and do it all over again a thousand times over. I know that, barring a miracle, we are most likely done having children, but I believe God is sovereign, even over surgical measures. If He were to choose Matt to be one of the very few men whose vasectomy becomes ineffective, I would rejoice in another pregnancy and would trust Him to take care of me. Humanly speaking, we have taken measures to try to spare my life, and yet I still pray the Lord's will be done. If I were to become pregnant after a vasectomy I, like Mary, would say, "Behold, I am the servant of the Lord; let it be to me according to your word" (Luke 1:38). Children are truly a gift from the Lord, and the blessing of a new baby is a joy like no other. I look ahead five years down the road to a time when we will no longer have little people running around our home, and I know that I will greatly miss their cute chubby fingers and toes and adorable little antics. I am going to be so excited when we are blessed with grandchildren!

Convictions about family size is a decision a couple must make before the Lord. Some will be convicted to let the Lord give as many as He will, and He gives the grace and all that is needed for that. I have a huge respect for that position. Like us, some families will have a huge openness to children and yet may put some space here and there and pray about the Lord's will between children. I do have a firm conviction against any kind of birth control that could be abortive in nature, and I think people should really research this matter and not just go on what a doctor says or the pills doctors are so eager to pass out. I would encourage mamas and daddies to do the medical research and not do anything that is questionable. Wherever you may fall on your convictions about family size, I would encourage you to not ask, "How many children do I want to have?" I think the question we all need to ask is, "Lord, how many children do you want us to have and how may we raise them for your glory?"

Furthermore, I encourage families to realize how quickly the child bearing years will fly by. It is such a privilege to have the health and ability to bring babies into this world, and that blessing will not always be here. Our bodies wear out and sometimes health crises occur. Certainly it is not enough to just have the children; that is the easy part compared to the lifetime investment of discipling them. I encourage ladies not to listen to what the world says about how children are a burden but to meditate upon what the Scripture says. The Bible says that they are a blessing and a gift. So many in our culture value material things and freedom from responsibility over the blessing of children. All material blessings and worldly pleasures wear out, but children born in one's youth are gifts for eternity.

I have also seen the blessing it has been for my older children to have younger siblings. They have received a wealth of experience in loving and caring for younger siblings. Their siblings have brought so much joy and laughter to them, and they have special bonds with them that are priceless. Even though large family dynamics can be challenging and exhausting it is so worth it, and I would not change it except to throw more little blessings in the mix if I could.

Courtship

Courtship was a big buzz word in homeschool circles back when I was a teenager in the nineties. I still hear people talking about following principles of courtship today, but the concept has lost some of its popularity. Joshua Harris' book *I Kissed Dating Goodbye* hugely spread the popularity of the idea of courtship versus dating. Actually several books by different authors have been written on the issue of courtship, and the term means different things to different people. In a nutshell, I would say it has to do with rejecting the worldly pattern or cycle of entering a romantic relationship with someone, growing tired of that person, breaking up, and moving on to selfishly have your emotional and/or physical needs met through someone new and more exciting and then repeating that cycle over and over. What I have just described is the pattern that our culture calls dating, and I do believe there is a better way. When people talk about courtship they are usually talking about a more purposeful process of entering an intentional relationship with the goal of seeking the Lord about a potential future marriage. Certainly God moves differently in different relationships, and not every courtship will look just the same. There are, however, some overall principles of wisdom that are Biblical and can serve as an aid in pursuing a godly relationship leading to marriage.

In the last couple of years the internet has been overcome with essays people have written on the topic of courtship vs. dating. Many of these articles do not paint courtship in a positive light at all. In my personal experience I was very much courtship minded in that I never dated until I dated Matt, who later became my husband. That is because my mom instilled in me the idea of saving myself in every way possible for the man I would marry. She had many talks with me about what I should be looking for in a husband. I firmly believed that I should not go out with guys "just for the fun of it." I did not want to date to break up and date another guy and repeat that process over and over. I felt that would be practice for divorce. I knew some basic qualities I needed to see in a guy before I would consider a date with him. I was not interested in casual dating that I felt could lead me to an emotional attachment with a young man who might not have the character qualities I was looking for. I wanted to first know that I saw certain character qualities in a young man's life and that I would consider him marriage potential before going out on a date. I felt my own emotions could get attached far too easily, and I could end up loving someone who did not have the godly qualities I knew I wanted in a spouse. Another thing that was important to me was to have my parents' approval over any relationship I might enter into. I valued their wisdom and knew this was an area I needed to receive wise counsel in.

One interesting opportunity I had as a young lady was speaking on a panel during an "I Kissed Dating Goodbye" conference. Joshua Harris recently began recanting some of what he wrote in that book, and so it is a bit uncertain where he stands on the issue at the present time. I would say that I am thankful that I "kissed dating goodbye" until it was time for me to pursue a marriage relationship. It spared me heartache and mistakes I could have otherwise made. I was able to pursue ministry and the things that were in the Lord's will for me until He brought Matt and the time was right for us to move towards marriage. I went on my first date about a decade after many of my friends went on their first dates. I just served the Lord until it was His timing for me to enter the season of marriage.

Now that I am happily married to a man who loves the Lord and his family and is my best friend I am so grateful that I did not play the dating game before he came along. One thing I regret, however, is that I was not more content during my high school and single years. I had always wanted to be a wife and a mommy, and I really struggled with watching friends date and get married at early ages while I felt left behind. There were more than a few times that I threw myself a royal pity party instead of trusting the Lord as fully as I should have. I did throw myself into ministry, but I wish with all of my heart that I would have rested in the goodness of the Lord more and doubted less. I wish I had not been secretly looking everywhere I went to see if "Mr. Right" might be there.

Because I had been involved in ministry my whole life and the Lord was using me to serve Him in my singleness, I had a fear that maybe the Lord did not intend for me to be married. That was a fear that crippled me and caused me much discouragement. I was recently explaining to my oldest daughter that I am grateful that I did wait for God's best for me, but I regret that I was not more content. I wish I could have had a still and quiet spirit in this area of my life. This is an area where I would like for my children to stand on my shoulders and not only wait for God's best for them but also wait with contentment.

I stated earlier that I was courtship minded, and yet when Matt came along we did not have what many would define as a courtship. We were both adults and had a very focused and purposeful relationship that quickly led to marriage. We were friends years before we began officially dating. Matt was my brother's friend and had spent much time at our home. My parents knew him well and approved of us dating, knowing that we were considering each other as marriage partners. One thing that my mom suggested early on is that we do some pre-engagement counseling with a mentor couple before we got too serious about engagement. There was a couple in our church that we really respected, and we asked them if they would begin meeting with us and going through some pre-engagement books from the ministry of Family Life. Those sessions were special and really helped us dig into God's Word concerning important aspects of marriage. We had individual study homework and sought the Lord in between sessions. We also read through some books and watched a Gary Smalley video series on marriage. We did a lot of preparation for marriage during some of our times together. Our dating did not particularly look like what many courtship books might describe. Matt did not ask my dad's permission to court me and we did not have chaperones go on dates with us, etc. However, our intent was not a casual dating relationship that would likely end up in a devastating break up. There was a time soon after we began dating that I began to feel concern that Matt would change his mind, and what if I had waited twenty-five years for my first date just to have him break up with me? I told him my concern, and I remember him assuring me that he was indeed going to ask me to marry him but just not yet. I share that to reiterate that our relationship was not casual but purposeful. We talked much and entered into our relationship with the end goal of marriage in mind. We committed our relationship to the Lord, prayed often, and sought out counsel through mentors and Biblically sound resources. Now that we have been married for seventeen years and have experienced a lot of life together, I see how important laying that foundation was. I personally am not as hung up on the terminology of a relationship, whether it is called dating with a purpose or courtship, etc.

What I believe to be the heart of the matter is that God's people honor and respect one another and do not enter relationships casually just to have personal needs met. The world's current pattern for dating is relationship without commitment. As in so many other areas of life it is important that God's people do things differently. Single young men and women do need to love their brothers and sisters in a way that protects their emotions and their purity.

When people say courtship, there are many different ideas about what that looks like. It can depend a lot upon the particular book you have read on the topic. I think that it often plays itself out differently in different relationships. Had I married a man who had grown up in the homeschool community and who was familiar with courtship principles, perhaps he would have approached my dad initially. If I hadn't already been halfway through my twenties by the time we started dating, some things might have lined up more with courtship-book suggestions. When the Lord brings people together, they are not always from similar backgrounds, and there are often varying circumstances. Courtship to me does not mean following steps one through seven from a book in precise order. I think of courtship more as following principles of wisdom to try one's best to keep from hurting a brother or sister in Christ. It includes an intentionality and seriousness that is not willing to play games with someone's emotions and not willing to put oneself in the compromising position of falling in love with someone who would not be a wise and godly marriage choice. I think it also is a position of the heart that values the sage counsel of godly parents or mentors who know and care about those involved. So often, parents can point out things in a potential spouse that a young, single person might be blinded to. My counsel to young people would be to seek the Lord wholeheartedly, to never consider missionary dating with a non-Christian (it is too easy to get attached and marry an unbeliever), to listen to wise counsel (especially from godly parents), to not play the loosey-goosey dating game with person after person, but to enter into any relationship knowing this relationship could lead to marriage. If a single person would not want to marry a potential date, then I think it would be better to never go on that date in the first place. Emotions can be tricky and very deceitful, easily confusing a young person. I would also encourage someone entering a relationship to not be afraid to cut things off if red flags arise. Just because one enters into a relationship with a seriousness that can foresee a possible future marriage does not mean they need to hesitate to back away if things come to light that are concerning. Seeking the Lord all the way to the wedding altar and beyond is vastly important. I am not as caught up on the term "courtship" as I am on the principles of a God-honoring relationship. Whether you call the process dating, dating with a purpose, courtship, etc., the principles I am talking about are the heart of the matter.

I have always been grateful for the preparation that Matt and I did even before we were engaged and throughout our engagement. The books we read on marriage, the videos we watched, the counsel we received from our mentor couple, and the time we spent praying together helped to set a foundation for our marriage. Gratefully, we discussed many common marriage issues before marriage and knew fairly well where we each stood on issues that often come as a surprise after marriage. One thing we look back on with amazement is a question our counseling book asked each of us to answer individually. The question was how many children we wanted to have. The amazing thing is that we both individually on our own wrote, "At least five or six." Those kinds of questions and discussions helped us to assess whether we were on the same page on important issues before we committed to marriage. If I had answered the question by saying, "At least five or six" and Matt had said "None," then that would have been a huge red flag that our life goals were not in harmony.

Seeking the Lord and godly counsel together set a precedent for us to take into our marriage. We were already in the habit of seeking out wisdom, of communicating, and of going before the Lord in prayer together. I cannot encourage young couples strongly enough to practice wisdom in their relationships before marriage as a foundation for after marriage. It is something I will always be grateful we did.

In recent years, I have witnessed several young people enter into courtships and into God-honoring marriages. Often these courtships have been short, because these young adults entered into the relationships with wisdom and purpose. It has been a beautiful thing to observe these new homes being established and the children the Lord is blessing these couples with. It has been an encouragement to my heart to see that Biblical principles do not become outdated. Even in a climate where there has been a lot of negativity about the idea of courtship, it has been sweet to see these couples shining as beautiful examples of how this can be done very well and in God-honoring ways. The ways of the Lord are faithful and true and work in every generation.

Farm Life or City Life

My husband grew up in the country on twenty acres and dreamed of one day raising his children on land. I, on the other hand, grew up a city girl who wanted to be sure I was in close proximity to a good mall. Before we were mutually interested in one another, Matt shared with me how he wanted to raise his children to do things like dig potatoes in the potato patch. As a single young lady, I didn't really have that vision. By the time we became mutually interested in seeing if the Lord had marriage for us my vision had grown to the idea of living on a few acres within close driving proximity to civilization as I knew it. It has been interesting to see how the Lord has taken a country boy and a city girl and united our hearts and vision for how we want to raise our children. We started out our parenting journey in a nice suburban area in a brand new apartment complex. Then we moved to our first small house where we brought home our second baby. After a few years in that house, we built a two-story home in a neighborhood with all the stores and conveniences around us. We brought home two more babies in that home. By this time we were really itching to purchase some land so that our four children would have wide open spaces to run and play. I also had come to the point in my mothering journey where I knew my place was at home and that we didn't need to be running all over the place on a regular basis. This was a time to give my young children the stability of being home as I worked hard at discipling their hearts to love and follow Jesus. We found 3.5 acres in an acreage community still within thirty minutes from our old stomping grounds. That was a good introduction to country life for our growing family. We were blessed with our fifth child shortly after moving to that home. While there, we raised some baby chicks and enjoyed fresh eggs until the raccoons ate our chickens. Someone down the road brought in peacocks some years previous to us moving there, and they could be seen roaming the road and in the yards of the street we lived on. The children enjoyed running and chasing after them, and visitors found them a novelty. We used to have a lawn service come mow our property, and on one occasion a guy from the crew took some of the peacock feathers from our yard. I have to say I found these birds annoying, as they are very loud creatures. We experimented some with gardening while there as well. Then, after a few years, we made a drastic move clear across town to our current farm, which is a good driving distance away from anything. Now we live on fourteen acres and are once again trying our hand at gardening and other farm adventures. I recently saw a sign that said something like, "Urban Farm Girl." I thought that pretty much sums my story up well. I have come to see the value of living away from the noise and rattle of city life and having a place where my children can learn about and explore the ways of God through His creation. Certainly, not everyone is called to live on land, to have animals, to grow their own food, etc. For our family, this has been a process and is a journey that we are grateful the Lord placed us on.

One thing that took me by surprise, starting with our 3.5-acre home and continuing on our fourteen-acre farm, has been the constant drama that goes with country living. There truly never is a dull moment, especially with a house full of children! We can recount many stories of experiences country life has brought our way. When we lived in our previous home we had a bat infestation in the attic, culminating in the dreadful event of a bat entering our home and flying around. We had to leave our home for a few days while it underwent treatment to get the bats out and keep them out. There have been countless battles with wasps and other flying insects entering our home as well. Then there was the time the neighbor's cow crossed a broken fence and entered our yard and the time another neighbor's donkey meandered over to our farm. Another memory happened soon after moving to our current farm. While Matt was away on a business trip my oldest son informed me that he saw a coyote running around in our pasture in broad daylight. I looked out the window and, sure enough, he was not seeing things. A day or two later we had that same coyote or another one walk right up to our back porch and stare at us through our family room window. Another incident was the time Matt saw a venomous cotton mouth snake in our house. He was holding the newborn baby on the couch when he saw the snake come out of the kitchen and coil up under the baby's car seat. Thankfully our newborn son was not in the carrier, and my brave husband was able to do away with that horrid creature. I have to say that these and other farm events were not exactly on my radar when I thought country life would be worth pursuing. I have been unnerved at times by these occurrences, but I have also grown some thicker skin and learned that such horrors do sometimes come with the territory. I pray regularly for God's protection over us as we live out where these kinds of run-ins with wild creatures can be more prevalent. At the same time, I also know that if we were back in the suburbs, we would face other challenges. The Lord has faithfully carried us through these farm incidents thus far, and we continue to look to Him to be our protector.

There are some huge benefits to living out and learning all there is to learn on a farm. Science lessons certainly abound as we learn about how things grow and about the ways of different animals, etc. I am grateful that we are away from many of the influences that we would have living in a suburban neighborhood. It would be harder for me to oversee the influences in my children's lives if we were surrounded by other kids who were growing up in homes that did not share our values. Also, when you live way out, you are forced to consider your outside commitments more carefully. I know that, unless I want to spend a great portion of our lives living and schooling in the van, we must be judicial in choosing our activities. For the most part we stay home during the week and do not overcommit to things. Even a few commitments here and there can feel overwhelming considering the drive time. It really keeps me accountable to considering the cost before committing to things.

Another benefit has been using our home as a ministry center. We have had far more people over since we bought the farm, and we usually try to have our guests join us in seeking the Lord through family worship, singing, and even through having our children sing or quote Scripture for our guests. People enjoy visiting a farm and getting away from the chaos of the city, so having our place has been a motivation to move more towards fulfilling Scripture's teaching to practice hospitality.

All of that being said, however, I would advise families to really be led of the Lord as to where He wants their family to live. As wonderful as it is to live away from it all, there are also some real challenges. For us, some of those challenges have been the long drive to get anywhere, finding enough help to manage everything, the never ending list of work that needs to be done, and less than optimal internet service. It is wise to count the cost when considering a lifestyle change of moving to the country and evaluating if one's family has the time and energy to manage the new challenges that come with country living. It is easy to look at country living with rose-colored glasses, thinking that life will be slow paced and restful in the country. It can have very enjoyable moments, but there is also a lot more work involved.

For some families their calling will be in the city ministering to neighbors and the community surrounding them. For others, like our family, we have been led to the country where we try to minister to people as we practice hospitality in our home. The Lord calls His people to proclaim His glories both in the city and in the country. I do not know if we will live in the country forever, but for this season, with all our young ones, it is a lovely place to allow them to run, play, and discover God's handiwork in the animals, the growing trees, plants, and even the bugs we have in abundance. I think living in a place where there is so much more work to be done forces us to teach them to work harder as well. There are many life lessons for us all on the farm, and we are grateful for this season of living and learning.

Church and the Homeschool Family

We started out in the church where my dad was pastoring. I had been in my dad's church my entire life, and in time, we felt the need to spread our wings and pave our own path for our family. Right after our second child was born we joined a large Southern Baptist Church. We enjoyed seven years there, but the Lord began birthing in our hearts the desire for a more family-integrated environment. In 2007 the Lord sent us to Germany with Matt's job for a couple of months. While we were there we attended the only gospel-preaching, English-speaking church we could find. It was a very small International Baptist Church. On any given Sunday there would only be a handful of people sitting around a circle. Our children would stay with us for the first half of the service as we knelt in prayer, sang, and heard passages read from Scripture. After that the pastor's wife would take them in a back room for a Bible lesson. As hard as it was to keep our little wiggly people still, we began to really value the sweetness of experiencing worship as a family. When we returned to the states we felt unsettled about putting name labels on our children's backs as we dropped them off in age-segregated nurseries and classes. We did continue with that for a while, but eventually we began attending a conservative Presbyterian church that was much smaller and we were able to keep our family with us. We were at that church for a few years and enjoyed good expository teaching and friendship with some sweet homeschool families. Having always attended Baptist and Bible churches there were a few differences, but overall we felt blessed and encouraged. Our hearts continued to grow towards the idea of family integration and when the Presbyterian church hired a youth pastor and started moving toward the youth group vision, we felt led to make a change. We had visited a family-integrated church off and on that was an hour across town. We eventually decided to commit to that drive to avoid youth group and enjoy family integration. Family-integrated churches can be a sweet option for the homeschool family, but be aware that there is every flavor from vanilla to chocolate. You will find all different stances on matters of theology, of practical living, of what sanctification should look like in the life of the believer, etc. It is important to make sure that the teaching is well balanced in matters of theology and sanctification. You don't want to be in a church where people are trusting homeschooling or lifestyle choices to be the Savior. Some churches can focus so much on outward behaviors that they miss the heart of the gospel, while others can focus so much on theology that the environment can feel academic, and teaching in practical life application can be amiss. It is hugely important that God's Word is taught faithfully and that the Word of God is elevated to a high level of prominence in the service.

"All Scripture is breathed out by God and profitable for teaching, for reproof, for correction, and for training in righteousness, that the man of God may be complete, equipped for every good work" (2 Timothy 3:16-17).

One thing we loved in the Presbyterian church as well as the family-integrated church was how much pure reading of Scripture was done in the service. In the Presbyterian church we would finish an Old and New

Testament reading every Sunday by hearing the pastor say, "This is the Word of the Lord," to which the congregation would say, "Thanks be to God." At the family-integrated church we appreciated having the fathers and older sons rotate in going up front and reading the Scripture passages.

"So shall my word be that goes out from my mouth; it shall not return to me empty, but it shall accomplish that which I purpose, and shall succeed in the thing for which I sent it" (Isaiah 55:11).

I am not saying that every church must do things exactly the same, but my point is that the high priority of hearing large passages of Scripture has given life to our family. It is something we have come to greatly appreciate.

"For it is no empty Word for you, but your very life, and by this word you shall live long in the land that you are going over the Jordan to possess" (Joshua 32:47).

As much as we wanted the family-integrated church to be permanent, we saw some areas that were shifting away from our family vision. We prayed much about it, and one Sunday the Lord made it crystal clear that it was time for our family to move onward. We had no choice but to prayerfully make a change. God in His goodness made the process a gentle transition, leading us to the church we are at now. Our current church is not family integrated by name, but it is very family friendly. Many families take their children of all ages into the service, the teaching is expository, there is no youth group, there is a sweet spirit of love for each other and joy in the Lord as well. It is a small Bible church, and our children are happy there. We appreciate the ministry of a true Titus 2 woman in the church who is working hard to disciple women of all ages, from the young girls to the adult women. We still love the idea of a family-integrated church, but there is not one around us that is likeminded with our family. Currently, we are finding a sweetness and healthy balance in this small Bible church. We have found that finding the right church for a large, conservative, homeschool family can be quite challenging. It is a matter to pray much over and to allow the Lord to lead your individual family in. It has been a journey for us, but I can say that we have learned a lot of lessons from each situation the Lord has taken us through. It has never been our desire to church hop, but, in our case, the Lord has taken us in and out of a few churches and we have learned a lot through this journey. One thing for sure is that there is no perfect church, but there is a church that is right for your family, and it is worth prayerfully seeking and walking in obedience to the Savior. The place where He lands you may not seem perfect, but it will be His perfect will for you at the time.

My encouragement for the homeschool family looking for a church would be to pray for a church that teaches sound doctrine. John MacArthur says the following on the importance of teaching sound doctrine:

> The basic task of the church is to teach sound doctrine. That is the task of the church. Not to give some pastor's opinion. Not to give you my opinions. Not to recite to you tear jerking illustrations. Not to try to play on your emotions. Not to be a fundraiser. Not to be running around doing this and that. Not to provide programs, entertainment, short little spiritual thoughts, weekly devotionals. The ministry of the church is to teach sound doctrine. To teach sound doctrine. Titus 2:1. See, here's another instruction to the one who's planning a church, "But speak thou the thing which become sound doctrine."
>
> And if it is to be pure, then there must be, on the part of the elders that lead it, a faithfulness to the Word of God. Not fuddling around in meetings, and conferences, and councils, and running up your gasoline bill. And it's so easy to do this, because some things are good, but they're just not priorities. As a minister of Jesus Christ, I and all others who minister in His name are responsible to God for the purity of the Word. We must teach it in its purity. We must preach it in its purity. We are responsible to protect you from false doctrine. We are answerable to Jesus Christ for how well we do, and how faithful we are to protect the flock and to nurture the flock. [9]

There is an increasing trend in many churches towards feel-good messages that aren't much more than a pop-psychology lesson. Many pastors focus on topics like self-esteem, good deeds, how to be happy, how to reach your full potential, and humanitarian service. These churches often fail to proclaim the good news of the gospel as central to all of life and often fail to teach on sin and the need for repentance. In looking for a church, you want to look for a church that is not wimpy in proclaiming truth.

"I am not ashamed of the gospel, for it is the power of God for the salvation to everyone who believes, to the Jew first and also to the Greek" (Romans 1:16).

"Speaking the truth in love, we are to grow up in every way into Him who is the head, into Christ" (Ephesians 4:15).

There is increasing pressure on pastors to back down and not give the full counsel of God's Word, especially as it pertains to sin, man's need for repentance, and the Lordship of Christ. So ask God for a pastor who is not a pansy but who is courageous to speak the Gospel of Jesus Christ with a heart of love! One good question to ask yourself when listening to a sermon is, how much is the pastor referring to Scripture versus how much is he rambling on with stories and illustrations? Is it a Word-saturated church?

I think there are some things to pray for in searching for a church or even in praying for growth in your current church. One would be for the centrality of the gospel to be evident in the church. The gospel of Jesus is the most important thing and should be proclaimed clearly and faithfully.

Similarly, you want to be a part of a Christocentric body of believers. That is a group of Christ followers that make Christ the center of all.

I would pray for a church that would support the values you are working so hard to teach your family at home. You want the church to fortify what you are telling your children in the context of your home and not work against it.

A healthy church will greatly value taking the light of Jesus into a dark world. It will not be content to just be a holy huddle but it will have a focus on evangelizing the lost. That is what Scripture tells us to do. We are to "Go into the world and preach the gospel" (Mark 16:15).

Scripture also calls us to be ambassadors for Christ.

"Therefore, we are ambassadors for Christ, God making his appeal through us. We implore you on behalf of Christ, be reconciled to God" (2 Corinthians 5:20).

So I would pray for a church where your family can serve as Kingdom warriors, working mightily for the furtherance of His eternal Kingdom.

It is so helpful if you can find a church where there are at least a few likeminded families that you can develop heart friendships with. In all of the churches we have been in, the Lord has blessed us with at least a few likeminded families who have enriched our lives and encouraged us to press on in the race for the high calling of God in Christ Jesus. You don't have to be in a church where everyone is a clone of your family, but, if possible, it is a great encouragement to have at least a few like-minded families. You see, if you are around lost neighbors, and their children are allowed to do things you do not allow your children to do, then you can share with your children that they are lost and you as a family are being a light for Christ to them. However, if you are in a church where all the Christians are living a different lifestyle from that of your family, and the church leadership is promoting a culture that is in stark opposition to that of your home, then your children can become discouraged and wonder why they have to be the odd Christians. So there is a balance. I'm not advocating that a Christian homeschool family must find a church where everyone talks the same, dresses the same, styles their hair the same, and pretty much looks like a group of clones. What I am saying is that, in our family, we have found it vitally important to be in a church where there are at least a few families who think like we think. Different Christian families are at different points in their journey towards sanctification and may land at different points on standards and personal convictions. If your family has had the blessing of being discipled and working out your sanctification more than others, then the Lord may have you planted in that church, wanting you to come alongside weaker families and help them grow towards a vision of holiness and sanctification.

So there are two sides to this equation. On one side, we as a family want to be leaders in righteousness, but, on the other side, we do not want to discourage our children by putting them in a stifling environment that lacks likeminded friendship and back up for what parents are trying to teach at home. We have not found any situation to be perfect and we continue to pray through these matters and seek the Lord, asking Him to raise up our children to love righteousness and turn from folly. We continue praying that they will be discerning as we try to guide them through wise choices in who they make their closest heart friends ... even at church! One day we will have perfect unity in Christ when we are praising Him in His eternal Kingdom. No church will ever be perfect this side of eternity. Choosing a church is an extremely important decision to be carefully thought through and prayed over. Convenience is not always the best criteria for choosing a church. Our last two churches have been an hour's drive, but we find it worth it to be in a place where we have some like-minded fellowship and where we agree with the vision the church is pursuing.

When choosing a church or evaluating your place within your current church, it is vital to consider where you may serve the body of Christ. Does this particular church offer opportunities for your family to grow in areas of service? This is not an area we have excelled in. We have always had our hands full and felt we were doing good just to navigate our crowd of little people around without a scene. Now a new awareness is being birthed in us of how important it is to TRAIN our children to serve. I think the best time to get our children excited about serving is when they are little. If we wait until they are old enough to do big things, they may have missed the window to really spark the excitement over serving. It is never too late to start and we are working on that, but with our younger crowd I am realizing now is the time to teach them to serve our local church, even in small ways, such as drying dishes in the kitchen or wiping tables after a fellowship meal. They can pick up trash off the floor, etc. As our children grow older they can help in bigger ways, but the training and heart for serving is formed as they begin to be faithful in small ways as very young children. If your family serves in more public ways, such as music, teaching, and being in prominent positions that put you in the spotlight, it is important to also teach your children to do the behind-the-scenes jobs that don't usually get the praise and admiration of men. This can help teach them the true heart of service and keep them humble at the same time.

In recent years there has been such a focus on making church relevant, entertaining, and appealing to the lost that I fear that this generation often feels they go to church to be entertained. Years ago, when we were in an age-segregated church, our daughter came home talking about playing video games in Sunday school. That did not settle well with us. We believe the Word of God has the power to transform lives without making church primarily about entertaining music, skits, videos, recreation rooms, etc. while just throwing in a little Scripture here and there.

Another matter of importance in considering a church is that of church leadership living under proper accountability. Church leadership and Biblical church government is very important. When looking for a church, it is important to know if the leaders are servant minded and humble. It is important that they are held accountable to others. Who is asking them the hard questions about their private lives? There are too many stories of church abuse when a leader is not under proper accountability. Also, how are decisions made for the church? Is there a healthy feeling about how the leaders interact with each other and with the church body? Is it easy to get answers to questions about the church, or does it seem like it is hard to talk with leadership and things are under cover? Is there an overall feeling of confusion as to who is making the decisions and why? Is the direction and vision for the church being clearly explained? If changes happen, are they explained to the people or are the people left scratching their heads in bewilderment? These are important matters to discern before committing to a church family. When joining a church, you want to join, not a perfect one but a generally healthy one.

One area that people might not often consider in choosing a church is proper church discipline. In too many churches today you have people in blatant sin without any church discipline going on. According to Scripture, if a Christian man or woman is living in immorality, whether married or single, measures of church discipline should be taken to turn the sinner from his ways. The same would apply for a man beating his wife and children. It is the jurisdiction of the church to hold the believer accountable in these areas, and yet you do not see this kind of ministry happening in most churches today. At the same time there needs to be a balance in church discipline so that people are not being disciplined for just somehow offending the leadership. Church discipline is a Biblical command and is for specific, clearly defined sin issues. It is not something that leadership should ever use in a heavy-handed, prideful, abusive way. I like the way our pastor talks about this subject. He says that he prefers to call it church restoration. That is because the purpose of the discipline is to bring the one being chastised back into restored fellowship with the Lord and with His people.

"Brothers, if anyone is caught in any transgression, you who are spiritual should restore him in a spirit of gentleness" (James 6:1).

Adjoining one's family to a local church is a huge responsibility and will have a huge impact upon the life of that family. The church is designed by God to be a blessing to the Christian family. Sadly, in our day of so much apostasy, it can be difficult to find the right church that is operating Biblically and that will support a family in Biblical principles. Even so, the Lord preserves His people and His church. Church is a matter to be prayerful over and to make a high priority in the Christian family.

Media

Media is a HUGE topic for today's Christian family. When I was growing up we did not even own a television for several years of my life, and then our grandparents gave us a small TV set that my parents closely monitored. I remember watching some Sesame Street, but television was not a big part of our family during my young years. As I grew older we watched more programs like *Little House on the Prairie* and then the VCR came on the scene and we were able to watch some carefully selected movies. When I compare that with what today's Christian family is up against with media everywhere we turn, the contrast is astounding. Just this morning I was eating breakfast in a hotel restaurant and noticed that there were at least three different channels playing on different screens. Screens are in our faces everywhere we go. Our children will be exposed to screens all over society whether we like it or not. There was a sense in which my parents' generation could shelter their children and choose what they saw and didn't see. With my own children, media is forced upon us everywhere we go—sitting in traffic, waiting in lines, going to the doctor, and a myriad of other circumstances. Additionally, we get to contend with the iPhones, iPods, iPads, laptops, etc. We may have a tight rein on what media is happening in our homes, but we have no control over the media other children are bringing to church and everywhere else.

My point is that we as concerned Christian parents have huge issues to contend with in trying to protect our children's hearts, minds and eyes. Before I go any further in talking about the negatives, let me say that I am grateful for the God-honoring media options we have to set before our children. Media can be a tool for teaching our children and encouraging them in the faith. One series we have enjoyed around our home is the animated Torchlighters' "Heroes of the Faith" series. Our family has been able to watch excellent biographical portrayals of heroes of the faith such as Corrie Ten Boom, Perpetua, Amy Carmichael, and many others. We have also enjoyed some of the historical animations from Nest Family Entertainment. We love the things put out by Answers in Genesis and Buddy Davis and also videos from Jobe Martin on creation, etc. There are some great resources out there that our families can learn much from and, for that, I am grateful. When thinking about media I realize that it is a powerful medium, and I want to use it in purposeful, beneficial, educational, and inspirational ways.

There are those times where we do watch something that is not deeply spiritual, but I want the majority of what I put before my children to be for more than mere entertainment purposes. Personally, I did not grow up watching tons of movies or very much TV. I don't think I saw Disney's *Cinderella* until I was an adult! When I had our first child I wanted her to be a girly girl, and I was excited about sharing Disney princesses and all things girly with her. We were very much into the classic Disney princess things when she was little. The classic Disney princess stories did have a lot of redeemable elements. For example, Cinderella was sweet, feminine, joyfully served others, was not vindictive, etc. In that movie a girl with character was made to be the hero. I can appreciate that. However, around the time the *Little Mermaid* came out I believe Disney began making a huge shift towards rebellion and feministic leanings. Ariel, in *The Little Mermaid*, rebels against her father and then the movie paints a happy ending. I'm not making a blatant statement here about Disney. Yes, we have watched some Disney videos and visited Disneyland. However, it has become very clear to me, especially by the things Disney has recently put out, that they have a strong agenda they are promoting in subtle and increasingly unsubtle ways. These ideologies, worldviews, etc. are not going to be a friend to the sanctification of our families. Now I'm not saying we have totally abandoned Disney. What I am saying is, if you watch something, talk through it, analyze it, dissect it, and talk through the message running through the video. Is it coming from a Christian worldview? If not, what is the worldview? Is it promoting God's roles for men and women? Is it promoting good or evil? Where you see feminism, talk through it. Where choices are in opposition to God's Word, point that out. Talk through disrespect to parents. When my son was little he loved *Finding Nemo*. There is a scene in there where Nemo says to his dad, Marlin, "I hate you!" How horrible is that! How destructive, especially if a loving parent doesn't pause the movie and share with his child that God's Word says that rebellion is as the sin of witchcraft.

In *Rapunzel* there is a scene where Glenrider tells Rapunzel that a little rebellion is good for you. That is a good time to stop the movie and ask your children what God's Word says about rebellion. God's Word makes it very clear that rebellion is never good for you!

"For rebellion is as the sin of divination" or, as the King James Version says, "For rebellion is as the sin of witchcraft, and stubbornness is as iniquity and idolatry" (1 Samuel 15:23).

While I am not saying, "Thus says the Lord, 'all Christian families need to abandon Disney,'" I am saying we *have* to be discerning. There is no formula for every Christian family to follow on matters of conscience like movies, music, etc. We have to, as a family, go before the Lord and ask His wisdom.

"If any of you lacks wisdom, let him ask God, who gives generously to all without reproach, and it will be given him" (James 1:5).

It is vitally important that we as Christian parents ponder these choices. Media is so powerful in our children's lives. We need to bathe these things in prayer. If you do allow some of these gray area children's films into your home, I would strongly recommend that you sit with remote control in hand and discuss these matters as they arise. In that scenario you can prayerfully accomplish some training in discernment with your children. There is certainly nothing wrong with completely cutting off these influences either if that is how the Lord leads. Sometimes parents have to choose the hills they are willing to die on. There are some things my children can pressure me on all they want and I will not cave in. However, if there is a certain Disney movie that they really want to see, I may or may not allow it. There are some that I definitely have not allowed at all. For those I may allow, I try to point out areas that do not align with our Christian worldview. It has been encouraging to me to see my older children growing in these areas of discernment as we have tried to talk through these issues. The other day we were watching something that I felt had some issues we needed to talk about. After watching it I asked the children to gather around so that we could talk.

My oldest asked if she could say something. Then she proceeded to bring up almost every point I was going to address with her younger siblings. My mommy heart swelled with gratitude for the discernment the Lord is building in her heart. What a huge backup to me as a parent to have our firstborn address all her siblings with principles and wisdom that she has learned. I'm picking on Disney a bit here just because that is where a lot of the hype is at for today's generation of young people, but these principles apply to any entertainment/media choices. This area of media and entertainment is a huge area of heaviness of heart for me. I pray much about it. It is one of those areas where the Lord keeps me needy and humble before Him. I think whether you choose to abstain from most secular media choices or choose to prayerfully and selectively watch some things with discernment and dialogue, we are all waging a huge battle and must be prayerful for the hearts and souls of our children. This is an area where we must not cater to the enemy and give up the battle. I will also say that I think there is a point in which Christians definitely need to draw a line in the sand and say we will not go over this line. In my own heart I know Disney is on a trajectory that is pushing our family closer to that line all the time. Already, there are some Disney animated movies that we have not and will not watch. Others, we have watched once with critical analyzation and chosen not to watch again. I think, more and more, the norm will be that we will not be interested in most of Disney's newest offerings, as they continue to incrementally push a new and progressive worldview message that rages against the Kingdom of God.

I have already made the point that whether we allow these things in our home or not, our children will see all kinds of media the minute we walk into a mall or a fast food restaurant. We are at a point in our culture where it is impossible to fully shelter and guard our children against the anti-Christian media so prevalent everywhere today. That is one reason we do allow our children to be exposed to some Disney films, etc. We want them to have the spiritual muscles of discernment to be able to view something through the lens of a spiritual worldview. At the same time, we need to ask ourselves how steady of a diet we want our children to have of these things. I can say for a fact that I do not want the values of Disney or most cartoons to be the prominent thing I am exposing my children to. Thankfully, there are an increasing number of family friendly, faith-building, character-building, educational videos being produced from a Christian perspective these days. Many Christian homeschool families are gaining a vision for putting out Christ-honoring video resources for Christian families. That is very encouraging, and we have been very blessed by some of these enriching videos. As these types of videos are available in increasing measure, I certainly feel less need for some of the other borderline options.

On the topic of videos, movies, etc., another point to be made here is everything with moderation. Too much of even a good thing can be problematic. I don't want my children's minds turning to mush or their creativity stunted by too much screen time of any source. Also, it is important that our children not have an ongoing appetite for constant entertainment. Our purpose in life is not to be entertained but to bring glory to God. There is a great quote from Saint Ignatius of Antioch that says, "Apart from Christ, let nothing dazzle you." [5]

There is a spiritual battle raging for lost souls, and time is too short to be wasted on a steady diet of entertainment. This huge area of media consumption is an area to take before the Lord and to be continually prayerful and discerning about. In the case of some popular animated films, we have chosen to give our children minimal exposure (like a one-time viewing) so that they do have a clue on how to interact with their peers on some of these things and not feel completely out of the loop. Additionally, it may be a helpful exercise for us to teach our children how to look for the underlying messages and practice Biblical discernment. However, once they have seen the movie and have an understanding of it, there is no need to *love* the movie and to watch it over and over. This is where we landed with *Frozen*. We watched it once at the theater and talked much about the messages being communicated in it. We did not, however, choose to buy it and watch it repeatedly and sing "Let It Go" which is, very sadly, a song reeking of rebellion. I totally did not want my little girls going around singing about testing the limits, turning away and slamming the door, or with the attitude of no right, no wrong, no rules for me.

I am still shocked as I read those lyrics, and I know that little bitty girls all the way up to teenage girls were taken by storm with that song. Dolls were made singing it, and it was all over radio stations and across the internet. Truly, if we heard that song out of the context of a children's movie, would we think those were helpful lyrics for our daughters? It is as if, because Disney put it out as a song in a children's movie, people don't see the rebellion screaming in it. I don't want my little girls singing, "No right, no wrong, no rules for me. I'm free." That is just not my vision for my daughters. Our children are born with hearts bent towards rebellion without us feeding that natural bent with unhelpful messages like that. We need to be vigilant to discern in matters like these instead of just following the flow of culture. So, with *Frozen,* we watched it once, we talked about it a whole lot, and we did not let it become a point of idolatry in our family. In the case of *Frozen*, I think it was good that especially my oldest daughter did watch it and was able to talk about it with other girls her age in an informed way. It became all the rage even amongst teenage girls, and if she had not seen it she would not have really known what to say about it. Because she saw it and we talked about it extensively, she was able to point out areas of concern to other girls. Now I certainly do not promote always exposing our kids to things just so that they can relate to other kids. I am also not trying to tell any other family what they should watch or not watch. In the case of *Frozen,* this is just an example of how our family chose to handle that particular movie and why. We have many dear friends who would disagree with us and we can agree to disagree.

My biggest point is that we must not be apathetic here. We can be homeschooling our children and trying to protect them from an ungodly education and ungodly influences, but if we are letting the TV, YouTube, videos, video games, iPod music, etc. run without monitoring and without keen discernment, we are inviting so much of what we are trying to avoid right into our own living rooms.

One way to think about this is to aim to create an appetite for the best so that our children will desire the best. If you feed someone tender, juicy steak on a regular basis and then offer them cheap, tough meat, they probably will be missing the steak. In the same way, when we offer our children the best in literature, music, movies, etc., our hope is that the twaddle, shallow stuff will be less intriguing. Whether we eat or drink or watch movies, let's make it our aim to do all to the glory of God!

Chapter 7

Legalism, Antinomianism,

and Holiness

What Legalism is Not

It seems to me that there is much misunderstanding these days as to what legalism is. When you talk to evangelicals or read many of their writings you will often hear the word "legalism" thrown around loosely. So what is legalism? Let me start by stating what I do not believe it is. I do not believe legalism is having high standards or Biblical adherence to the law of God. Obedience to Biblical mandates and commands is a good and right thing. God expects no less from His children. Yes, we fail often and that is why the Gospel is such good news! When we sin we can go back to our loving Lord and repent. We can ask Him to help us as we continue to aim for obedience to His Word in our lives. Having personal high standards of holiness is a part of being sanctified, of putting on the Lord Jesus Christ, and of being conformed to His image. It seems that in our culture today, however, if a person tries to live in a countercultural, sanctified, "set apart," devoted-to-Christ kind of way, the ugly word "legalist" gets slapped upon his back. It seems that many people cry "legalism" when they smell anything remotely different from what they choose to do in their own lives. For example, if Mrs. Christian A wants to wear a bikini to the pool and Mrs. Christian B wears a modest swimming alternative, in many cases I've seen Mrs. Christian A accuse Mrs. Christian B of being legalistic. This is just one example, but my point is that many people are quick to judge others of being legalistic when others do not do certain things that they do.

Now if Mrs. Christian B in her modest swimming attire has a harsh, unloving, judgmental attitude, all the while sporting a self-righteous haughtiness, then she may very well be a legalist. If her assurance of God's acceptance of her is rooted in her modest attire rather than in Christ's work on the cross, then she would be falling into legalism. However, it is her attitude of trusting in her modesty while having unloving attitudes towards others that condemns her as a legalist, not the fact that she is dressing modestly. If her assurance of her acceptance with the Father rests in Christ's atonement, and she is dressing modestly out of love for her Savior, then her modest dress is an act of worship and obedience, not legalism.

89

Additionally, speaking the truth in love is sometimes confused as legalism, but it is not the same thing. The Bible instructs us to warn, to disciple, and to exhort one another.

"Rather, speaking the truth in love, we are to grow up in every way into him who is the head, into Christ" (Ephesians 4:15).

"My brothers, if anyone among you wanders from the truth and someone brings him back, let him know that whoever brings back a sinner from his wandering will save his soul from death and will cover a multitude of sins" (James 5:19-20).

"But in your hearts honor Christ the Lord as holy, always being prepared to make a defense to anyone who asks you for a reason for the hope that is in you; yet do it with gentleness and respect" (1 Peter 3:15).

In the book of Mark, chapter eleven, we read an account of Jesus correcting the money-changers in the temple. As my husband has pointed out, "If correcting sin were legalism, then Christ Himself would have been guilty of legalism."

> And they came to Jerusalem. And he entered the temple and began to drive out those who sold and those who bought in the temple, and he overturned the tables of the money-changers and the seats of those who sold pigeons. And he would not allow anyone to carry anything through the temple. And he was teaching them and saying to them, "It is written, 'My house shall be called a house of prayer for all the nations.' But you have made it a den of robbers." And the chief priests and the scribes heard it and were seeking a way to destroy him, for they feared him, because all the crowd was astonished at his teaching (Mark 11:15-18).

Jesus had no qualms about calling out sin. He spoke truth and, in this case, He did it with firmness and fervency. It is not legalistic to speak truth. Do you see that Jesus supported His reprimand with God's Word? "It is written, 'My house shall be called a house of prayer for all the nations.'" As He pointed out their sin He used the Word of God to show them why. This is critical! It is *not* legalistic to point out sin when it is clearly defined in the Word of God. So, we are told to "speak the truth in love" to "bring back the sinner from his wandering." We see this example of Christ correcting wrongdoers saying, "It is written." Clearly, lovingly bringing God's truth to others and rescuing the perishing is not legalism.

90

It seems that the masses of believers today take the viewpoint that most everything in life, outside of our salvation in Christ, is an area of neutrality. Maybe it is the relativism of the day bleeding over into Christian culture. Society at large worships the idea of relativism that each person decides for himself what is right and wrong. Unfortunately, I see this attitude prevailing in much of evangelical culture as well. So many are antagonistic against any kind of a call to holiness, and if you touch specifics at all you are judged as an unloving legalist.

In a way it reminds me of the deism that was prevalent in the early 1700s. Deism differs from atheism in that it does acknowledge a Creator God but it denies His involvement in our lives today. Practical deism is a lifestyle that denies God's activity in our lives. A deist does not see that all we know and believe about God has implications for how we live the nitty-gritty details of our daily lives. Practical deism acknowledges the gospel while denying its power. A deist can worship in church on Sunday and yet feel free to live any way he wants during the week. Basically, he has separated his orthodoxy from his orthopraxy. What he believes about God does not affect how he lives his life.

In today's Christian climate it seems people are very quick to call you a legalist if you offer any kind of exhortation to others. The Scriptures, however, tell us to teach, admonish, and spur one another on to good deeds. The Titus 2 principle of older women teaching younger women is very important, and it is not legalistic for an older godly lady to come alongside a younger lady and share Biblical wisdom when this is done in love and humility.

"And let us consider how to stir up one another to love and good works" (Hebrews 10:24).

"Older women likewise are to be reverent in behavior, not slanderers or slaves to much wine. They are to teach what is good, and so train the young women to love their husbands and children, to be self-controlled, pure, working at home, kind, and submissive to their own husbands, that the word of God may not be reviled" (Titus 2:3-5).

If I have a friend who is in an extramarital affair, I would not be a legalist to bring the law of God to her and share God's truth. We see in Leviticus 20:10 how seriously God takes adultery. Under the Levitical law a person was to be put to death for breaking covenant with their spouse. Here is what God's Word says about an extramarital affair:

"If a man commits adultery with the wife of his neighbor, both the adulterer and the adulteress shall surely be put to death" (Leviticus 20:10).

"He who commits adultery lacks sense; he who does it destroys himself" (Proverbs 6:32).

"Let marriage be held in honor among all, and let the marriage bed be undefiled, for God will judge the sexually immoral and adulterous" (Hebrews 13:4).

"Or do you not know that the unrighteous will not inherit the kingdom of God? Do not be deceived: neither the sexually immoral, nor idolaters, nor adulterers, nor men who practice homosexuality, nor thieves, nor the greedy, nor drunkards, nor revilers, nor swindlers will inherit the kingdom of God" (I Corinthians 6:9-10).

Christ takes us to a higher standard by saying that even looking at a woman with lust is adultery.

"But I say to you that everyone who looks at a woman with lustful intent has already committed adultery with her in his heart." (Matthew 5:28).

If I really love my friend and care for both her soul and her welfare, then the loving thing would be to confront her about her sin. I would need to remind her that the Bible says that the marriage bed should be undefiled, that marriage should be held in honor among all, and that adulterers will not inherit the Kingdom of God. Again, my confronting her and pointing out her sin would not be legalistic. Why? Because I would be sharing God's Word, which is the absolute authority. This is not my standard; this is what the Word says.

What Legalism Is

Now that I have told you what I think legalism is not, let me attempt to share what I think legalism is. Legalism is a heart attitude that says I'm right and you're wrong based upon my own personal standards. For example, if I strongly believe that eating chocolate chip cookies is a sin and I go around judging everyone I see that enjoys chocolate chip cookies, then I am being a legalist. It may be very true that the Lord has given me a personal conviction that I should abstain from chocolate chip cookies for a personal reason, but that does not mean that this is the standard that everyone I know must follow. Now this is a ridiculous, fictitious example to stress a point. This would be legalistic because I cannot back this up by God's Word. You can try all you want, but you will not find a command anywhere in the 66 books of the Bible that condemns eating chocolate chip cookies. This silly example definitely falls within the bounds of Christian liberties. In areas where the Word of God does not speak specifically, such as eating cookies, we need to be careful not to impose our own personal standards on others. Conversely, in areas where the Scripture is clear, we can speak on the authority of the Word of God.

Also, legalism is an effort to win God's favor by outward behaviors. Those outward behaviors may very well be good and Christ honoring, but if a person is trying to win God's favor or merit through those behaviors, this becomes legalism. All other religions in the world are based upon a legalistic code, because whether it be Muslims, Buddhists, Hindus, Mormons, or Jehovah's Witnesses, these religions are all based on earning God's favor. None of them teach salvation by grace and faith alone. On the other hand, outward good behaviors are not legalistic when they are done out of love and devotion to Christ. When a believer truly grasps the beauty of the gospel and what Christ has done on his behalf, then living a life of holiness will flow out of a heart of gratitude and worship. In other words, the freeing goodness of the gospel should compel us to live godly lives in Christ Jesus.

Antinomianism

I have seen many young people from Christian homes reject the godly standards their parents tried to impart to them. In many cases, these young people chalk up godly standards, Biblical wisdom, and the teaching of their parents as legalistic. It is easy to excuse sin by crying, "Legalism!" In these cases I have seen droves of people go to the polar opposite extreme of legalism, which is antinomianism. There are many definitions defining antinomianism but, in simple words, an antinomian is one who leans very heavily upon cheap grace while ignoring the need to walk in obedience to Scripture. Paul addressed this when he asks:

"What shall we say then? Are we to continue in sin that grace may abound? By no means! How can we who died to sin still live in it?" (Romans 6:1-2).

The book of Hebrews gives a strong warning against treating God's grace as a license to sin.

"For if we go on sinning deliberately after receiving the knowledge of the truth, there no longer remains a sacrifice for sins, but a fearful expectation of judgment, and a fury of fire that will consume the adversaries. Anyone who has set aside the law of Moses dies without mercy on the evidence of two or three witnesses. How much worse punishment, do you think, will be deserved by the one who has trampled underfoot the Son of God, and has profaned the blood of the covenant by which he was sanctified, and has outraged the Spirit of grace?" (Hebrews 10:26-29).

There is a beautiful and delicate balance in Scripture of grace and truth. Both are essential. Yes, legalism can choke the life and joy out of the believer, and yet to run to the opposite ditch of antinomianism and party with the world is presuming upon God's grace. As believers, we should be in a process of ongoing sanctification where we are putting off our old self, our old habits, and gaining victory over sins of the flesh. In this process of transformation, we should be putting on the new self—becoming more and more like Christ. Colossians puts this beautifully:

> If then you have been raised with Christ, seek the things that are above, where Christ is, seated at the right hand of God. Set your minds on things that are above, not on things that are on earth. For you have died, and your life is hidden with Christ in God. When Christ who is your life appears, then you also will appear with him in glory. Put to death therefore what is earthly in you: sexual immorality, impurity, passion, evil desire, and covetousness, which is idolatry. On account of these the wrath of God is coming. In these you too once walked, when you were living in them. But now you must put them all away: anger, wrath, malice, slander, and obscene talk from your mouth. Do not lie to one another, seeing that you have put off the old self with its practices and have put on the new self, which is being renewed in knowledge after the image of its creator (Colossians 3:1-10).

As I have observed both hopeful and discouraging results from various Christian homeschool families over many decades, I am trying to make heads and tails of it in my own mind. How is it that one family launches several well-adjusted, well educated, visionary, Kingdom-minded adults into society while another set of parents tries with all their might and ends up wanting to run and hide in a closet due to the shame their grown children have brought to them? I don't want to oversimplify this complexity, and I do not have all the answers. I believe there are some things that we can take warning from and there are some good examples to look to as well. Mostly, it is a somber reminder that I am not in control of the final outcome of my children. I do not like that fact, but it is reality. I will absolutely be held accountable for how I raised my children, if I faithfully taught them the ways of the Lord, if I loved them well, if I shepherded their hearts, if I set a good example, etc. However, while it is my responsibility to do my best under the leading of God's Holy Spirit working through me, there is only so much I can do. This is why I find myself pouring out my heart to the Lord in increasing measure as my children are growing older. I pray that God's Holy Spirit will bear fruit from what I am teaching my children. Oftentimes, as I sit down to study Biblical truth with my children, I will say a prayer under my breath asking the Lord to bear fruit in their lives.

As my mind surveys the last several decades of the homeschooling movement, I believe that I see where some families erred on the side of legalism. That is, they focused too heavily on law, rules and externals without capturing their children's hearts. Many of these parents had good intentions and yet missed balancing the truth with grace. Perhaps the children felt their parents' demands were greater than their love. Perhaps they did not feel their parents liked them and enjoyed being with them. Also, sometimes these families were so focused on proper behavior and discipline that fathers and mothers used their God-given authority in a harsh manner that sometimes crossed the line into abuse. While I firmly believe that parents are to lead children and not the other way around, parents are to lead in a Christ-like manner demonstrating the fruits of the spirit. They should steward their authority and their leadership and not use it in destructive ways. Yes, there should absolutely be loving discipline, consequences, and training, but rules without relationship lead to rebellion. Sadly, in some of these scenarios, I would think that the extreme focus on externals and behaviors eclipsed the focus on the gospel and the position of the children's hearts towards Christ. If the primary focus was so honed in on polishing up the outside in manners of behavior and dress that there was not sufficient attention given to the inside heart of the children, then the outside could look impressive while the inside was growing with the ugliness of an unregenerate, sinful heart. I have to ask myself if many of these homeschool rebels, who have rejected all they were ever taught, may possibly have never come to saving faith in Christ. Could they have thought they were saved because they prayed a prayer at a certain time in their lives and looked good on the outside? Perhaps people praised them a lot and they grew prideful. Perhaps Satan himself deluded their minds to think they were in the faith because they were so moral and outwardly looked much better than their peers. These are things to ponder and traps to be careful of. Certainly, these things do not apply to all families; these are just my thoughts concerning the wayward, disgruntled, bitter adults who hate their homeschooling experience and are walking in ways contrary to the Scripture. In my mind's eye, I am picturing the young people who once upon a time looked super conservative and sweet and now look edgy, hard and worldly.

Aiming for a Biblical Balance

Now here is the problem I see lurking in much of the homeschool movement today. For some reason our human nature tends to want to go from one ditch to the opposite ditch. What I am observing in the Christian evangelical and homeschool atmosphere of the present time is a huge leap from legalism to liberty. So many in our churches and in homeschool circles are railing against legalism and proclaiming Christian liberty. It is to the point that sometimes it seems that what defines these people is their "freedom" to do whatever rather than salvation and sanctification through Christ. In some cases, these people have truly suffered under the burden of legalism, and yet many times I believe people are using the ugly word "legalism" as an excuse for sin. There is a popular movement in Christian circles today that promotes messy, worldly, edgy, raw realism and neglects to offer the hope and victory Christ offers His children. We need to be discerning about the influences we allow our children to be shaped by. Things like media, music, books, friendships, modesty, or the lack thereof really do matter.

As Christians we are not to wallow in sin and love the things of the world. Neither are we to excuse carnal attitudes and behaviors. We are to have an ongoing, growing relationship with our Savior that is transforming us from the inside out. J.C. Ryle put it well when he said, "Sin forsaken is one of the best evidences of sin forgiven."

So practically, what am I saying here? As I see it, in past decades I think some parents missed the mark by neglecting heart matters while scrubbing their children up on the outside. While these kids grew up looking outwardly shiny, the muck and mire in their hearts, their anger against the rules, and their anger towards harsh parents bubbled over into some shocking outcomes. These days I am seeing the contrast of masses of permissive parents who have very few standards to live by, expect little respect and obedience, and who do not have much of a vision for their families to look different from the ungodly culture around them. They are so freaked out about "legalism" that they are afraid to raise the bar and live differently from the world. These families are very much integrated into the world around them, loving its entertainments and marching to its drumbeat.

Here is an example of what I am talking about. Perhaps a few decades back, a young lady was raised with the value of modesty being taught in her home. Her mother taught her to dress in a chaste way that brought attention to her countenance rather than her body. She was taught to be feminine and carry herself in an appropriate way through the way she sat and spoke, etc. She was raised to be meek in spirit rather than overly flamboyant and loud. I would agree with all of that and am trying to encourage my own daughters in the same regard. Let's say that this young lady's heart was never quickened by the Holy Spirit and she never made these convictions her own. She only did what she was taught to do to avoid displeasing her parents and receiving discipline. Inwardly, her unregenerate, sinful heart grew bitter at what she viewed as "rules," and she grew to hate the idea of modesty and femininity. At some point, she made friends with girls who did not grow up like she did, and they fed her desire to rebel against these virtues. This became a slippery path for her, and as an adult she ended up dressing in a post-modern, edgy, immodest, feministic form of dress. She changed her mannerisms to be hard, sarcastic, proud, and edgy. I personally have seen this happen way too many times. What is the problem here? Were her parents at fault for teaching her what the Scripture says?

"But let your adorning be the hidden person of the heart with the imperishable beauty of a gentle and quiet spirit, which in God's sight is very precious" (1 Peter 3:4).

"Likewise also that women should adorn themselves in respectable apparel, with modesty and self-control" (1 Timothy 2:9).

I believe her parents were absolutely right to teach her to dress modestly and to carry herself in a feminine manner which honors God's design for women. It appears that the root problem is of the heart in this situation. Unfortunately, this young lady did not accept God's Word as her standard and failed to make modesty and femininity a conviction in her own heart. This could be because she was never saved. Maybe her parents were harsh, or perhaps some of her questions about the whys of the "rules" were not adequately answered. Parents do need to be careful about setting standards and only having, "Because the Bible says so" or "Because I said so" as their only answer. I have heard too many rebellious adults say that their parents had tons of rules and never explained why or answered their questions. It would behoove us to take our young peoples' questions seriously and have heart to heart discussions with them, showing them from God's Word where we are getting the convictions we hold in our families. These talks need to transpire in a loving, safe environment where our kids know that we are for them and not against them. We are not the enemy seeking to make their lives miserable. Instead, we are in their court, fighting for them, and sacrificing our time and emotion for their well-being. It is important that they understand that our "rules" are not something we made up or just something some conference speaker recommended. We need to take them straight to the Word of God and show them what His infallible Word says on any given topic. At this point we should not be preaching at them and cramming verses down their throats. We should rather be speaking the truth in love and reminding them that our goal is their good. What is going to be good and lead to blessing in their lives will always be following God's plan laid out in His Word no matter how vastly different that may look from the culture around us. From time to time we as Christian parents need to assess whether our children are adopting our teaching and making it their own heart conviction. Is the baton of faith being passed from one generation to the next? This is a very important question.

First John 5:3 tells us that, "For this is the love of God, that we keep his commandments. And his commandments are not burdensome." As parents wanting to disciple our children and have their hearts we need to consider carefully how we present and lead our families in God-honoring standards. In a business there are effective and ineffective ways to lead employees. It is the same in a family. We want to be the kind of parents that our children desire to follow. It is true that we do not want to throw Biblical standards to the wayside, but we need to be wise in our leadership. God's commands are not meant to be burdensome. There is joy in obeying the Lord, and we want our children to grow up serving the Lord with gladness. We cannot accomplish this in our own strength, but the Lord can do this through us as we lead with love, always point to Scripture for answers, make ourselves available to talk and listen, and resist the urge to enforce rules by harsh leadership.

I think it also needs to be said that sometimes parents do everything "right" and their children still rebel. I have brought out some areas in which parents contribute to the problem, but I am in no way saying that every prodigal points to a parent who did things wrong. I believe we are living in a day of strong apostasy, and there are no guarantees in parenting. It is imperative for us to remember that we cannot save our children or give them a heart to follow Christ in righteousness. We must prove faithful to be Biblical in training our children and yet remember the most important work is the work that only the Holy Spirit can do to woo our children to Himself. There are some prodigal kids whose parents were exemplary in how they raised and discipled their family for Christ. Hence I am in no way pointing judgment on anyone who has a wayward or struggling child. I am only trying to point out some observations that I think can be helpful to me and to those still raising small children. The reality that there are no guarantees in parenting should keep us faithfully on our knees. Also, for those parents who do have struggling prodigals, it is never too late for the redemptive work of the Spirit of the Lord in our families. There is always hope, even for the prodigal child.

98

Holiness and Sanctification

So what is the Biblical balance between legalism and antinomianism? Well, I believe the Lord calls his people to holiness. God is perfectly holy which means He is without sin. Of course, we will never be without a struggle with sin in this life, but one day we will be fully sanctified in the presence of our Savior. As we journey through life, the Lord desires to continue the process of ongoing sanctification in our lives so that we become more and more like Christ Jesus. Sanctification is that process of the Lord setting us apart for His Kingdom and glory. As He sanctifies us we begin looking and acting more like the character of Christ, and our values will be shifting away from worldly, temporal desires and becoming more eternally focused.

I pray for an awakening in the hearts of Christian parents, that many will desire to consecrate all areas of their homes and families to reflect the purity and goodness of the Savior. I pray that there will be a new crop of Christian families who seek to approve the excellent rather than wallow in the muck and mire of worldly mediocrity. How exciting it would be to see masses of Christian families experiencing true revival and bowing the knee to the Lordship of Christ in their homes. This ongoing work of consecration and sanctification is what my husband and I pray for in our own family and what we desire to find in fellowship with others.

"Strive for peace with everyone, and for the holiness without which no one will see the Lord" (Hebrews 12:14).

The book of First John tells us that we will not love the world if the love of the Father is in us. Christians often argue about what the definition of worldliness is. People will ask, what is worldly? I have heard people say that it is hard to define worldliness. I think First John chapter two helps clarify this.

"Do not love the world or the things in the world. If anyone loves the world, the love of the Father is not in him. For all that is in the world—the desires of the flesh and the desires of the eyes and pride of life—is not from the Father but is from the world. And the world is passing away along with its desires, but whoever does the will of God abides forever" (I John 2:15-17).

I believe this passage indicates that the main components of worldliness are the lust of the flesh, the desires of the eyes, and the pride of life. The ungodly are those who march to the drumbeat of this world rather than look to Christ for their marching orders. When considering what is or is not worldly or what is and is not holy, we can ask questions such as:

1. Does this thing appeal to the lust of the flesh?
2. Does this thing appeal to the desires of the eyes?
3. Does this thing appeal to the pride of life?

For example, in considering a movie, does the movie stir up lustful desires? Does it make me covet what I do not have? Does it promote a worldview of pride? These questions can certainly be applied to media, clothing, relationships, entertainments, attitudes, materialism and most any area of life. I believe worldliness is following after the broad road of destruction that the ungodly are running down. I believe part of holiness is not delighting in that which is sinful, lustful, prideful, and following the narrow path that leads to life. Holiness is God setting us apart from sin and to Christ. This is something we cannot do in and of ourselves. This is done by the power of Christ in us so that He will receive all the glory. It is not a popular message but we all must decide if we will pursue worldliness or holiness. Jesus said:

"Enter by the narrow gate. For the gate is wide and the way is easy that leads to destruction, and those who enter by it are many. For the gate is narrow and the way is hard that leads to life, and those who find it are few" (Matthew 7:13-14).

Pursue Unity

The topics of legalism, antinomianism, and holiness are explosive topics in today's Christian climate. People often enter these conversations with very biased opinions and strong emotions. It is important to keep going back to Scripture and basing our beliefs on the Word of God rather than the opinions of man. I do not want to close this chapter without touching on one more point, and that is unity. As Christians we are called to love one another.

"A new commandment I give to you, that you love one another: just as I have loved you, you also are to love one another. By this all people will know that you are my disciples, if you have love for one another" (John 13:34-35).

I strongly believe in the pursuit of holiness and sanctification and yet it is important to also seek love and unity with other believers. We will not all see eye to eye on the gray areas in life, on every theological point, on styles of church worship, etc., but we should seek to pursue peace with one another. When we understand that we will spend eternity with all Christians, it brings perspective that we are truly the family of God and need to learn to get along. I know when my children have conflicts with one another it makes my heart sad. I think the heart of God must also sorrow over so many believers who war against one another. A huge dose of humility can go a long way in promoting unity, love, and peace among God's people. This does not mean that we turn a blind eye to sin, but in areas of Christian liberty and personal convictions we need to be gracious with one another. Those who are more seasoned in their Christian walk need to seek to disciple newer believers in a spirit of love. Every person and every family is on a personal journey with the Lord and we need to prayerfully and lovingly seek to spur one another on towards love and good deeds. We should look for what we do agree upon and unite around the blessed news of the gospel of Jesus Christ. In a day when persecution of Christians seems to be moving closer our way we would be wise to not splinter and divide over every petty issue but to humbly love our brothers and sisters in Christ. We will often gravitate to people who are more likeminded with us for our closest heart friendships and yet it is important to seek peace with all men as much as it depends on us.

"Live in harmony with one another. Do not be haughty, but associate with the lowly. Never be wise in your own sight. Repay no one evil for evil, but give thought to do what is honorable in the sight of all. If possible, so far as it depends on you, live peaceably with all" (Romans 12:16-18).

Let us pray that our families and the body of Christ at large will pursue Biblical unity, holiness, and love. By God's grace may we all be moving closer to loving what God loves, hating what God hates, and having our hearts broken over what breaks the heart of God.

Chapter 8

No, Character Training is Not the Gospel, BUT It is Important!

I am thankful to have grown up in an environment where training in godly character was like the air we breathed. I was taught from my youngest years to obey, to respect adults, and to treat others in honorable ways. I am extremely thankful for this legacy, because as I look around, I see culture coming apart at the seams. I believe much of this is because character is a rare find. My grandmother recently went home to be with Jesus, but she imparted much love and many life lessons to me. One thing I remember her saying is, "I believe in smiling at people and speaking to people." She was known and loved in her small town of Longview, Texas for her friendliness, loyalty, and kindness towards others.

As a young girl I loved story books that taught various character traits, either through animal stories or stories about other children. Sadly, I have noticed the rise in popularity of a parenting philosophy that discourages focused character training in fear of creating little Pharisees. I believe this ideology is a knee-jerk reaction to parents who groomed their children to look almost impeccable on the outside, while in some cases not doing such a good job working on heart issues. We need to address the heart as the foundation with our children, but we must not neglect to also train them in godly character. This character training needs to begin with correcting their attitudes and disobedience as little tots and should be an ongoing work in process as they grow older. Both the Old and New Testaments have many verses about training and disciplining children.

"My son, keep your father's commandment, and forsake not your mother's teaching. Bind them on your heart always; tie them around your neck. When you walk, they will lead you; when you lie down, they will watch over you; and when you awake, they will talk with you" (Proverbs 6:20-22).

And have you forgotten the exhortation that addresses you as sons? "My son, do not regard lightly the discipline of the Lord, nor be weary when reproved by him. For the Lord disciplines the one he loves, and chastises every son whom he receives." It is for discipline that you have to endure. God is treating you as sons. For what son is there whom his father does not discipline? If you are left without discipline, in which all have participated, then you are illegitimate children and not sons. Besides this, we have had earthly fathers who disciplined us and we respected them. Shall we not much more be subject to the Father of spirits and live? (Hebrews 12:5-11).

"Discipline your son, and he will give you rest; he will give delight to your heart" (Proverbs 29:17).

"Children, obey your parents in everything, for this pleases the Lord" (Colossians 3:20).

These verses are just a small sampling of the many verses in Scripture that talk about obeying and heeding parental instruction. In fact, there is a serious warning that, if we neglect to train and discipline our children, we will destroy them. Regardless of how much we talk to them about their heart and the good news of the gospel, we do our children a great disservice if we do not also train their character and teach them the necessity of obedience and surrender to God-ordained authority. We are actually disobeying the commands Scripture gives to us as parents. We are not being faithful to what God has required of us as parents.

"Whoever spares the rod hates his son, but he who loves him is diligent to discipline him" (Proverbs 13:24).

Discipline is definitely required, especially with little people. They need to understand that obedience brings blessing, but disobedience brings trouble or consequences. That is something I have often reminded my children of. It might even be a little phrase you would want to have your young children repeat back to you. Even though discipline is a necessary part of child training, it is great when we can prevent the need for it by training ahead of time. If we can talk through various scenarios and practice good behaviors, politeness, and right responses, then some of the need for discipline will be cut out as our children will be ahead of the game because of the time we spent training them. Of course each child is born with a sin nature and will sometimes choose to yield to that nature, creating the need for consequences as well. Young children must be taught to yield to and obey their parents with respect. This is training for them to learn to respond to their Heavenly Father and obey His voice.

If a child is not taught to be honest, kind, polite, work hard, etc. when he is young, he will not suddenly have those virtues when he is older.

With that being said, it is worth raising a caution here that we be careful to not let our children believe that they are righteous based upon the

104

development of commendable character. Their hope should never be in their good works or right behavior but solely upon the work of Christ in their behalf. They must understand that moralism will not save them, but that does not at all negate the need for character training. First and foremost, they must understand that they are sinners and that they have a great need for the good news of the gospel. In addition to teaching them of their need for Christ and salvation we must also be training them from their earliest days to work on obedience and all the other character traits that we can see in the life of Christ. It is our goal to be like Jesus, and that training should start from the time our children are little bitty. I believe parents can miss the mark if they focus only on the character and outward performances but ignore the heart of the child or if they focus only on the love of Christ and the gospel message while ignoring their responsibility to train the character of their children. It is possible to raise up a child who looks very impressive on the outside but has a stinky, selfish heart inwardly. So, while genuine salvation is the highest goal, basic character training should also be worked on from the time our children are babies. The two go together. When a child realizes he cannot measure up to God's standard, which is perfection, then he is better able to see his great need for a Savior. Also, when genuine conversion has happened, it should propel the child to want to follow the Biblical command, "You shall be holy, for I am holy" (1 Peter 1:16). In my observations I have noticed that many parents today are running from what they see as a legalistic approach of trying to solely clean up the external appearance of their children while ignoring their hearts. I believe the problem is that many of these well-meaning parents are overcorrecting and have become afraid of any kind of character training at all. Some of these parents focus so heavily upon the heart that they have lowered the bar to a very low expectation of obedience and respect from their children. There is a delicate balance needed here. If our children never learn to obey us as parents, how will they ever know how to bow the knee to the Lordship of Christ? If they never learn to respect us as God-given authority figures, how will they come to reverence and respect the Lord Jesus in their lives? If they think they rule the universe, how will they see the need for King Jesus to rule in their lives? I see two extremes that are both dangerous. We must not just clean up our kids outwardly and ignore their hearts. We cannot let them think they are righteous before God just because they are well behaved. This will indeed produce pharisaical children. However, a pendulum swing in the opposite direction is also very dangerous. To raise children and only focus on their hearts while failing to train them in the way they should go is a recipe for disaster. We cannot just tell our children how much Jesus loves them without balancing that by teaching them that the sovereign God of the universe is a

God of justice and has commands that we are to obey. His commands are for our good and are not burdensome.

"By this we know that we love the children of God, when we love God and obey his commandments. For this is the love of God, that we keep his commandments. And his commandments are not burdensome. For everyone who has been born of God overcomes the world. And this is the victory that has overcome the world—our faith" (1 John 5:2-4).

Our culture today has so elevated foolishness, frivolity, and entertainment that godly character is hard to find. Many companies have a hard time acquiring employees they can trust to put forth a decent effort, to be trustworthy, and not to steal from their employers. Have you noticed how rude people often are in public? It is astonishing! Sadly, our society has lost sight of the value of each person as made in the image of God. We see the devaluation of life in the manslaughter of the abortion industry and in practices such as euthanasia. When we lose sight of the fact that each life is made in the image of God and created for His purposes and glory, society loses respect for life. As culture implodes itself with sin and debauchery, character is lost, and people treat each other with little respect and courtesy.

It doesn't take rocket science to see that something is wrong with the unhealthy relationships that are common place in our society. People go into marriage with the philosophy that they can discard their spouse if it doesn't work out. There has been a huge unraveling of the nuclear family, and many parents farm out their children at every possible opportunity for more "me time." Masses of children are growing up disrespecting their parents and other authorities. In many cases social media is replacing real life relationships, youth is idolized in our culture, and the youth fail to see the value of learning from the insight of their elders. In general, people think they owe no one respect but themselves. This is depicted in the t-shirts that say, "It's all about me." I have heard it said that this millennial generation is the most narcissistic generation yet. Truly, it is disturbing when you realize the trajectory society is on. Many people think only of themselves and think nothing of hurting others. The culture is becoming more animalistic in behavior all the time. When you look at Scripture, this is not the way God created mankind, made in His image, to exist. He said:

"Then the LORD God said, 'It is not good that the man should be alone; I will make him a helper fit for him'" (Genesis 2:18).

Adam valued the gift God gave him in Eve. "Then the man said, 'This at last is bone of my bones and flesh of my flesh; she shall be called Woman, because she was taken out of Man'" (Genesis 2:23).

Verse 24 goes on to say that the man and wife should leave father and mother and hold fast to each other. This verse exemplifies a connection and loyalty first to parents and then transferred to spouse. This is not a flippant, disposable relationship.

"Therefore a man shall leave his father and his mother and hold fast to his wife, and they shall become one flesh" (Genesis 2:24).

Much of relationship breakdown is due to two things. First, it is obvious that much of our nation has apostatized from the faith and rejected the Lordship of Jesus Christ. Secondly, when we do not follow Christ Jesus as Lord, godly character is broken down and lost. This is where I believe our nation is at. Praise the Lord there is always a remnant of Christ followers who do not just claim Christ but also bow the knee to Him. As parents may we be constantly taking our families to the cross, bowing our knees there, and obediently following our Savior.

If our goal is to teach our children to love Christ, to obey Christ, and to make Christ known, we would be greatly amiss not to train our children in Godly character. What I am talking about here is the careful, strategic training of our children in the ways of the Lord.

Some time back, I was shopping at a local store when I heard a team leader address an employee and say, "Thank you for leading by example." It struck me that even in the secular business world people recognize that right character should be encouraged.

In way of reiteration here, I will make the point again that teaching our children godly character does not save them. Our justification in Christ is by grace through faith alone and not by any works we have done. Our children need to be reminded of this often.

"For by grace you have been saved through faith. And this is not your own doing; it is the gift of God, not a result of works, so that no one may boast" (Ephesians 2:8-9).

While I see the dangers of focusing too heavily merely on externals, it has been much to my dismay to see the rapid growth of the popular Christian parenting philosophy that discourages purposeful character training in our children. This philosophy abounds in many circles and tends to run thick in some reformed theological circles. I hear things like, "Since I, as the parent, do not see fruit of regeneration in my child, I would be teaching him to be a hypocrite if I require character that is not coming from his heart. I better just sit back and wait for the Holy Spirit to save my child and then my child will want to do right from his heart." In my opinion that is a hyper-Calvinistic perspective on parenting that is unhealthy. Scripture does not add the prerequisite of salvation to training their children.

There is a balance needed in these philosophies. Yes, the Holy Spirit is the only one who can change a child's heart, draw him unto Himself, give him repentance and faith, and energize him to walk in obedience. However, parents are also given a responsibility to "train up a child" (Proverbs 22:6), to discipline a son (Proverbs 29:17), and to teach all through the day (Deuteronomy 6:7), etc. Ephesians commands children to "obey their parents," and Proverbs tells a son to "honor his father and mother." These verses do not say, "if the child has been regenerated." They show a certain way a child should be brought up. It is as if we should bring them up with the expectation that God will save them. How exciting that we as parents get to partner with the Lord in this calling. He is the one who saves, but He uses us to gently nurture, train, discipline, lead them to the cross, and engage in ongoing discipleship. While we teach our children right from wrong and engage in ongoing character training, we must stay focused on showing them their need for the Savior and sharing the good news of the gospel with them over and over again. When they show a character deficiency, such as rudeness instead of kindness, we can gently remind them that this is yet another reason they need to repent of sin and put their trust fully in Christ. Character training without the good news of the gospel will leave children feeling either defeated or proud. They will either be proud of how perfect they think their behavior is or defeated that they cannot measure up. Character training rooted in the gospel is the goal. We want our children to know that there is a standard in God's Word for our behavior. It is because we are powerless to attain that standard that God has sent us a Savior through His Son and a helper through the Holy Spirit.

Children are Born with a Bent Towards Foolishness

"Folly is bound up in the heart of a child, but the rod of discipline drives it far from him" (Proverbs 22:15).

The Lord has given parents the job of training their children away from foolishness towards character that honors Him. He has given us our children for a season, and the training should begin early as that season passes very quickly. In the process of training and teaching our children, they are given the opportunity to see more clearly just how much they do need a

Savior to help them in their character deficiencies. Godly character will not save our children, but parents must remain faithful and obedient to what Scripture says about bringing up children in the way they should go.

Chapter 9
Marriage Within the Context of Homeschooling

I have known of and heard stories of Christian homeschooling couples whose marriages have not survived the test of time. I have known many more that have survived but have not thrived. This breaks my heart as I know so many of these couples were probably trying with all their might to do the best they could for the children and families and yet their marriages suffered. Most marriages begin with two people coming together with hopes and dreams of a happy life together, and it is very sad when these dreams are dashed and a couple is anything but happy. It comes as a huge warning and reminder to me that homeschool daddies and mamas need to keep working at their marriages. I know that, whether you homeschool or not, life can get very busy and chaotic as your children grow older. Through the years I have heard many people talk about how the busyness of their children and keeping up with their activities eventually strained their marriages. In the homeschooling context it is important to be extra vigilant to fight against this scenario. Oftentimes, daddies and mamas are working overtime to teach their children at home and, sometimes, there are a lot of children in the picture. Consequently, life can get very busy, and communication can break down in the marriage relationship.

Matt and I are no exception in that we have to prioritize time for us to communicate and stay connected. One thing we have done in recent years is to enjoy a date night at home. For us, this has meant that, after Matt arrives home from work, usually on a Friday night, I will leave and go pick up fajitas from our favorite restaurant. He will get the children to bed while I am gone so that we can have a quiet dinner together when I return with the food. This has been a good way for us to have a time where we can talk without interruptions on a weekly basis. Occasionally, we have the treat of having a babysitter come, but there have been many weeks when our date night at home has had to suffice.

At other times, we have put the children to bed and taken a walk around our farm. If the children need us they can call us on the walkie-talkies. Or sometimes we wait until the children are in bed and then we sit on the porch swing or rockers with bowls of ice cream. What is most important is that some way, somehow, time is carved out for couples to have time to talk, communicate, and pray about things together.

We are now in a new season where we have a couple of young people who are old enough to babysit for us. When we first started leaving our oldest with her siblings we started very small and only left the house for about an hour, eating dinner very close to home. Over time we have worked up to longer stretches of time and have ventured out farther from home. I remember the first night we left Lauren at home to babysit. I told Matt that it had been such a long time since we had enjoyed the freedom to go to dinner without hiring a babysitter! It felt strange and wonderful all at the same time!

Matt and I try to pray together before bedtime when it is possible. It has become more challenging the more children we have and the busier our lives have become. I am grateful, however, that Matt keeps pursuing me to pray with him when we have the opportunity. His prayers are comforting to me as I hear him address concerns he knows weigh upon my heart. I appreciate his leadership to keep working at seeking the Lord together even when it is not as easy to be as consistent as it once was. I am thankful he does not give up and keeps making that effort to share prayer with me at the close of the day.

As hard as it can sometimes be to prioritize the marriage when life is spinning at lightning speed, it is vitally important to the overall health of the family. I have heard it said many times that one of the greatest gifts we can give our children is a strong marriage. When they know that Daddy and Mama are committed to each other and love each other, that gives them a strong sense of stability. It is our job to model for our children an example of what a loving, Christ-centered marriage should look like. For better or for worse, they are learning from our example. They will naturally pick up many of our patterns of relating to our spouses. In turn, they will likely default to many of the same ways of dealing with their future spouses one day.

When a mama has committed her life to staying at home and homeschooling her children, this vision can easily take her all, and it can be easy to let the priority of a healthy marriage slip to the back burner. I believe that our enemy, the devil, has employed this strategy to bring down some Christian marriages within the homeschooling community. We need to be aware and vigilant. Marriage is worth fighting for and it is worth working at. Let's pray for hearts to keep working at building strong marriages that display the beauty of the gospel for our children and those around us to see. Christ chose marriage to be the image of His relationship with His church. Marriage is a powerful way to display His glory, and that is why Satan has an all-out attack on it today. Everything testifies to something, and God ordained it that the oneness in our marriages should testify to the unity and love between Christ and His church.

"Therefore a man shall leave his father and mother and hold fast to his wife, and the two shall become one flesh. This mystery is profound, and I am saying that it refers to Christ and the church, However, let each one of you love his wife as himself, and let the wife see that she respects her husband" (Ephesians 5:31-33).

One thing that has been life giving to our marriage has been taking little getaways together. I am very aware that not every season of parenting affords busy parents this blessing and yet, in our case, we have had the blessing of being able to do this occasionally. Usually a getaway involves a lot of hassle to make it happen. The arrangements for the children can be overwhelming, along with packing and all the added stresses of travel preparations. Sometimes it can feel like it is just too much to even try, but it has been very good for Matt and me. We have not been able to do this every year, but the Lord has been good to provide opportunities off and on. We have enjoyed a couple of Weekend to Remember events put on by Family Life, and those have been really great in reminding us of Biblical truth and vision for a God-honoring marriage. It has been a good tune up each time and an opportunity for us to talk, pray, and communicate. A getaway with your spouse is an opportunity to create memories and build relationship with the one God gave you to journey through life with. It is helpful to have that one-on-one time without distractions to focus just on each other. Planning a couple nights away is a helpful way of refreshing the marriage when the stresses and demands of life can be so intense. The Lord may or may not choose to give a time away in a given season, but if you can make it happen and feel confident your children are in good care, then it is worth the sacrifices to prioritize marriage getaways. The marriage is the foundation for the family and needs to remain strong. If the foundation starts cracking, it does not go well for the rest of the family. Regardless of your stage of life, I would encourage you to prayerfully making sure that your marriage does not get ignored but remains a high priority. Even if you cannot do anything more than have a date night at home, do not ignore your marriage while being swallowed up in homeschooling children and raising a family. One day the children will fly away and you want to be sure that you still like and enjoy your spouse. Marriage is the first institution established by God, and it is very important to Him and is designed to bring Him glory.

Chapter 10
Life Lessons from the Amish

When I was young and had free time, I used to read Christian fiction books about the Amish. Being a conservative girl at heart, I fell in love with these stories. There was something about their simple, conservative, family centered values that resonated with me. I formed this inward dream that I would one day love to go and visit Lancaster County and see it all with my own eyes. My dear husband knew this and, many years into our marriage, he suggested that we take an anniversary trip to Pennsylvania and visit Amish country. We stayed in a quaint, antique Bed and Breakfast and toured the community during the days we were there. I remember my ecstatic excitement as we were driving into Lancaster County and I saw a real-life Amish daddy playing outside with his real-life Amish children on a Sunday afternoon. I was taken with the beautiful winding farm roads, old farm houses, dresses hanging on massive clotheslines, and the beautifully manicured lawns. I seriously fell in love with it all and felt like I was leaving my heart behind when it was time to return home. I had to leave, but I did not forget all that I had seen there. It left me hungry to see and experience more.

The Lord blessed us the following year with another opportunity to get away for our anniversary. Now let me be quick to say that these opportunities to get away together come few and far between, but the Lord has been good to grant us this blessing from time to time. It just so happened that we were able to go two years in a row. At the time, we had frequent flyer miles from Matt's many overseas trips, so we could choose wherever we wanted to go. My heartstrings were pulling me back towards Amish country again, and so my sweet husband told me to pack my bonnet and be ready to visit Ohio Amish country this time. I was elated and fell even more in love with Amish country the second time around. This time we hit it at the peak of the fall foliage, and I learned just how beautiful fall can be. Wow! There was a beautiful glow radiating from the beautiful Maple trees in deep yellow, orange, and red hues. The abundant flowers and other trees were truly magnificent. One day Matt and I rode a small train, winding around a picturesque lake with October blue skies above and radiantly colored trees surrounding us. This train was driven by an older Amish man and we had such a lovely time. Ohio is the largest Amish community in the country, and the landscape was picturesque. We rented a car and popped in a CD of Fernando

Ortega singing hymns as we drove those beautiful backroads admiring sprawling farmlands, white houses, and large silos. Our trips to Amish communities have included history tours, tours of homes, school houses, gardens, buggy rides, plays, and shopping in quilt shops and other cottage industries. We also experienced the yumminess of whoopie pies in different flavors that are oh so scrumptious!

There is a precious tranquility in the air in these communities. You often see signs or crosses with Scripture posted around the community. The people in these communities value character, their faith, their families, hard work, and they seek to be good neighbors to others. It is so refreshing to go into a place where, for the most part, you see respectful and obedient children and a community of tight-knit families who are seeking to live in godly ways. I have been very curious and gone in with a watchful eye to see what I could learn. I don't think you have to be Amish to learn a great deal from their way of life. In so many ways they have their priorities straight in areas most of us Englischers (the name Amish people call Non-Amish people) struggle to keep in balance.

My next visit to Amish country took me on a trip to Shipshewana, Indiana. This was a personal retreat where I was able to enjoy the Amish country, write some in this book, and visit the ministry headquarters for Revive Our Hearts, about an hour away in the neighboring state of Michigan. The night I drove from the airport into Shipshewana happened to be the night the town lit up its square for Christmas. People were singing special music, and a pastor was praying over the microphone in Jesus' name. It was refreshing to stand and watch this ceremony and see how Christ honoring it was. Amish, Mennonites, and other members of the surrounding areas were gathered together for this warmhearted, special occasion. It was a celebratory environment to enter into and to experience the heart of the community, which is much more Christ centered than most communities. While there, I enjoyed shopping for Christmas gifts, taking a tour at the Menno-Hof museum on Amish and Mennonite history, taking a car tour with an audio CD explaining the history of the area, feasting on Amish cooking, etc. I was there on a Sunday morning and visited a conservative Mennonite church where I made a friend who shares the name Ruth with me. The area has such a small-town feel that she asked which hotel I was at and dropped off a gift sack for me later during my stay. In the sack she left some locally made cheese and popcorn and a sweet note of encouragement. I have loved keeping up with her since that time. It was neat to experience how the community was small, warm and welcoming in so many ways. Once I had been there a few days some ladies started recognizing me, and I enjoyed chatting with different ones. It was a refreshing contrast to the large city rat race I normally deal with when I go out to do errands. I remember being in my hotel room at night diffusing my essential oils and writing in this book. It really was a wonderful retreat that I have fond memories of.

Well, after these adventures in Pennsylvania, Ohio and Indiana, and loving every minute of them, I was in complete shock when I was shopping at Costco one day and got a text from my husband saying he saw what looked like an Amish couple in a buggy not far from where we live. I absolutely could not see how this could be possible. I had done plenty of research to know that the only Amish community in Texas is in Beeville, around seven hours from us. The Amish have not traditionally settled in Texas very much. Every now and then I will see a conservative Mennonite somewhere in the Houston area, but I don't remember ever seeing an Amish person in Houston. Only the Lord knows how much I have wished I could have an Amish friend or even a pen pal. When I got home from running errands that night I did a google search to see if I could find out whether any Amish had moved into our area. My search was not giving me any leads so I began periodically driving down the road my husband had seen this couple on. There was one building where I saw a horse and buggy. Many other times I would go by and not see a buggy at all. It was a huge mystery that I could not figure out. I was speculating in my mind what the possibilities were. Had my husband seen a movie in the making? Had he seen Amish traveling through and gone forever? Why was that buggy at that building sometimes but not there when I drove by at other times? I was in quite the state of confusion until one morning I was driving down the highway and saw an Amish couple beside a horse and buggy having a bake sale! I quickly pulled off the highway and introduced myself to them. The young man explained to me that the couple my husband had seen was his parents and that he and his wife and children were visiting from Virginia. He told me there were indeed two Amish families living under ten minutes from our farm! We exchanged phone numbers, and he invited our family to a hymn sing that coming Sunday night. I was ecstatic about this invitation, as I was familiar with the idea of Amish hymn sings through books I had read. That Sunday night, my husband and I went to our first Amish hymn sing with our nine-year-old Annagrace and our baby Ella Ruth. It was a potluck-style gathering, so we brought some taco soup in our crockpot and entered into a gathering of very sincere people who welcomed us into their midst. We loved hearing them sing some of their hymns in German out of their hymnal called the *Ausbund* and also singing along with them when they sang in English. We were impressed with their heartfelt singing and beautiful harmonies. When we complimented them on their harmonizing they were quick to share with us that what is important to them is making melody in their hearts to the

Lord. One thing that I have found so refreshing about the Amish culture is their humility and sincerity. I found myself that night rocking my baby in an Amish-made rocking chair, holding a genuine Anabaptist hymnal, and singing with new friends who warmed my heart. After the singing time, someone read a passage of scripture and we had a time of everyone going down on their knees and praying. You would have to be there to experience the beauty of such simplicity and devotion. There was nothing fancy about the gathering; it was just a relaxing time of sweet worship and fellowship. Well, that was not our only hymn sing. We have continued to develop friendship with these families and have enjoyed meeting other Amish people, as various groups have come for a visit from out of state. I have had the privilege of driving some of them in our van and have greatly enjoyed getting to know these sweet neighbors.

Perhaps you do not know much about the Amish and Mennonites and maybe you wonder what touches my soul so deeply about these people. On the other hand, perhaps you have read books, visited Amish country, or have known some of these people yourself. I think sometimes the Amish are deeply misunderstood when people do not take the time to learn about them and why they live in some very set apart ways from the rest of culture. What some people fail to realize is that, oftentimes, when the Amish have a way that is different from the rest of society, it is not because they think a particular thing like vehicles is sinful but, rather, they are choosing alternate ways in order to preserve a simpler, less frazzled lifestyle. They are also seeking to honor their heritage and maintain family-centered priorities. They are a people who value helping one another out and living in a tight knit community. The beautiful thing that I have observed is that they are often very welcoming to outsiders but resolute in who they are. They have chosen not to follow the modern culture off the cliff of annihilation. They are trying to preserve a lifestyle of honoring God, loving others, raising respectful adults, and holding onto principles of godly character. When we have traveled out of state and taken historical tours of farms and museums, we have been reminded that they are people like the rest of us and that sometimes they face troubles in their homes and communities as well. Overall, however, it seems the Amish are doing a good job of keeping their children's hearts and growing strong, God-centered families and communities.

My trips to Amish communities, and now my experience with Amish neighbors, has been encouraging to me. It has been reviving to my heart to see people who display character, who honor God, who live in wholesome community, who train their children in character, and who strive to live according to Biblical principles. Of course they do not do this perfectly, because none of us do everything perfectly, but the general trajectory of these communities seems to be something very unique and special.

Many of the Amish value the Word of God and esteem it highly. They believe it to be the infallible and relevant Word of God. They encourage reading it daily and memorizing passages to help resist temptation. They prioritize reading the Bible as a family as well. They also value children knowing that earthly things will pass away but children are eternal souls that last forever. The Amish value traditional roles for men and women. The women are generally keepers at home and are never the preachers in their churches. They believe in the Biblical authority structure for the family. In the book *Our Amish Values: Who We Are and What We Believe*, Lester Beachy explains:

"I believe the greatest responsibility lies on us men. If we love our wife with a sacrificial love, she will find it easier to let us lead, and thus to fulfill her role. As we fulfill our God-given role, we find that it works. God's plan is always best." [10]

They also value freedom, particularly in light of their history of persecution going back to the time of the Reformation. Again quoting from the book cited above, Lester Beachy says:

"We value honesty. We simply trust each other. We try to speak the truth. We value integrity and moral purity. We value community, and strive to help each other in time of need. We value our heritage and pray that we can instill these same values in our children."

What have I learned from studying the Amish and from my friendships with them? I feel like I have learned and am learning many things. For one, I am challenged to look at my life and consider where I am too busy and where I need to simplify. I am encouraged to make my marriage, my children, and my home the priority that the Lord calls it to be and to center my focus on eternal values. I can easily get caught up in shopping for just the right whatever or feeling I have to have a Pinterest perfect this or that or I have to have things looking a certain way, etc. I'm not saying that all these things are wrong, but I am saying that I have been challenged to look at my priorities and to consider where I sometimes am tempted to get out of balance with temporal things. I have at times, especially when I had fewer children, been too busy letting my feet run about here and there when I should have been more faithful in the keeping of my home. I am also seeing that, oftentimes, the simpler things are the most beautiful things. We can spend our short lives running after changing trends and trying to keep up with whatever or we can pour our lives into things that will have eternal value. Things that will count for eternity are things like relationships with our family and those the Lord brings into our lives, things like discipling our children and Titus 2 mentorship of other women, things like loving and feasting on the Word of God, things like sitting around and singing hymns after dinner rather than turning on a movie, things like working hard and seeing the fruit of our labors, and the list could go on and on.

Since the name Ruth is a very common name among the Amish, I have laughed and said that my parents gave me a good Amish name. I think I would have fit right in had I been born Amish. Well, God did not choose for me to be born Amish, but He has graciously allowed me the blessing of learning from them and enjoying friendship with them. I do highly respect them and feel quite likeminded in many areas. Even though there are some cultural differences, I feel far more likeminded with them than I do with the liberal progressive, brave new world emerging around me today. I am grateful for my experiences with the Amish and for the things I am learning from their beautiful, simple way of living. I am reminded of the old hymn that says:

Turn your eyes upon Jesus
Look full in His wonderful face
And the things of Earth will grow strangely dim
In the light of His glory and grace—Helen Howarth Lemmel

Chapter 11
Treasuring the Ancient Paths
in a Progressive World

"Thus says the Lord: 'Stand by the roads, and look, and ask for the ancient paths, where the good way is; and walk in it, and find rest for your souls'" (Jeremiah 6:16).

The ancient paths are found in the Word of God. They are beautifully described in this hymn by Lynn DeShazo.

Holy words long preserved
For our walk in this world
They resound with God's own heart
Oh, let the ancient words impart
Words of Life, words of Hope
Give us strength, help us cope
In this world, where e'er we roam
Ancient words will guide us home

Ancient words ever true
Changing me and changing you
We have come with open hearts
Oh, let the ancient words impart
Holy words of our Faith
Handed down to this age
Came to us through sacrifice
Oh, heed the faithful words of Christ

Holy words long preserved
For our walk in this world
They resound with God's own heart
Oh, let the ancient words impart
Ancient words ever true
Changing me and changing you
We have come with open hearts
Oh, let the ancient words impart [11]

In thinking about ancient paths and godly legacies, I cannot help but ponder how fast culture is changing all around us. In recent years I have seen an acceleration of fast-paced, major cultural transformations in technological communications and interactions between people. I have also seen major shifts in cultural perceptions of reality, morality, and ethics. I believe we are living in a time of widespread rebellion against God and His Word. The speed at which technology has altered the way we live has almost been too much to keep up with. While some of the technological advances have opened incredible doors for ministry, much of it also seems to be leading the culture at large into deeper decadence and fracturing family relationships. We live in the information age and have stimuli and information coming to us at faster and faster speeds all the time. Personally, I find my brain is often trying to function in overload status, as all day I've been bombarded with not only the constant stimuli from the family I live with but also with a huge amount of media content. All day I have email, Facebook, Pinterest, radio, video, texting, podcasts, and other forms of media pulling at my thoughts. It is not unusual for me to have Facebook updates, new texts, a voicemail message, and several children competing for my attention all at the same time. All of this busyness can leave my soul feeling weary, and it is vitally important that I take daily time to be still and remember that He is God.

"Be still and know that I am God. I will be exalted among the nations, I will be exalted in the earth!" (Psalm 46:10).

Even when one tries to be intentional about setting priorities and not allowing media to consume their life, there is still a constant buzz going on, especially if you are out in society at all. It seems culture is in a state of craziness where real relationships are being replaced by social media, where families are disconnected and often times do not even gather together around the dinner table at the close of the day. People are on the go, and the results are evident. People are stressed to the hilt, children seem disgruntled and unhappy, and families are being torn apart right and left. As I view this landscape my heart feels burdened and concerned. This is a generation where many children are missing the traditional stability and security of the nuclear family. Basic routines like the family dinner and a decent bedtime are often not provided and, instead, children are pacified by media as they are drug all over the place. I see signs of this everywhere I go and more so all the time. A couple of years ago, our family was attending a large homeschooling conference in Texas. During one of the workshops, I found myself walking our baby around in the back of the room trying to keep him quiet. It jolted me a bit when I saw a family sitting on a row, and one of their children was actually watching a movie on an iPad while the speaker was talking. A few years back, a child would have had no option but to color with some crayons but now he can tune out the speaker completely and watch a movie. I don't say this to be critical; I am just trying to make a point that technology is changing our world. It is changing our lives, and if we are not intentional, I fear we will be sucked into a cyber-based, false reality and miss so very much in our real lives. My heart hurts for this new generation of children growing up knowing nothing but constant media stimulation and noise, which is often replacing real relationships within the family. For example, consider the newer baby bouncy chairs that have iPad holders to entertain babies while they sit. All our baby bouncers have had little toy bars, and yet even toys are often being replaced these days with media gadgets. I also have reservations and concerns about health ramifications for babies and children who are in constant close proximity to so many devices. I know many studies have been done about brain development and how media is harmful to young developing brains, but I also have concerns about the exposure to electric-magnetic fields.

There has been a massive shift in culture over my lifetime, and the media explosion has swallowed up culture very quickly like a raging wildfire. I was a teenager before our home had a computer, and my first cell phone came as a wedding present when my husband and I were married. Over the years, and in increasing measure, we have observed both the blessings and the curses that this media explosion has brought to society. I do recognize that much good has come through the technological advances and, to be honest, I really enjoy a lot of it. Social media also offers great opportunity to share the gospel and Biblical truth with others. I told my husband that if I were not sharing Biblical truth on my Facebook, I do not know if it would be worth my time. Yes, I share family pictures and updates, but a lot of what I use Facebook for is to share Scripture, great quotes, and links to uplifting and inspirational articles and posts. I think of the verse:

"So, whether you eat or drink, or whatever you do, do all to the glory of God" (1 Corinthians 10:31).

I think this could be paraphrased as, "So whether you text or Facebook or whatever you do, do all to the glory of God." I am discouraged with the snarky, cynical backlashing and attacking I see, even amongst Christians, on blogs and other forms of social media. It seems people think they can lash out with those they disagree with and say things they would never say to their face. I think a little social media courtesy would go a long ways. I personally have felt the bite and sting of that kind of behavior, and I think it does not reflect well on the name of Christ when believers are having online wars, expressing themselves in unloving ways in front of the lost. What

I am talking about here is the spirit and heart in which people oppose others on social media. I am all for "speaking the truth in love" (Ephesians 4:15), so my admonition is that we who call ourselves Christ followers would share His truth in a tone that reflects upon all that He is.

Another thing about living in this new age of the World Wide Web is all the contradiction on any topic imaginable! It has been frustrating to me personally to look to blogs and ministry websites on a given topic and find vastly different ideologies and perspectives. Even more so when evangelicals are attacking one another in critical tones and lacking grace toward one another. Whether the topic is politics, parenting, theology, homeschooling, or any other topic, you will find vastly different counsel, advice, and interpretation as you hop from one site to another. I have often felt weary by this scenario and struggled to know who to listen to. I think there is a huge lesson to be learned here. Jesus sent His Holy Spirit to indwell the believer and to be his guide.

"When the Spirit of truth comes, he will guide you into all the truth, for he will not speak on his own authority, but whatever he hears he will speak, and he will declare to you the things that are to come" (John 16:13).

So even though we may often look to websites to help us gain greater knowledge and understanding, we should be abiding closely in fellowship with the Lord so that His Spirit will help us discern truth from error. Additionally, the Word of God is our guide.

"Your word is a lamp to my feet and a light to my path" (Psalm 119:105).

Christian blogs and ministry pages should never replace the living and powerful Word of God in our lives. The men and women who write on the internet are human, but God's Word is divinely inspired and is our true north, helping us to avoid pitfalls and false teachings. Let's fill up on His Word before looking for guidance from what others have written.

With the internet and the explosion of technology, I have also seen the world change with things becoming far more global. When I was a little girl, I would have never imagined that my husband would one day be flying back and forth to various continents, all the while connecting with the family through Skype and FaceTime. This Texas girl has seen a lot of changes in her lifetime, and the jolting thing is that all the transformation does not seem to be slowing down. I am not against progress or technological advances, but what concerns me is that the world seems to be changing faster than people know how to responsibly keep up with the changes. I am concerned about the fracturing of human relationships in exchange for online relationships.

Scenarios like seeing a group of kids gathered together all texting on their phones instead of talking face to face is an alarming reality. What about the family that sits down at a restaurant and the whole family pulls out their own phones while maybe the little ones play games on their personal iPad? On a recent date night with my husband, we observed a family being seated next to us. There was a grandparent in this group and a preteen-aged boy. Sadly, the boy in the group was given an iPad to play games. It was sobering to me to think about the wisdom the grandmother might have to offer this young man if he hadn't been escaping the reality of dinner with his family in preference of playing a fictional game. If this flood of media concern is not enough, how about the fact that you are hard pressed to walk through a mall or dine in a food court or a restaurant without larger than life screens flashing all kinds of things in front of your eyes? Recently, I went to a restaurant and noticed that the large TV screen they had inside the restaurant was not enough, so the restaurant decided to also place screens outside the restaurant. Now for me it is exhausting and too much stimuli, but I have huge concerns about how all of this plays into shaping the hearts and minds of my children. I do not want to sit down at a food court and feed my children while there are raunchy, seductive videos playing on the screens above. Because of this I feel like I am always on high alert, trying to be discerning as to the environments I take my children into.

It is almost as if our culture is drugged by our media gadgets and constant noise that makes "old-fashioned conversations" hard to engage in. Are we losing the ability to put distractions aside and look those we love in the eye while engaging in meaningful conversations? Do we not know how to sit still and be quiet? Do we know how to cultivate a quiet heart so that we can hear His still small voice? I think about the verse that says that Mary contemplated all these things in her heart. I'm concerned that people are losing the ability to sit, be still, and listen. I do what I can to shield my children and make wise choices, but there are very real limits to my ability to protect them. Am I able to control what the vehicle in front of ours is playing on their video screen as we wait at a stop light? The challenges seem to be constantly increasing.

Here is another one I cringe at. What about the kids bringing phones to church? Yes, the sad fact is that even church is not a safe place when kids are carrying these gadgets around. We have chosen to instruct our children not to look at other kids' media screens on phones, iPads, etc. We have told them to tell other children that their parents do not want them looking at others' screens. That might seem extreme to some, but we have no idea what other kids have on their screens and what they might want to show our children. At home we are selective and try to have careful oversight over what comes on any screens. Why then would we allow them to flippantly look at some child's screen without our knowing what is on that screen? When I was a child, all of these concerns were not even on the parenting radar. This world has changed drastically in the last few decades. In fact, I would say the most rapid changes I have seen have been in the last fifteen years since I have been married and begun raising our own children.

It is of paramount importance that we take a careful evaluation of where the culture is and compare what we observe with God's blueprint found within His holy Word. What kind of life does God call His people to? What is His design for the family? I think we should, as Jeremiah 6:16 says, "Stand by the roads, and look, and ask for the ancient paths, where the good way is; and walk in it, and find rest for your souls."

There is a saying that if you shoot for nothing you will hit it every time. So, as Christian families, and, specifically, as Christian home educating families, what are we aiming for? What is the vision? What is the end goal? Will we go with the flow, the philosophies, the cultural norms, and the idols of this society? If so, why are we even homeschooling?

I am not suggesting that we should throw out our phones, computers, etc. but I am saying that we should prayerfully set boundaries. We must be watchful and guide our children through all of this. If we do not manage it, then the media will manage us. It can easily seize our children and grip them tightly. It can easily become that "sin that so easily entangles" (Hebrews 12:1) and become a huge idol, not only for our children but for us as well. I have to be very careful that I do not let my iPhone, Facebook, blogs, etc. steal my limited time from seeking the Lord. I am part of the first generation that is having to wrestle with all of these media issues with their children. May the Lord grant a special grace as you and I try to tame the media monster and teach our young people how to handle media responsibly. Media is not all bad; it can certainly be used for the glory of God and to advance the gospel. It is, however, an area for the Christian family to be alert in and to use great intentionality in the use of it.

Just like technology and media, culture is rapidly shifting and changing. As our nation is losing its moral compass and embracing ungodliness, we need to continually look for those ancient paths. Let's search for the good way and walk in it. Let's fight getting swept up in the current of a degrading culture and letting our families be washed away to destruction. God's ways are eternal. They are never outdated. Let's stand and look for those proven paths and go against the tidal wave of secularism and apostasy.

Throughout time our Lord has always laid out a path that is the good way for His people to walk in. Today, we have His instructions for us written in His holy Word, which should be our guidebook for life. His Word does not change with the trends of culture but remains faithful and true for all generations. Unfortunately, as we consider history, we see a cyclical pattern of God's people gladly receiving His Word and obeying it, then disobeying His Word, followed by facing consequences. Because God is a loving and redemptive God, He also provides the way to get back onto the right path through the means of godly repentance.

Things were much the same in the days of the prophet Jeremiah. The Jewish culture of his day had apostatized from the ways of the Lord, and the northern ten tribes had already been carried into captivity by the Assyrians. God sent Jeremiah, known as the weeping prophet, as the last prophet to deliver warning to the two southern tribes of Judah and Benjamin. He spent many decades delivering an urgent message that they must repent of their sin and idolatry. Sadly, the people remained stubborn and unrepentant, even after all of Jeremiah's pleading, warning, and proclaiming of the divine message that the Lord was ready to remove them from their home by a pagan king He called, "my servant" (Jeremiah 27:6). These Israelites were too hardened and their senses too dulled to listen and respond in repentance.

In our own country I believe we are at a similar crossroads where God has sent godly men to preach His glorious gospel and yet America has rejected Biblical truth for a lie. Today, truth is not accepted by the masses. Paul told Timothy that this would be the case.

"For the time is coming when people will not endure sound teaching, but having itching ears they will accumulate for themselves teachers to suit their own passions, and will turn away from listening to the truth and wander off into myths" (2 Timothy 4:3-4).

I am in my early forties, and all of my life I have heard men of God preaching and pleading for our nation to repent of sin and turn back to the ways of the Lord. Much like the people of Jeremiah's day, it seems most Americans today are too blinded and numb in their sin to respond to the call for repentance and revival.

A look back at the founding of America reminds us that this is not the way our nation began. When you read the writings of the great Pilgrims and Puritans, it is clearly evident that their desire in coming and founding America was to fear God, worship Him, and disciple their families to know, love and honor the Lord. Just a look through the Mayflower Compact sheds light upon the intentions of those who sailed to America seeking religious freedom for their families. The Mayflower Compact says that their voyage to America was for the glory of God and the advancement of the Christian faith!

> In the name of God, Amen. We whose names are underwritten, the loyal subjects of our dread Sovereign Lord King James, by the Grace of God of Great Britain, France, and Ireland King, Defender of the Faith, etc. Having undertaken for the Glory of God and advancement of the Christian Faith and Honour of our King and Country, a Voyage to plant the First Colony in the Northern Parts of Virginia, do by these presents solemnly and mutually in the presence of God and one of another, Covenant and Combine ourselves together in a Civil Body Politic, for our better ordering and preservation and furtherance of the ends aforesaid; and by virtue hereof to enact, constitute and frame such just and equal Laws, Ordinances, Acts, Constitutions and Offices from time to time, as shall be thought most meet and convenient for the general good of the Colony, unto which we promise all due submission and obedience. In witness whereof we have hereunder subscribed our names at Cape Cod, the 11th of November, in the year of the reign of our Sovereign Lord King James, of England, France and Ireland the eighteenth, and of Scotland the fifty-fourth. Anno Domini 1620 (The Mayflower Compact).

Here is a quote by William Bradford who was one of the signers of the Mayflower Compact and also a long-term governor to the Plymouth colony.

"May not and ought not the children of these fathers rightly say: 'Our fathers were Englishmen which came over this great ocean, and were ready to perish in this wilderness but they cried unto the Lord, and He heard their voice, and looked on their adversity, etc. Let them therefore praise the Lord, because He is good, and His mercies endure forever. Yea, let them which have been redeemed of the Lord, shew how He hath delivered them from the hand of the oppressor. When they wandered in the desert wilderness out of the way, and found no city to dwell in, both hungry, and thirsty, their soul was overwhelmed in them. Let them confess before the Lord His loving kindness, and His wonderful works before the sons of men." [11]

Our nation was established by many God-fearing men and women who made it their ambition to establish religious freedom for their families and to advance the gospel. Unfortunately, just like the Israelites, our country has wandered far off track. Most children today are not being taught the spiritual heritage of our nation, the fear of God, the law of God, nor a Biblical worldview. In fact, in America's public schools it seems that just about every religion and worldview is tolerated today except that of Christianity.

In a similar way to the early pilgrims of America, a group of grassroots parents, including my own, propelled the Christian homeschooling movement forward several decades ago. Just as the pilgrims valued teaching their children the ways of the Lord, many of these pioneering homeschool parents chartered difficult waters in a brave effort to raise up a godly generation of young people who would know and fear the living God. I am immensely grateful for the Christian legacy my parents left to me. Not only were they willing to be brave trailblazers in the early modern homeschool era, but more importantly they imparted God's everlasting truth to me from infancy.

From my earliest days, even while in the womb, I had the blessing of parents who were praying for me and purposing to lead me in the ways of the Lord. Once I was born, I was taken to church three times a week (at least) and taught to revere the Lord and walk in His ways. My parents, due to lack of example from their own upbringings, could have excused away their God-given responsibility to disciple their children. It would have been easy to just think that they didn't know what to do because they were not taught. They did not grow up in homes that operated under Biblical principles. Even though my dad was taken to church his home was dysfunctional, and he did not come to know the Lord until he was in high school. My mom's parents did not know the Lord at all during her growing up years. When my parents married and started a family, they were starting out like first-generation Christians. The Lord took their hearts and their intentionality and used them to raise me to love and know Him. My parents were trying to figure things out as they went along, and things were not done perfectly. Even so the Lord delights in showing Himself strong in our weaknesses. He took the little my parents knew and blessed their faithfulness as He continued to teach them. This is encouraging to me as I know I make mistakes daily in parenting my own children. I am grateful that God sees the heart my husband and I have for our children, that He hears our prayers on their behalf, and that He is working in their lives. He is using us as His vessels, but, ultimately, He will have His way with them with or without us. I pray that He will raise them up to be mighty men and women of God in spite of my failures. Isn't it freeing to know that God is able to make all grace abound in our families even though our best efforts are often flawed? For that I am incredibly grateful. When I contemplate such a rich heritage I realize that the Lord in lovingkindness was drawing me even from a very young age.

"The Lord hath appeared of old unto me, saying, Yea, I have loved thee with an everlasting love: therefore with lovingkindness have I drawn thee" (Jeremiah 31:3, KJV).

I, like Timothy, was taught the Scriptures from my infancy.

"And how from infancy you have known the Holy Scriptures, which are able to make you wise for salvation through faith in Christ Jesus" (2 Timothy 3:15, NIV).

I consider this faithful Christian upbringing to be the best gift my parents could have given me.   They led me to my Savior, and this is a legacy I am endeavoring with all of heart to pass on to my own children.

When I think about it, my ultimate parenting goal is that my children know, love, and serve the Lord Jesus and that they be with me in Heaven for all eternity.

"We will not hide them from their children,
   but tell to the coming generation
the glorious deeds of the Lord, and his might,
   and the wonders that he has done.
He established a testimony in Jacob
   and appointed a law in Israel,
which he commanded our fathers
   to teach to their children,
that the next generation might know them,
   the children yet unborn,
and arise and tell them to their children,
   so that they should set their hope in God
and not forget the works of God,
   but keep his commandments" (Psalm 78:4-7).

I pray that my children will take the baton of faith and then tell the wondrous deeds of the Lord to my grandchildren who are yet unborn.

"I have no greater joy than to hear that my children are walking in the truth" (3 John 1:4).

Chapter 12
Homeschooling When Life Gets Tough

One of the beautiful blessings of homeschooling is that it offers us the opportunity to bend and flex with the different seasons, trials and blessings of life. Homeschooling families face all of the same pressures in life that others face, but, at times, homeschooling itself can make normal life pressures even heavier to bear. That is simply because there is more responsibility, more to juggle, more to manage, etc. I have learned in my own journey as a homeschooling mama that some seasons feel more manageable while others can thoroughly overwhelm me. I have had many times where I have known that if the Lord did not sustain us and carry us through, we would surely sink. It is helpful to remember in these intense seasons that He who called you is faithful.

"He who calls you is faithful; he will surely do it" (1 Thessalonians 5:24).

Homeschooling Mama, here is a word of encouragement I want you to remember. The same God who called you to homeschool will be faithful to complete what He started in your family. This is something I have to remind myself of when the going gets hard.

"And I am sure of this, that he who began a good work in you will bring it to completion at the day of Jesus Christ" (Philippians 1:6).

This may not be humanly possible but in His strength all things are possible. He can supply a supernatural wisdom and strength, and He can provide for the needs in ways we could never imagine.

One of the personal challenges we have faced as a homeschooling family has been that of seasons where Matt has travelled a lot with work, leaving me at home alone with many young children. There were times when Matt would be leaving again for another two- or three-week trip, and I would be unnerved about how I would make it that long with so many children. We lived in the country in an old house where something seemed to always be breaking. As I look back the Lord was faithful and provided help even when I did not know where the help would come from. It was faith building to see the Lord supply help and encouragement during those times when I felt in over my head.

Another challenge for us has been very painful pregnancies for me. I have spent years of my homeschooling journey in intense pain as I carried another baby inside of me. For some reason, this has worsened through the years and turned into ongoing chronic pain issues that come and go even when I am not pregnant. This has been hugely difficult as we have had more children, and I have found myself limping around in terrible pain. Again, the Lord has carried us through each time and provided people to help in various ways. As our children have grown older they have also been able to help out during these times.

For some reason we have also struggled with selling houses. We have already spent three years of our marriage trying to sell one house or another. Without going into great detail, building, buying, and selling houses has been something the Lord has allowed us to have a lot of practice at. We have had some situations that looked utterly hopeless, but the Lord, in His timing and not ours, stepped in and worked miracles before our eyes. These times have been beyond trying, as often painful pregnancies coincided with times of trying to show a house, move, etc. Let me just say that showing a house for over a year while pregnant and homeschooling a house full of children definitely fits a stress category all its own. The point in all of this is that, even though these times have been stressful, we have lived through it and our faith has been boosted in seeing the Lord move mountains in our behalf. The last move we made, we put our house on the market before I became pregnant with Nathaniel. We continued to show our house all through my pregnancy, and we did not actually close on the sale of the house until about a week and a half after he was born. We brought him home from the hospital to a house full of boxes since we were about to move. Then we closed on the house we were selling and the house we were buying and moved an hour away to our farm within two weeks after his birth. This was a huge feat for us after a painful pregnancy, a newborn, and still parenting five other children. The Lord used so many people to help us through that move. People helped pack up our home, provided food, helped with our children, etc. It felt like the Lord was carrying us through something that was much bigger than we could handle. By His grace we made it through and transitioned into our new home.

By far the biggest struggle was right after the birth of our last baby. Again I experienced much pain with the pregnancy and was hardly able to walk by the end. This time an ultrasound showed that our Ella Ruth was transverse. I went to the chiropractor to see if we could get her to move head down, and we prayed that she would get into the right position for birth. Another ultrasound showed that she was still not positioned right, so my doctor said we should plan a Version (External Cephalic Version) and deliver earlier than we had thought. We went into the hospital early in the morning and my doctor performed the version on my stomach and got Ella Ruth's head downward. At this point we proceeded with the induction and hoped to deliver our little girl soon. Things did not seem right, and after a while we had another ultrasound to check her position. She had turned transverse again. It was at this point that my doctor, who had delivered all my other babies vaginally, told us she thought we needed to go to a cesarean before the situation became dangerous. The whole situation was becoming overwhelming, and I remember shaking like a leaf in the operating room. I was freezing cold and really scared. My epidural had not worked properly, and I was so nervous and cold that I opted to be put to sleep for the cesarean. Unbeknownst to me that meant Matt could not come in the operating room and had to wait in the hall. Once my doctor opened me up she saw what the problem was. I had a baseball-sized fibroid tumor blocking the way so that Ella Ruth could not descend and that is why she was transverse. Her first horizontal cut was right into the fibroid and she could not take the baby through this cut. She had to make a second vertical cut in order to get the baby out. My uterus was cut in the shape of a T. I was cut horizontally on the outside to get into my uterus and a horizontal and vertical "T" cut inside to get the fibroid tumor and baby out. All of this made for a severe cesarean surgery. My first memory of Ella Ruth is when Matt put her up to my face in the recovery area. I sensed my baby by my face and remember having such love and admiration for my wonderful husband who was there taking care of us both.

The pain after the cesarean was so much worse than the other six births. I learned what a big deal a cesarean is, especially one of the magnitude I had. I was intensely sore and could barely sit up or walk as every move hurt. They had me on intravenous morphine. When I began to hurt too much I could punch a button that would deliver a small amount of morphine into my system. We thought that the worst was behind us and that I would heal, but we were in for many overwhelming and painful days ahead.

Things began to go wrong beyond the abdominal soreness. My hemoglobin had dropped really low as I had lost so much blood in surgery that I needed a blood transfusion. After that I began to show other signs of illness. Somehow, I picked up a violent intestinal superbug called Clostridium difficile (C. diff) while in the hospital. My body's immune system was already so compromised from the pregnancy that it could not fight the C. diff, and my body began breaking down on multiple levels. Once I was diagnosed with C. diff, I was quarantined within the hospital, and no one could go in and out of my room without suiting up in a gown, gloves, and a mask. Shortly after finding out I had C. diff, Matt had to take our newborn baby girl home, and we could not bring her back to be exposed to this superbug. One nurse told me that if Ella Ruth got C. diff it could kill her. At one point in this story I did go home, but we had to go back to the ER within a few days because I had edema so bad in my legs and feet that I could hardly stand. My legs were red and hot to the touch. I was taking Lasix, but it was only worsening. At this point I was readmitted to the hospital and separated from Ella Ruth for another nine days. Within a few days' time my colon was decimated and there was a real scare that my colon would have to be removed. During this second hospital stay things became very critical, and Matt and I faced some of the scariest days of our lives. I ended up in the ICU for three days. Over the duration of my time in the hospital, I was given four blood transfusions and many transfusions of Albumen. Albumen is a protein that removes water from your blood. The doctor said my Albumen was the lowest he had ever seen in somebody that did not have liver failure. I also had extremely low blood pressure, tachycardia, mouth thrush, edema, and red, burning, weeping skin. Eventually I was given a sigmoidoscopy to see what was going on with my colon and why I was not improving. The results of that test were horrifying and the doctor's report to Matt was not good. He explained to Matt that I was a very sick lady and possibly the worst case he had ever seen. He found that my colon was black, bleeding, and oozing pus. He said that he was going to start a new line of treatments for me that would include getting a PICC line put in my arm to start intravenous nutrition. He also put me on an anti-inflammatory used for Crohn's disease and also a new antibiotic called Fidaxomicin. He said that, after the new treatment, we would see one of three outcomes. The desired outcome would be that we would try these new treatments for a few days and see improvement. The second option was that I would not improve and that they would be forced to remove my colon. The third option was that my colon could rupture at any time and I would most likely not survive. Since having my colon removed was a very real possibility, my GI doctor had me consulting with a surgeon daily. I told the surgeon that it was nice to talk to him in my room, but that I did not want to see him in the operating room. By God's grace and the prayers of many I did turn a corner after a few days on the new treatments. We are so grateful that I did not lose my colon and that the Lord has restored health to my body. All in all I spent eighteen days in the hospital, and most of that time I was separated from my children and my newborn baby. My body was completely broken, I faced daily pain and suffering, and my heart was torn apart from being separated from Ella Ruth. I do not know when I have ever been so broken physically and emotionally. Before being discharged from the hospital I was warned that restoration of health would take months, and it did. Even though we would never have planned things this way, and even though I would do anything to go back and change it if I could, this trial allowed us to see the Lord carry us through the fire without allowing us to be consumed.

"When you pass through the waters, I will be with you; and through the rivers, they shall not overwhelm you; when you walk through fire you shall not be burned, and the flame shall not consume you" (Isaiah 43:2).

For months we had an amazing outpouring of love and support from family and friends, such as we had never before been the recipients of. If you had asked me previously how we would stay afloat if I was in the hospital for weeks I would have said we would sink. We live so far out from most everyone, and I would not have imagined the sacrifices people made on our behalf. As it turned out people drove an hour to bring us meals, we had a rotation of friends coming in to help with our children for weeks, we had close friends who were at our house managing things on a daily basis, people mowed grass and brought groceries. Others sent us paper goods, such as diapers and paper plates through Amazon, and it goes on and on. It was incredibly moving to see the Lord move through those who would be His hands and feet to carry our family through.

We are also grateful for an amazing amount of prayer support. It has been astounding to hear how so many people were praying that did not even know us. Slowly over time my white blood cell count normalized and I regained strength, but it did take months to recover. This trial was enormously hard on my husband who had to carry the weight of it all on his shoulders. He did an amazing job of taking care of me at the hospital by day and taking care of our children and our infant through the night. This was not an easy thing for a large homeschool family to go through and yet the Lord was faithful. The Lord sustained us and allowed us the sweet blessing of seeing His provision through those who stepped into our lives to help. He allowed us to see His mercy in sparing my life and my colon and in allowing Matt and I to continue through this journey of life together. When I think that I could have died and Matt could have been left a widower with seven children, my heart swells with gratefulness to my Lord Jesus for His mercies to our family.

Life can be hard, and homeschool families are not immune from the turbulent waters in the sea of life. We can, however, rest in the fact that we serve the God who calms the winds and the raging seas. He can say, "Peace be still," and He will carry us as we stay faithful to His call.

Chapter 13
Practical Tips I've Learned
Along the Way

"So teach us to number our days that we may get a heart of wisdom" (Psalm 90:12).

What to Do When Daddy Travels or the Season is Otherwise Intense

At the time of writing this I have been homeschooling for around ten years. We have had enough time in this journey to experience quite a few different seasons and challenges. Honestly, sometimes life is hard and the name of the game is survival. There can be any number of circumstances that can add extra stress to a homeschooling family. Moving, illness, travel, pregnancy, having a newborn, extended family crises, broken appliances or vehicles, and the list goes on. One of those survival mode times for our family has been when my husband has been in seasons of a lot of travel with his work. At times he has been gone for weeks at a time or had back to back trips where he would come home and turn around and leave again. When this was happening a lot we were in a season with many children who still acted like children, and we didn't have teenagers who could offer the kind of helping hand that I appreciate with my older ones today. I remember how challenging it was, and I am here to say that the Lord was faithful to preserve us through those challenging times. In the process of walking through such seasons, I have learned a few survival strategies that can be implemented at times when daddies travel or when life is otherwise challenging.

An automatic in our house is that, if Daddy is traveling or coming home late, the children get ready for bed very early. I'm talking preferably before dinner. The reason is that sometimes things go crazy in the chaos of dinner and clean up. If unexpected things occur I do not want to be giving baths and putting a pack of children in jammies late at night when I am exhausted and running on fumes. It is easier for me to get all the little people in their pajamas early in the evening and then be able to plan for a special video or story time after the dinner time clean up. In fact, I have at times asked my older daughter to help me with getting her little sisters ready for bed while I was preparing dinner.

Back when Matt traveled a lot I would look for new, wholesome videos to show our children when he was away. This worked out well, because it gave them something special to be excited about since it was a real bummer that their daddy was gone. We had lots of pizza and video nights. At times we used paper plates, bowls, cups, etc. to make clean up easier. It is a small thing but it can help. There were nights when I would roll up the rug in our family room, roll the high chair in there, and let the children have a pizza party on the living room floor while we watched a new video.

On other nights I would send them to their rooms really early and make visits to each room to spend some special time with whoever slept in that particular room. Since my oldest daughter loves books I would often read a chapter or two out of an inspiring book with her. With my little girls I might go to their room and read a picture book and sing a song or two with them. I would also read to my son in his room. I tried to be intentional in picking books that would sharpen them and turn their hearts toward Biblical truth. Sometimes we might talk more than read, but the purpose was to encourage their hearts with a little extra Mommy time since they were missing Daddy. My end goal on these nights was to ideally have a little bit of time at the end of the long day to refresh my own spirit. Often, that would mean turning on a podcast that would renew my mind and sharpen my perspective for the next day. I think the challenge in this scenario with a daddy traveling is that the mama is trying to be both parents to the children while the children are extra needy and Mama is extra tired. Getting everyone ready for bed in the late afternoon or early evening allowed me to give extra time to my children and still be able to go to my room at a decent hour. I find that, for my personality type and energy level, it is very helpful for me to have some recharge time where no one is talking to me if I am going to go strong again the next day.

When I reflect upon those long days and nights, I remember the exhaustion, tears, and fears that sometimes gripped me. In hindsight, I see that I was learning a lot about the faithfulness of the Lord and about finding strategies that work when things are intense.

Occasionally hiring a responsible babysitter/mother's helper helped me during those times as well. If Matt was gone two or three weeks, it was very helpful to me to be able to get out once a week and run errands in order to clear my head from all the noise and chaos. I am, however, wise and cautious as to whom I hire to come in and spend time with my children. If I am going to be gone for the day, this person is going to have a big influence, and I want it to be an influence that supports the values I am working so hard to impart to my children. At times I was able to hire a mature young lady to come stay with us for a few days and serve as a mama's helper. That was a blessing, and my children enjoyed such times as well.

I also learned that children get down about their daddy being away just like Mamas do. It helped if I had some special things to do at home and, at times, a special outing. I learned the hard way, however, that having too many special outings at one time can defeat the purpose. If I planned outings such as a zoo trip, children's museum, play dates with friends, etc. back to back, it left me exhausted and caused us to not get our bedtime routine done early, leaving me worn thin. I had to learn to pace myself. It was helpful to pass the time with some special outings, but wearing myself to a frazzle was not a good scenario.

I remember one time when Matt was going to be leaving yet again for another trip and I felt really disheartened. I came up with what I thought would be a great idea to take the children on a mini vacation to San Antonio for a few days. I will just share with you that that was the only time I ever came up with such a plan. We did have some good times, but Mama was worn slap out! From then on, we stayed home when daddy traveled, and I did my best to strategically and intentionally plan out our time when he would be gone. I learned what worked and what did not work, and I worked hard at holding to a schedule that carried us through.

Careful preparation and planning for these times when Matt was away helped things go a lot smoother. It was important for me to do a thorough shopping trip before he left so that we had the food and supplies we would need during his absence. It is never a good thing to run out of an essential food or needed item and have to drag a van full of children down the highway to the nearest store.

Overall I found that, when I knew he was leaving, I needed to think through everything that would transpire while he was away. If I planned our days ahead of time (lining up sitters, planning our outings, maybe planning a few surprises like a craft or outdoor activity, coordinating any outside help from others, and being prayed up), it brought some peace to an otherwise stressful situation.

Our family is immensely blessed that my husband makes discipleship times with our children a high priority. When he traveled it was tricky to figure out how he could continue to lead the children spiritually in the Word of God while he was overseas and in a different time zone. If we timed it just right Matt often engaged in FaceTime with the children, enabling him to still conduct a Bible time with them. Depending on the time zone he was in, he sometimes was able to call right before he went to bed, while the children were having breakfast. There were mornings where they would sit and eat breakfast while they watched him read from the Bible or ask them catechism questions on basic Bible doctrine. They would sometimes sing a hymn with Daddy, even while he was across the world. This helped to keep him anchored as the spiritual leader of our home and they enjoyed seeing their daddy while he was away. With all the vices of modern technology, there are also some huge blessings, and this has been one of them for our family.

All of these ideas are not going to fit all families, but these are some of the things that have helped us.

Organization and Scheduling

I wish I were super organized and that I loved schedules, but I have to be honest in saying that this is not my reality. I grew up in a small home with only one sibling, so I entered my marriage with much to learn about managing the large family. This is an area I struggle in, because I am not naturally the super woman type. I am also not one who can go without sleep. I desperately wish that I could function without sleep, but that is not realistic for me. If I push my body and neglect my need for sleep, my immune system screams at me and I end up sick. As much as I love organization and long for a peaceful, orderly home, I also struggle to keep afloat with all the ongoing busyness happening in our abode. With so many people dwelling day and night in our home, keeping order and organization has proved to be a huge challenge for me. This is an area where I pray for wisdom from the Lord and also an area where we are continuing to try to do better. Now if I lived alone I think I would be organized, because I really do pine for a tidy home and orderliness. Although I desire to know where things are when I go to look for them, the problem is that, with seven children, I put something in one place and who knows where I will find it when I go to look for it. We have nine people living in our house, and even though I keep picking it up, it is far from magazine perfect. I'm always working towards creating better organization and trying to train my children towards that end, but the struggle is real when you have this many people living in a house all the time. I definitely try to keep clutter out, but it seems that no sooner have I dropped off things at a donation center than my family drags more items into our home. It seems to be a never ending process of hauling things off and having more things appear. It is my practice to evaluate what I see in our home and get rid of things that do not have a useful purpose or deep sentimentality. Hopefully by God's grace and through the ongoing training of the children, our family will improve in organization as time goes on.

I have a hard time sticking to a rigid schedule, because life happens and I often cannot keep up with a tight schedule. What I have found the most helpful for us is an overarching outline of our day or a loose schedule. This means that I do not have every thirty-minute block of time planned out for every member of the family every day of the week. Some mothers have successfully created and implemented such schedules, but up to this point that has not worked for us. What I mean by a loose schedule is that we know the basic pegs that our day hangs on so to speak. We know about what time meals are going to be and when we have nap time/rest time. We know the overall flow of our activities throughout the day such as getting up and eating breakfast and then moving into chore time, followed by a circle time where we all meet together before the children start piano practice, etc. So meal times, nap time, and bedtime are huge pegs in our day, and then we have an order to our other activities. This allows us some flex room when interruptions and unexpected things occur in our day. This is not a perfect system, but this is what has worked for us. I think if you can implement an even more detailed schedule then that is great, but at this point in our homeschooling journey a loose schedule has been more realistic for us. One thing I have learned is that my children thrive on consistency. They like to know what to expect in our day and when we do what. I think consistency helps provide feelings of security and assurance for my children.

It seems to me that the more children in a family, the more need for systems and organization, but this is also harder to pull off the larger a family grows. I find myself praying often for wisdom in this area of organization and streamlining for maximum efficiency. I know there are many people who are so much more gifted in these areas than I am, but in this section of the book I'm just throwing out ideas that have helped in our home. Below I am going to list some strategies that have helped us out with family management and organization:

Drink Bands. Because we do not want to dirty up a cabinet full of glasses and cups every day we use drink bands. I bought the children some stainless steel cups from Amazon and purchased different colors of drink bands that slip around the circumference of the cups. Each of my children has a different color drink band, which makes identifying their cup an easy process. Even my young children can set the cups out on the table for me at the appropriate seat because everyone in our family knows which color goes to which child. This really has helped a great deal.

Blessing Charts

Each of our children has a small blessing chart on a bulletin board in our kitchen table area. When a child does something that I want to encourage them for I will give them a sticker on this little chart. Once they fill up a row they get a jelly bean, and once they fill up the chart they get three jelly beans. I reward them with stickers for anything that I want to encourage them in. It might be for a good attitude or for helping and serving without being asked or for being kind to a sibling, etc. Sometimes we use these charts and sometimes we forget about them, but it has been a neat way to encourage them along the way.

Counting Blessings

Whenever I take them all out in the van, I will count my blessings— one, two, three, four, five, six, seven blessings—just to make sure we are not leaving anyone behind. With this many children, I want to make sure that someone is not behind the van or left in the house. It is also a sweet way for them to hear me remind them that they are blessings.

The Buddy System

Due to living so far out in the country we do not go out as a large group a whole lot, but when we do I will sometimes implement a buddy system where an older one is asked to hold the hand of a younger sibling, especially crossing a road or walking in a store.

Housework Help

At different times the Lord has provided various forms of housework help for me. When we lived closer to town, we had a cleaning service that came and cleaned our house from top to bottom every week or two. That was very helpful in keeping on top of the dirt and grime that can build up very quickly. The house felt really nice and clean after it had been cleaned. Now that we are so far out I have not found a reasonably priced cleaning service, but I currently have a homeschool graduate who comes each week for a day of cleaning. She does a boatload of laundry, picks up, cleans bathrooms, and does whatever I ask her to help me with. This is a huge blessing that I am thankful for. I struggled for some time with feeling like I wanted to be able to keep my own home and surely I should be able to find a way to juggle everything, but I finally had to listen to my husband who told me that he wanted my energies to be on discipling our children and to get the help I could get for the housekeeping. Now I am still totally swamped in housework because we mess our house up and create a massive amount of new laundry daily, but I am thankful for whatever help the Lord provides as He has been faithful to do through the years.

Shopping Trips

I rarely shop with all of my crew. I usually go when I can have a sitter at the house or when my husband is home. Because we live far out it takes a good while to get to a town to shop. Taking all seven children that far and running errands would be so very hard and time consuming. When I do go to town to shop, I try to get as much done as I can. I am starting to see how cooking from scratch and growing our own food will be helpful in that I will not have so many things to buy from the store. Buying tons of processed foods, snack foods, etc. is a never-ending process. As soon as I bring in a van full of these foods, it seems like it is time to restock. My family will go through these things so fast, and I have to spend so much time buying these in bulk when I go to town. It is our goal to grow more of our own food, and our oldest daughter is starting to cook more from scratch. She recently asked me to stop buying breakfast bars and breads and to let her bake these things from scratch. I have been more than happy to oblige her on that request. Not only is it less that I have to buy when I go to town, but it tastes better, costs less, and is better for our health. We are on a journey in figuring out life on our farm, and our shopping and kitchen processes are being tweaked as we go along. Additionally shopping online is a huge help especially to families like ours who are so far away from the stores. These days you can order almost everything you could need except perishables and have it delivered to your door within a couple of days.

Small Paper Sacks

Even though I do not take all of my children out very often we do all travel to church on Sundays, and one thing that has helped is to have a package of small paper sacks stashed away in the side compartment of either the driver's or the passenger's door. The little sacks are wonderful if we go through a drive-thru and I have food to pass out to all our passengers. This way I can divvy up chicken nuggets and French fries or whatever our food is and pass the bags to the back. We have been using these paper sacks in this way for years and it is such a life saver. Also, we keep a small trash can with a flip lid in between the front seats in our van. It is very helpful to have a place to throw trash while we are on the road. Then, when we return home, a child will empty the trash can and put it back in the van.

Travel by Ziploc

Homeschoolers often like to travel and learn by visiting historic sites and beautiful places that proclaim the mysteries of the Creator's hand through nature. Many homeschool families also enjoy traveling to conferences and conventions. One thing that has been helpful to our family is to divide up each child's clothing by day and place it in a gallon or jumbo-sized Ziploc bag. I will label the bag with the child's name and the day they are going to wear it. Sometimes I have color coordinated our family clothing by the day, which helps us to keep up with one another when we are out and about. It also makes for some nice family pictures while we are traveling. I may use a jumbo-sized Ziploc for all a child's underwear and pajamas for the entire trip. The Ziploc bags have helped us to stay a little more organized on long trips rather than clothes being thrown all over hotel rooms while trying to find a particular piece of clothing. It takes time initially when packing the family up, but it is nice to know who is wearing what once we are crammed into hotel rooms. Some of my girls have learned my packing method and really like to help me pick out the clothes and put them in the labeled bags. Sometimes they slow me down a bit but they are learning and eventually will be able to take over the job for me.

Kitchen Helpers, Freezer Meals and Snacks

Feeding the family is a huge part of a mama's daily life. Over the years I have found a few helps in this department. I have found out the hard way that giving young children too many food choices is not a good thing. When there are too many choices, it is prime opportunity for sibling squabbles about who gets what food, and it can cause wastefulness as children may sample many different things, wasting the food they don't prefer. Also, it is more work to put it all out and then have to put it away. I finally decided the children were going to have one kind of cereal, or two at the most, on a given morning, and that simplified the whole process. When I was the one setting out the breakfast in the mornings I would not allow my children to come out of their rooms until I called them. That gave me a moment to get things together before children started running through the house and slowing down the process of setting the table. Now that my son is the one setting the table, I have him and his little brother come out first and then they can call their sisters once the table is set. This has helped me because I am not a morning person. Having too much chaos first thing in the morning does not help me to get off to a good start.

I have my second oldest daughter prepare lunch, and this past year, I have had a lunch menu posted that tells her what to make on each day of the week. Having a plan in place has cut out disagreements amongst the children as to what lunch is going to be. Instead of one child wanting corn dogs while another wants pizza, we have a plan that they all understand.

Along this same theme I do allow my children to have a snack in the afternoon. Like breakfast, it is one snack for everyone. Take it or leave it. I do not negotiate about what they can have for snack. I choose some particular thing and it is their choice if they want to have it or not. Now there are days where I give them a choice of a few things, but I don't allow it to be this big deal of the kids getting into all kinds of different foods. Chaos ensues when everyone is grabbing and opinionated about what they want. If I let them decide, we end up in scenarios such as there are only three granola bars but five children want one, etc. It makes things easier to say, "Today's snack is (whatever I choose)."

For dinner I have fallen in love with crockpot freezer meals. This requires me to make a massive grocery shopping list for a lot of these meals. Then, when I am able, I do the assembly part where I dump the ingredients for each meal in a gallon-sized Ziploc bag. I place all the ingredients into the bags uncooked. I usually make two to four of a particular meal at one time. I mark the date I assembled it on the bag and the instructions for cooking it. I mark whether to cook it on high or low and for how long it needs to cook in the crockpot. I like to stock as many of these meals in my freezer as I am able to get assembled. This has helped me so much as it eliminates the stress of late afternoon cooking. I just pull out a freezer bag in the morning, dump the contents in the crockpot, and let it cook throughout the day. My oldest daughter often enjoys making a bread to accompany the main dish, and I will sometimes make a salad or a side as well. It is so much easier for me to start dinner in the morning than to wait until late afternoon and then try to figure out what's for dinner at a time of day when things tend to get a little crazy anyway. The other beautiful thing about the freezer bag meals is that I can share them if someone has had a baby or is in need of a meal. These meals have also been helpful when we have been going to a potluck or something of that nature. The freezer meals have been a win-win situation in many ways.

Room Time

One of the biggest sanity savers for me through the years has been nap time/room time. This is not going to be a good fit for every family but for us it has been great. I have observed different mothers implement this concept in different ways according to the layout of their homes, number of children, homeschool schedule, etc. The basic idea is that, if a child is too old for a nap, they still take a quiet time of reading, playing, or doing other individual school work while the nappers sleep. For some families everyone will go to their own room during this time, and for other families several children and a mom may share different locations in a big open area. The idea, however you work it, is that this is a quiet time for quiet activities where Mom is not to be disturbed. Some mothers will try to get things accomplished during this time, while other mothers will lay down and take a rest while the children rest. This is often when I get a quiet time in with the Lord, respond to emails, etc. Some days I am exhausted and choose to get in a nap while my little ones are napping. My older school-aged children generally work on individual work such as math and writing assignments during this time. My children do not always delight in this time, but I will say that it has been a real help to me, especially through many years of pregnancy, waking up in the night with babies, health issues, and having a husband who has traveled a lot. I do indeed look forward to this quiet spot in my afternoon.

Miscellaneous

At certain times in our day I will rotate having my older three children watching and playing with a younger sibling. This usually happens during their piano practice time. For example, my older three each practice for twenty minutes a day. While one of them practices, another one will watch the toddler and the other one may help with a chore. They will rotate so that, during that hour, they each practice for twenty minutes, do a chore for twenty minutes, and watch a little sibling for twenty minutes. Sometimes we will do something similar right before dinner as well. They might all be outside playing, and I may ask different older siblings to rotate watching their younger sibling or siblings for the hour leading up to dinner.

With babies it is helpful to have various ways of carrying them and various places to station them. I have used various kinds of baby carriers with the Ergo being my favorite. I carried Nathaniel in the Ergo a lot when he was a baby. I even learned to carry him on my back which helped when I was busy in the kitchen. With my last baby I have not used the Ergo much at all. I feel like, as much as I would love to wear her, my back cannot hold up to it. I also learned somewhere in my mothering journey that strollers are not just handy outdoors. I will stroll Miss Ella Ruth around the house when she is happy sitting in her stroller, and this saves my back some when I am working. Now that she is mobile and crawling around, we bought a very lightweight playpen by Summer that is collapsible and can be moved to different locations very easily. We have also loved wagons with our little ones. When we lived in a suburban neighborhood, the wagon was a fun ride down the sidewalk to the mailbox and, of course, wagons are handy for hiking around country property as well.

Another helpful tip for the homeschooling mama is to teach children to work from as early of an age as possible. I wish I had taught my older children a better work ethic when they were young. I did learn some things along the way and have tried to start earlier with my younger children. It seems that when they are young they view work as something enjoyable. That is the time to pull them onto the family team and enlist their help while they are excited about it. I have found that my younger girls LOVE helping in the kitchen. It keeps them occupied and out of trouble and is such good training for their future. The trick is to give them jobs they can handle without making too big of a mess. Some things that I have found to work well with my little girls are washing fruit and scrubbing dishes. Grapes are great, because you can teach them to wash them and pick them off the stem and drop them one by one into a bowl. This can be long tedious work that will keep them busy for a while. My girls have also enjoyed taking a spray bottle filled with homemade all-purpose cleaner. I use a mixture of water and essential oils. It is safe for them to get on their skin. They like to spray the table and chairs and wipe with towels. Sometimes they have been excited about spraying and wiping other surfaces such as counters and even the tile floor! You could put them to work on the baseboards and door frames as well. A few times things have gotten a little out of control with them spraying too much water, but for the most part they really enjoy the job and it keeps them occupied. My little ones have also enjoyed playing with brooms and lightweight vacuum cleaners. At first they weren't doing much good, but with time they turn into pretty decent sweepers. They will never learn if we don't give them opportunity. The best time is when they are excited to help you! You also build such a sweet connection with your little ones when you affirm their efforts. Even if they aren't accomplishing a lot you can praise them and tell them how much you appreciate them contributing to the good of the home and family. You can tell them that you can see that they are one day going to be very good homemakers taking care of their own homes. This also births vision in their hearts to see being a keeper at home as a noble position if the Lord so blesses them with future spouses and children. This culture is not going to affirm these values, and I strongly believe the time to instill a heart for these things is when they are very young.

There is a lot to juggle when you are homeschooling, trying to disciple children's hearts, running a household, and trying to be a loving wife and mother. Anything that can be done to simplify life and to simplify ongoing routines is a good thing. I have much to learn in this department, but the above things are some strategies that have helped us along the way.

Chapter 14
Keep the Main Thing the Main Thing!
(Discipleship)

Discipleship is the Most Important Goal

Homeschooling can be a very difficult, all-consuming job. Do I think it is worth the sacrifice and hard work? I absolutely do, but I think we need to count the cost and really analyze what are our top priorities for homeschooling? For me, the main thing is doing all I can to disciple my children. I honestly would rather they only know the basics of reading, writing, and arithmetic and love the Lord with all of their hearts than that they be geniuses with no heart for Christ and no depth of character. Now it is totally possible for children to be both brilliant and passionate about the Lord, but I think it is helpful for any homeschooling parent to know where things fall in order of importance. From experience, I know that many days do not go as smoothly as planned and can feel like a fight for survival. On those days, I have to ask myself if I am going to let academic pressure trump Biblical training and discipleship. I will admit that when we started out homeschooling I found myself thinking we had to get school done, and I sometimes failed to have a regular Bible time with my little ones. By God's grace He has shown me that this was not His plan for us, and that there is great blessing when we put Him first and trust Him to add everything else that we need.

At this juncture in the book I am going to share a lot of things that I think are important for us to keep in mind as we disciple our families. I want to remind my readers, however, that I am not laying out these things as a list to be checked off or as a formula to produce a certain desirable outcome in our children. I think these things are important but, again, we need to remember that we do not rely on a checklist to guarantee a godly outcome. Any godliness in the lives of your family or mine will be by the Lord's strength and not our own.

"Not by might, nor by power, but by my Spirit, says the Lord of hosts" (Zechariah 4:6).

Seek Ye First

"But seek first the kingdom of God and his righteousness, and all these things will be added to you" (Matthew 6:33).

Through the years the Lord has been opening my eyes to His priorities for our homeschool. I have come to clearly see that, on a priority list, spiritual discipleship is at the top of our homeschool goals. In fact, for the last several years I have had the experience of going to the Lord and asking Him to show me what our next homeschool year should look like. What should we keep the same? What should we change? What learning style or styles should we employ? What curriculum should we use? And on and on. These prayers have usually been in the summer as I have contemplated the next school year. As I prayed, I have felt the Lord directing me to "Add more of My Word, add more Christian worldview and apologetics, add more Scripture memorization and training in godly character qualities." He has also directed me toward curriculum choices, but, overall, I have felt that He has impressed upon my heart that training my children in godly wisdom is the most important thing.

"The fear of the Lord is the beginning of knowledge; fools despise wisdom and instruction" (Proverbs 1:1).

Knowledge alone can be dangerous. If a young person grows up without the fear of the Lord but with great academic understanding, they could potentially use their knowledge to do great harm. Nero, Hitler, Mussolini, and Stalin were no dummies. They were intelligent men who could have used their abilities to God's glory. Instead, they destroyed lives and brought devastation to many. The vision my husband and I have is that our children will possess wisdom and knowledge. We want them to have the wisdom first to know how to handle the knowledge they are entrusted with. We want our children to know the Lord and His ways. If we cannot fit everything into a day, we try to let the science lesson slide and get into the Word of God. I am walking in faith that if I help my children "seek first His kingdom," then all the other things they need will also be added. Does this mean that we don't take academics seriously? No, we are doing the best we can to teach them all that we can but we are striving to keep our priorities straight. By the way, this teaching of wisdom begins while they are still in the womb as we are praying over them and continues from their earliest days as we seek to teach them and lead them to Christ.

Delegate Academics

Unfortunately, I only have so many years to teach and train my children in the ways of the Lord, to teach them academics, to teach them to serve, and to teach them life skills, etc. It can be very hard to juggle teaching and training them in all these critical areas of life. In considering curriculum choices, I try to select things that do not take too much of my time, because I want to spend my energies teaching them about Christian worldview, discipleship, serving, etc. I mentioned in a previous chapter that my oldest is currently taking a writing course where she has a writing tutor giving her assignments and grading her papers. This has been a huge blessing as she is growing in an area we feel she is gifted, and it is not consuming my time. If I have to choose between teaching my daughter to write or discipling her to be a godly young woman, I would rather spend the time going through a book study on Biblical womanhood with her.

Our three oldest do a math program on computers where they can watch a tutorial on how to work the math problems, and then their daddy can check their grades. This also frees up time for me to teach them other things. I would rather gather my children in the living room and read a biography of a great Christian than labor through teaching them math. What I am trying to express is that what is burning in my heart to teach my children has everything to do with equipping them to live lives for the Lord. I also want to teach them life skills like gardening, sewing, canning, etc. In addition, I want them to know it is a joy to serve the Lord and to minister to others. I want them to be mission minded and to have a heart for the massive needs in our own country and abroad. I love the way Ann Dunnagan puts it when she says, "God's mission is for your family to expand His family." [12]

Because of this I find myself looking for ways they can learn the academics with as little of me as possible. That is because there are numerous ways they can learn their academics but I, as their mama, only get one shot at teaching them to love and serve Jesus and to prepare them for life.

Focus on the Basics

Truly, if we cover the basics of reading, writing, and arithmetic, we are giving our children a strong foundation. If they are equipped to read well, they can teach themselves anything they need or want to learn. There are so many extras that we may want to focus on, but the longer I homeschool the more I realize the three R's are central to a solid education. I would add character training to the core basics. In fact, if I had to pick only two areas to focus on in teaching my children I would say that the two most important things for me would be training my children to understand the ways and character of the Lord and growing strong readers. Again, if they can read and love to read they will teach themselves all kinds of things. Now we may be able to teach far more than these two subjects, but for us these two things are at the heart of our family goals.

Teaching In Pockets of Time along the Way

I have already established that my time is very limited between running a household, living on land and the work that ensues, homeschooling, training my children in the ways of the Lord, being a wife and helpmeet to my husband, and leading my children towards character and a focus on ministry. We have walked through different seasons, and what worked last year might not work this year or vice versa. Using small pockets of time for instruction can go a long ways. One thing that sometimes works for us is utilizing meal times to go over academics or discipleship materials. Sometimes this goes over more smoothly than others, but overall it has proved beneficial to try to teach something during meal times. That is because everyone is gathered together and occupied with eating. I will also say it has helped to cut out some of the problems with silly chatter, as we have a focus and they are expected to be attentive. At times I have eaten before the children so that I am free to be reading to them while they eat.

At one point we were doing a study on godly character traits during breakfast. We used a topical study book called *Parenting with Scripture.* Each day we discussed one character issue, such as kindness or truthfulness. The book gave us several Bible verses for each topic, as well as some discussion questions and application ideas. It was short and sweet and a good way of starting our day.

At times we will also go over picture vocabulary cards during breakfast. We have streamlined the subjects of vocabulary and spelling by using vocabulary cards that we put on a board above our kitchen table. We have used many lunch times to read history or our Christian worldview material. Sometimes I will also throw in a picture study at breakfast or lunch. That may sound intimidating, but it is not. All I do is hold up a picture of a famous piece of artwork. I may tell my children a few facts about the artist or the picture. I then ask them to stare at it for a short period of time (maybe one or two minutes). Then I take the picture away and they recite to me what they can remember from the picture. Then we may hang the picture on the wall, fridge or a bulletin board. It can stay there until we rotate with a new picture the next week or whenever we get around to it. That is just a super quick and easy way for them to be exposed to some pieces of art that are lovely and admirable. The same thing could be done with a classic piece of music while naming who the composer was, etc.

At dinner, my husband takes the reins as he is currently doing family worship right before or during our evening meal. He usually leads us in a study of the Scripture. (We are currently doing a study through Psalms.) At times, he has also used this time to review catechism questions with our children. We see value in teaching catechism because it is a question and answer method of rooting our children in sound theology and great doctrines. Noah Webster's 1828 Dictionary defines a catechism as:

"A form of instruction by means of questions and answers, particularly in the principles of religion."

For example we have taught our four-year-old to answer the question, "Who Made You?" She answers us, "God made me." Just reviewing a few questions at night goes a long way. We have also found that teaching a catechism through music is an effective way for us all to memorize it. It can be easier to remember when set to a catchy little tune. These catechisms that we have memorized often come up in our conversations with our children. They even come up in my mind as I think about things. Sometimes we will be discussing something pertaining to the Bible or a Christian worldview, and one of the older children will bring up a particular catechism that deals with that exact issue. We have all been blessed, and our family conversations have gone deeper because of taking time to work on catechisms. You can make it fun, and the drilling does not have to be a dry, endless drill where the children are bored to tears. Just work on a few at a time, then add more and review from time to time. Honestly, though, I think we have all learned more easily through the catechism songs than through drilling. There are also some good books you can buy entitled, "Truth and Grace Memory Books" by Tom Ascol. These books are a series of little memory guides for teaching the catechisms systematically.

My husband also likes to review Scripture verses we are memorizing during this family worship time. We do not always cover it all every night, but rotating what we are reviewing works as well. We end our dinner time by singing a hymn. Incidentally, our little Nathaniel has been a singer ever since he was a baby. More so than I remember our other children being at his age. I believe it is because he is the first baby with whom we have had this dinnertime tradition of closing our meal with a hymn. I think that, because this has been the norm all of his little life, he sees his family singing and he wants to do likewise.

Circle Time

One way that I am currently attempting to make sure I spend quality time with all the children and am getting in core things I want to teach them is by having what we call our morning circle time. I have also heard some mamas call this their morning basket time. The reason for calling it morning basket is because, often, a mama will put a lot of different books and resources in a basket, gather up the children, and do a hodgepodge of reading and instructing. I keep my teaching resources either in a basket or on a shelf beside my rocking chair. This morning time has become one of the dearest parts of the day to me. This is when I gather my children and pray, sing, read, and instruct them all together. At times, if something pressing is on our hearts, we will go down on our knees right there on our family room floor and lift up special prayers to our Lord. Once the day get going, things can often spin out of control and it is easy for good intentions to go by the wayside. By gathering all the children together in the morning I am able to prioritize the most important things before the day runs away from us. We do our circle time after breakfast and morning chores. Our morning basket activities vary, but some of the things we include are a hymn of the month, quickly going over some vocabulary words in the context of sentences, review of math concepts, reading history aloud, reading through topical Bible studies, praying together, doing a study on a character quality, and more. Usually this time lasts about an hour to an hour and a half. It can be challenging at times with our little ones in our midst, but is also a good time of training for them to learn to be quiet and listen with their older siblings. I often allow my little people to play with toys, blocks, learning manipulatives, etc. while we read. At other times I will hold them if they are being too distracting. Often, my older ones like to be drawing or doing a handcraft during this time, and it is a good way for me to connect with them and be able to cover some things that I want to be sure that we are squeezing into our day. Our circle time usually ends up being partially academic but mostly discipleship oriented. I have really come to treasure this time in our day with all of my children gathered about me. Even though it can be challenging to get through circle time with all the interruptions, diaper changes, corrections, etc., I really believe it is worth the investment of energy and time to make it happen. I have seen some good fruit from this time and appreciate that it draws us all together at the start of our day.

Be Creative in Discipling and Training Along the Way

Deuteronomy chapter eleven tells us to train our children as we walk along the way, as we lie down, as we get up, etc.

154

"You shall teach them to your children, talking of them when you are sitting in your house, and when you are walking by the way, and when you lie down, and when you rise" (Deuteronomy 11:19).

With intentionality we can prayerfully ask the Lord to help us to teach our children in the process of doing life with them. Here are some ideas:

For one of our daughter's last birthdays, her daddy read a verse that coincided with her birthdate. Her birthday falls on the eighth, so he read verse eight of a certain chapter.

You could also read a verse coinciding with a particular time of the day. For example: "Children, here we are at the lunch table, again enjoying God's faithful provision for our family. The time is 12:15. Let's read Proverbs 12:15 to match the time we are eating." Then you would open Proverbs 12:15 and read, "The way of a fool is right in his own eyes, but a wise man listens to advice."

We sometimes do the Proverb of the day: There are 31 Proverbs, so if you read one a day you will have one for every day of the month. Think of the nuggets of wisdom we could be giving our children if we did this with them monthly, every other month, or quarterly. After a while, the Proverbs would become very familiar to our children. By the way, the book of Proverbs can be a very handy training manual to instill wisdom and character into our children's lives. The heart of the book of Proverbs is a father seeking to have his son's heart and teaching him what character traits he should pursue, what situations to avoid, what kind of friends he should have, what kinds of women he should avoid, what the condition of his heart should be, etc. I don't think we can give our children enough of the Proverbs.

It is always a wonderful thing when we can teach Scriptural principles as we learn academic subjects. One such example would be teaching the alphabet, ascribing a verse of Scripture that starts with each letter. The early colonists to America taught their children academics, with Spiritual instruction and discipleship in mind. In the New England Primer, the first reading primer designed for the American Colonies, pictures and Biblical rhymes introduced children to their alphabet with maxims such as, "In Adam's fall we sinned all." [13] The primer taught the alphabet, catechisms, and moral lessons that reflected a strong Puritan attitude and worldview.

Cookie Night

Going back to my own childhood I recall ways my dad displayed intentionality in discipling me as we drove in the car. When I was little I

155

remember him telling me "Little Suzy" stories. These were fictional stories he would make up about a pretend scenario where little Suzy made a right choice or a wrong one. I would be engrossed in the story, and there would always be a great lesson I could learn from the life of "Little Suzy." Now and then he would ask me to go with him on visitation. Perhaps he would be visiting someone who had visited the church or at times he would take me and we would go from house to house, leaving brochures on people's doors. The brochure would tell them about our church and extend an invitation for them to visit. I enjoyed those times with my dad. He would talk to me in the car about the ways of the Lord, and, often, he would pull off and take me into a health food store where he would purchase a package of cookies that we would share on our way home. I remember watching every turn he made to see if I thought our path would lead to a store to buy cookies. As a little girl, I was just enjoying time with my father and hoping for a cookie, but my dad had bigger purposes in mind. He was creating a memory and training me in the ways of the Lord along the way. My mother would do similar things in taking me shopping or staying up late at night talking to me. Whatever we did and wherever we went, my parents were always pointing me to the ways of the Lord.

Pancakes and the Bible

Another normal life activity that we lace with Biblical training is Saturday morning pancake breakfast. My sweet husband faithfully gets up and makes pancakes or waffles every Saturday morning. I believe this is part of our family culture that our children will reflect upon with fond memories. My little ones often ask me, "How many more days is it until daddy stays home?" and somehow it seems like the pancake breakfast is an instigator of that question. We could just have a tradition of pancakes, but my husband has taken it a step further. After everyone has full tummies, he gathers us in the family room where we sing and read Scripture and whatever book our family is reading through at the time. Currently, our book is *Foxe's Book of Martyrs*. We usually end that time on our knees in prayer.

The Lord's Day Prayer

Remember, we are talking about teaching as we walk through our day and, sometimes, in just short segments. One example of this is, after church on Sunday, our children know to gather in our family room. My husband will often ask them how their time was at church, and we might discuss the sermon or something that happened that day. Sometimes he will share an overview of what our week is going to look like, and, occasionally, he will have some kind of exciting news to share such as a family trip coming up. We will then pray and we're done. It doesn't have to take long, but it is being purposeful to establish that family tradition and to take a few minutes for family discipleship.

Changing Table Chalk Board

When our Nathaniel was a baby, I bought an adorable chalk board that says "Bible Verse of the Week" at the top. I asked my husband to hang it right above my son's changing table. I could write any verse I wanted on the board and then read it to Nathaniel during diaper changes. The verse that I put on the board was Ephesians 6:1: "Children, obey your parents in the Lord for this is right." I also know a song to that verse that Steve Green put on one of his *Hide 'Em In Your Heart* Bible memory songs CDs. While I changed Nathaniel's diaper I would sing the verse to him. Sometimes he was fidgety and did not want to be still. At times I would use different voice inflections to catch his attention, and he enjoyed the singing too. The wonderful bonus is that, often, I would have other young children who followed me into his room and they would get to hear the verse as well. It did not take my younger girls long to catch on to this new routine and, at times, they would remind me to sing the verse to Nathaniel.

Intentional Read-Aloud Times

As hard as it can be to carve out the time for reading aloud, I have found it to be a rewarding practice to read through great books together. One thing that really helps is to have a time set aside that everyone knows is reading time. There are many excellent, faith-building, life-giving, inspiring books that are wonderful to share as a family. Missionary biographies can really inspire us to live sanctified lives dedicated to the service of our Lord. Also, great allegorical stories such as *Pilgrim's Progress* and *Hinds' Feet on High Places* have rich lessons we and our children can learn from. Our children have read children's versions of these books, but as they grow older, they are ready to read the unabridged classics. We have read books about martyrs of the faith with our children and also shown them animated videos from the Torchlighters' "Heroes of the Faith" series. These animated videos tell the stories of people who loved the Lord and were faithful even unto death.

"And they have conquered him by the blood of the Lamb and by the Word of their testimony, for they loved not their lives even unto death" (Revelation 12:11).

I believe that, when we lift these kinds of men and women up to our children as heroes, it shows us all how petty our problems really are. When we think of Perpetua who was torn from her baby and eaten by beasts in a Roman theatre, complaining about petty inconveniences takes on a different perspective. It is recorded that Perpetua's dying words to her brothers in Christ were, "Stand fast in the faith and love one another."

I pray that, by being exposed to great men and women of the faith, our children will think and act out of a bigger eternal perspective. Proverbs 22:15 tell us that, "Foolishness is bound up in the heart of a child." I think we could also say that *selfishness* is bound up in the heart of a child. Two ways I know of combating the self-absorption so prevalent in our day are to make heroes of great missionaries, martyrs, and heroes of the faith and also to teach our children to serve: to teach them to get out of themselves, to see the needs of others, and to emulate those who have walked before us and given their all for the sake of Christ.

I have found it beneficial to try to read aloud to individual children as I can. Children love to have one-on-one time with a parent, and great books can open the door to meaningful conversations. You may want to read a book with each child and take turns on different days or whenever the opportunity presents itself. I can often sense where my children are with attitudes and overall demeanor. Sometimes I can tell one particular child needs some one-on-one time, and I will grab the book I am reading with that child and say, "Let's read together." They love that attention. My oldest has often sweetly grabbed some lotion and offered to rub my feet as I have read to her. These read-aloud times have been a sweet bonding time where I have utilized a good book to help me convey ideas and teachings my children need to hear. For example, I have been reading books to my oldest on Biblical womanhood and issues of purity, etc. Often, she will stop me even as I am reading and start sharing things that are on her heart.

Sacred Music

Playing melodic, sacred music in our home is another way of discipling our children along the way. They will begin picking up on great doctrinal truths as they sing the hymns they have learned. I have the sweetest memories of Christian radio playing throughout my home on a daily basis as I was growing up. Every day, our home was filled with the familiar voices of saints such as Elisabeth Elliot, John MacArthur, and many others. Every day, radio personalities would read Scripture over the airwaves and continually point us back to Jesus. To this day, my heart is stirred when I hear songs that were played on this radio station throughout my growing up years. My brother and I went to bed many nights with Christian radio playing in our rooms. This Christian radio station was a huge part of the atmosphere of my home during my growing up years and made a huge impact on my life.

Memory verses set to music are also an easy way to saturate our children in the Word of God. Somehow, what children are exposed to in their formative years seems to really stick. When they are young and their minds work like little sponges is the time to saturate them in truths they will remember and draw from for the rest of their lives.

Childhood is a small window of time and a beautiful opportunity for us to be intentional in pointing our children to the ways of the Lord. There are so many creative ways of doing this. Formal times of instruction are helpful and, yet, we should not limit ourselves to family Bible times. While family worship time is important, we want to go beyond that and look for opportunities to proclaim the greatness of our Lord as we walk along the way, as we lie down, and as we rise up. Every day and all throughout the day is the perfect time to be discipling our families for Christ. Homeschooling affords us extra hours in our day to talk to our children about the wondrous ways of the Lord and teach them His ways.

Chapter 15
Important Things to Teach Our Families

We Cannot Teach What We Do Not Possess

We can know the things that we should teach and impart to our children and yet lack the power to do what we desire to do. We cannot faithfully train our children to love and obey Christ if we are not loving and obeying Him. Our children will not likely be excited about the Word of God if they do not see us treasuring it and applying it in our own lives. Discipling our children day in and day out is hard work, and it cannot be done in our own strength. We need to be Word-saturated and prayerful parents in order to give our families the spiritual legacy that we desire. If we try to do this in our own strength we will fail miserably, but if we allow the Lord to flow through us He can do great things in spite of our weaknesses. It is good to have goals and lists of things to cover with our children, but let us never delude our minds into thinking that we can produce spiritual fruit by human effort. Let us cast ourselves humbly upon the Lord daily as we go about teaching our children.

The Gospel

The Gospel is the good news that, though we are born dead in sin, God has provided a way of atonement for that sin through the finished work of Jesus Christ on the cross. Through repentance of sin and faith in Christ's atonement for it, we can be made alive in Him. According to Part 1, Question 30 in "A Catechism for Boys and Girls," sin is "any transgression of the law of God." [14] It can also be further described as an independent spirit that resists surrender to the Lordship of Christ.

> And you were dead in the trespasses and sins in which you once walked, following the course of this world, following the prince of the power of the air, the spirit that is now at work in the sons of disobedience—among whom we all once lived in the passions of our flesh, carrying out the desires of the body and the mind, and were by nature children of wrath, like the rest of mankind. But God, being rich in mercy, because of the great love with which he loved us, even when we were dead in our trespasses, made us alive together with Christ—by grace you have been saved— and raised us up with him and seated us with him in the heavenly places in Christ Jesus, so that

in the coming ages he might show the immeasurable riches of his grace in kindness toward us in Christ Jesus. For by grace you have been saved through faith. And this is not your own doing; it is the gift of God, not a result of works, so that no one may boast. For we are his workmanship, created in Christ Jesus for good works, which God prepared beforehand, that we should walk in them (Ephesians 2:1-10).

"For all have sinned and fall short of the glory of God" (Romans 3:23).

There is a price to be paid for sin.

"For the Wages of sin is death, but the free gift of God is eternal life in Christ Jesus our Lord" (Romans 6:23).

Every human being is born in sin, but our just and loving God offers a way of escape from eternal judgment. The only way is through His Son Jesus.

"Jesus said to him, 'I am the way, and the truth, and the life. No one comes to the Father except through me" (John 14:6).

This is very good news indeed and the most important thing that we can ever teach our children! We need to show them the way of salvation and disciple them to have a thriving relationship with Christ. I so wish that I could repent and believe for my children. I wish that I could break their hearts over their personal sin and give them an undying faith in Christ and a desire to surrender their lives to His Lordship. If I could, it would be a done matter for all of my children. The thing is, however, that each person is held personally responsible for repentance and faith and for the stature of their own heart before the Lord their Creator. This prayer from centuries past expresses it so powerfully:

> Lord, it should be the first thing, that we would presently do for our children, to make them Thy children. But it is beyond us, it is above us. A very distinguishing stroke and beat of a perfect heart is a faith in the only Savior, a flight unto Him for His great salvation. but whose gift is this! We are told in Ephesians 2:8: It is the gift of God. We are elsewhere told more than once that God gives repentance. A perfect heart, which is always a very tender one, it is a stone turned into flesh. Who but the almighty God can do such a thing as that? Create in us a clean heart, O our God. It is a creating work, to make a perfect heart. None but God the Creator of all things can do such a thing. "This is My glory," says the Lord, "And My glory I will not give unto another." [15]

It is of paramount importance for Christian parents to be teaching their children the gospel faithfully. We need to be constantly preaching the good news of the gospel in our homes on a daily basis. We can use times of discipline and correction as a time to share the good news of the gospel once again. When a child is in trouble we can share with him or her that they were born in sin and, because of Adam and Eve's original sin, they inherited a heart that wants to go its own way. They inherited a sin nature.

"All we like sheep have gone astray; we have turned—every one—to his own way; and the Lord has laid on him the iniquity of us all" (Isaiah 53:6).

We can paint a picture of the hopelessness of sin and what a problem they have. Once they understand that they have a problem that they cannot remedy, then we can offer them the hope that is possible to help them in Christ. Although they have a problem that they can do nothing about, they are not without hope. They can call upon the name of the Lord Jesus Christ and be saved (Romans 10:13).

The Lord graciously gives us our children for eighteen or more years. He gives us years to speak truth into their hearts and lives and to teach them what they need to know to walk successfully through their adult years. Of all the things that we need to teach them, absolutely nothing is as important as that of the glorious good news of the gospel. It is the best news of all news!

Because we cannot save our children, parents need to be prayer warriors, petitioning the Lord that the hearts of their children will bow to the Lordship of Christ. My husband and I regularly pray that the Lord will draw our children's heart to Himself and save them. We take seriously our responsibility to teach them the ways of the Lord, but we are humbled in knowing that we cannot save our children. The Holy Spirit has to reveal Himself to each one of them and woo their hearts, granting them the grace of believing faith. We see it like this: Our children are not really ours; they are on loan to us from the Lord. He has asked us to teach them His Word, His truth, His ways, and their need for the gospel of Jesus Christ. That is our part. We have to walk a road of faith, trusting Him to do what we cannot do. When it comes down to it there is only so much that we can do. Convicting them of sin, wooing their hearts, and regenerating their hearts through faith and repentance is something that only God can do. It is a scary thing to know that we cannot accomplish saving faith for our children. This keeps us humble and keeps us on our knees. The great nineteenth-century preacher Charles Spurgeon said it like this:

"My soul, never be satisfied with a shadowy Christ. I cannot know Christ through another person's brains. I cannot love him with another man's heart, and I cannot see him with another man's eyes ... I am so afraid of living in a second-hand religion. Lord save us from having borrowed communion. No, I must know him myself. O God, let me not be deceived in this ... I must know him on my own account." [5]

An appropriate prayer for our children would be that they will know Him with their own brains, love Him with their own hearts, and see Him with their own eyes. I think it is behooving to Christian parents to take caution against their children thinking they know Christ just because they live in a good Christian family with godly values. Although this is a blessing in their lives, their faith should not rest in the family they were born into. Often, homeschool families spend so much time together that they become like one big unit or entity, which can be a great aspect of homeschooling. I often tell my children that we need team work when we have to go somewhere or accomplish something, but when it comes to salvation, this is not a team effort. Salvation is personal between each individual and their Maker. Each of our children have to own their own faith; their family and their parents will not get them to heaven. Only by personal repentance from sin and faith in the atoning work of Christ on their behalf will new life spring forth in their hearts. May we be found faithful in fervently praying that each of our children will bow the knee to the Lordship of Christ.

On a practical note, what are some of the ways that we can bring the gospel to our children and help them to understand eternal truths? I already said that moments of correction and discipline are a great time to lovingly remind our children of the gospel. Also, faithfully reading the Scriptures as a family is a powerful way as the Holy Spirit speaks to our hearts through His Word. Some resources for children also do a good job of explaining the gospel. I look for resources that make God the focus and not man. It is not because I am so lovable that God chose to save me but rather because God chose to extend mercy and love to me.

When I was a little girl, people often used the Wordless Book to explain the Gospel. I still appreciate this approach and used this with two of our children as the Lord was drawing their hearts. The book uses colored pages to explain the basic concepts such as black for sin, red for the blood of Christ, white for cleansing and forgiveness, etc. I think there are even puppets that you can put on your hand, and I have also seen colored beaded bracelets. These are creative and engaging ways to talk through the steps of understanding sin, repenting, receiving cleansing, growing in Christ, and our eternal home in heaven.

164

Another way of presenting the gospel to our children is to faithfully take them to a church that rightly divides the Word of God (2 Timothy 2:15) and makes the gospel a strong focus. God speaks to us through His Word and through the preaching of His Word. It is important to be discerning in the churches we choose. Some churches preach feel-good messages that are little more than a pep talk or psychological advice. For our family we want to be in a church where the Word of God is honored as the source of all truth and where the preaching is centered around what the Scripture teaches and not around the opinions of man.

"How then will they call on him in whom they have not believed? And how are they to believe in him of whom they have never heard? And how are they to hear without someone preaching?" (Romans 10:14).

As mentioned elsewhere in this book, missionary stories of people such as Jim Elliot and others who went so far as to die for the sake of sharing the gospel can be helpful. I think missionary stories and stories of great Christians can do a lot to paint a picture to our children of the beauty and supreme importance of the gospel.

The urgency in which we share the gospel with our families is an indication of how much we value it in our own eyes. Do we continue to marvel at the gospel or are we blinded by the cares of this world? Let us seek to have an eternal perspective to see what really matters and let go of lesser things, that we may have clarity and focus for what matters most. When all is said and done, the world and its desires will pass away. The only lasting thing that can go with us into heaven is our families. What matters most to me is that all of my family be together for eternity.

Ongoing Repentance

It can be said that when Martin Luther posted his 95 Theses on the church door in Wittenberg Germany on October 31, 1517, it started the Protestant reformation. Item number 1 of the 95 states, "When our Lord and Master Jesus Christ said, 'Repent' (Matt. 4:17), he willed the entire life of believers to be one of repentance."

Repentance is a change of heart and mind that propels us to align ourselves in obedience to God's commands. We need to help our children to understand that repentance is not a one-time event at the time of salvation. Repentance should be happening every time we are made aware that we have violated the law of God. When our behaviors and attitudes go against His Word we need to repent. Matthew Henry said the following:

"Many mourn for their sins that do not truly repent of them, weep bitterly for them, and yet continue in love and league with them." [16]

It is crucial that our children understand that repentance is not mourning the consequences of our sin but rather sorrowing that we have offended our loving Lord. Many times children will be sorry that they got in trouble; this is not what we are looking for. We should pray that they will be caught in their sin and that the Lord will give them godly sorrow that leads to repentance and restored fellowship with Him.

"For godly grief produces a repentance that leads to salvation without regret, whereas worldly grief produces death" (2 Corinthians 7:10).

Prayer

One thing about this parenting journey that has been true for me is that the farther I have gone into it the more prayerful I have become. I realize in increasing measure that I cannot parent Biblically apart from the help of the Lord. I think that not only should we be constantly in prayer for the faith and repentance of our children, but we should also be teaching them to pray and modeling prayer before them. It is important to share with our children answers we have seen to prayer and remind them of the faithfulness of God. Below are some ways that we can be purposeful in making prayer more and more a part of the ebb and flow of our lives.

Prayer Walks

Occasionally I have taken a child by the hand and gone for a walk with them outside. Sometimes we will talk and then I will pray with them as we continue walking. It is a good time to have them open up to me and share what is on their hearts and then to model prayer before them as we walk and pray together. It is also quality time spent together which helps to bond our relationship. This is a good thing to do when I know a particular child is struggling with a behavior or attitude problem. Sometimes just some focused time hearing that child's heart and praying can help a lot.

Prayer Tab Jar

A jar where prayer requests can be kept on little tabs or pieces of paper is a creative idea. As a family you could pull out one paper and pray for whatever request you draw out of the jar.

Christmas Card Pictures Prayer

I have heard the idea of keeping the yearly Christmas card pictures and praying through each card through the month of January. Each day you would take a new picture and pray for the family and needs represented.

Prayer Board

Having a bulletin board and/or dry erase board hanging near the kitchen table and listing prayer requests is a good way of remembering needs you want your family to be praying for. We have listed needs on our white board, and we also hang our church prayer requests and/or weekly bulletin on the bulletin board. This way we have a visual reminder to guide us.

Prayers for National, State and Local Government Leaders

Our previous church had people on all three levels of government that we would pray for on a monthly basis. It is a good rotation plan for teaching our children to pray for those in authority.

"First of all, then, I urge that supplications, prayers, intercessions, and thanksgivings be made for all people, for kings and all who are in high positions, that we may lead a peaceful and quiet life, godly and dignified in every way. This is good, and it is pleasing in the sight of God our Savior" (1 Timothy 2:1-3).

A good idea is also to have your family write a letter to different men in positions of leadership telling them that your family has prayed for them.

Pray All Throughout the Day

This is an area I want to improve in. When we have challenges arise throughout our day I want to be quick to stop everything and lead our children into prayer, asking the Lord for His guidance and help. It doesn't come naturally to stop in the chaos of life and call together a prayer group but I see the need to do more of this. Rather than plowing through the difficulties, I want to show our children that when things are burdensome we need to have a default called prayer. It is also a great thing to stop with a child when they come to us complaining about something that is bothering them personally. If we stop and say, "Let's pray about that," then we are teaching them to go to the Lord with their concerns.

Pray Through Sibling Rivalry

Here is another perfect opportunity to go to prayer when two or more children are not getting along. Again, this does not come naturally for me as I usually step in and want to tell them what to do. I see the need to grow in this area as I perceive how much more effective it would be to just make them stop and start praying through the fruits of the spirit and for softened hearts, all the while reminding them of God's truth through the process of prayer. The Lord is able to do so much more in their hearts through prayer than a parent can do by lecturing them in the moment.

More Than Just Blessing the Food

I know that we often feel in a rush when sitting down to eat, but this is a prime opportunity to pray over things happening in our families and homes and for needs that are arising with people we know. I have tried to grow in this area of not just blessing the food with a quick amen but praying more intentionally at our meal times. At lunch I might thank the Lord for His provision and for the things we were able to accomplish through our morning. Then I might pray that the Lord will give us strength through the afternoon to work hard, to love Him and to glorify Him throughout the remainder of our day. My prayers will change from day to day, but I think, since mealtime prayers are already built into our routine, they are a great opportunity to go deeper with our children, modeling a greater humility and dependence before the Lord. Some ideas would be to pray for the family to serve one another, to love one another, that the children will be diligent in their work, that they will look out for one another, that when you go out in public your family will shine like stars in a dark world. Pray that your family will love the Lord Jesus above all else. Pray that they will love God's Word and live in obedience to it. Pray that the Lord will bless the work of Daddy's hands as he is at work and that he will be a light in his business and around those who do not know the Lord. Additionally, if I hear of a need in the life of a family member or friend, I will sometimes share that with the children when we sit down at the table and we will add that to our mealtime prayer. Usher your children into the presence of the Lord at every opportunity, leading them to the throne of grace.

"Let us then with confidence draw near to the throne of grace, that we may receive mercy and find grace to help in time of need" (Hebrews 4:16).

Cherish, Read and Trust the Word of God

Our children need to be raised to honor and love God's Word. From their earliest days we can talk about God's Word with joy and enthusiasm. We can sing that old Bible song to our little people, "The B-I-B-L-E." Did you grow up learning this song?

The B-I-B-L-E
Yes, that's the book for me

I stand alone on the Word of God
The B-I-B-L-E!

Even in utero we can start reading God's Word to our children and holding it in high regard before them. As is the case in so many areas, things are often better caught than taught. Our children are more prone to catch an enthusiasm and reverence for the Word of God when they see us talking about it, reading it, studying it, meditating on it, and joyfully bringing it up in the context of everyday life. Studying it and teaching it is vitally important, but we do not want to impart only a stale head knowledge. Instead, we want to teach them to delight in the law of the Lord.

"But his delight is in the law of the Lord, and on his law he meditates day and night. He is like a tree planted by streams of water that yields its fruit in its season, and its leaf does not wither. In all that he does, he prospers" (Psalm 1:2-3).

It is not enough for our young people to just say they love God's Word. We need to encourage and exhort them to dig into it for themselves to see how the Lord will direct their paths. Solomon admonished his son to look for wisdom, understanding, and insight as if he were searching for hidden treasure. There is no better place to look for this kind of wisdom than in God's Word.

"If you seek it like silver and search for it as for hidden treasures, then you will understand the fear of the LORD and find the knowledge of God" (Proverbs 2:4-5).

Teach Them to be Defenders of the Faith

So we start out teaching our youngsters to love and respect the Bible and then go on to teach them to thoughtfully study the Bible. As they grow older we need to make sure that they understand the history and inerrancy of the Word of God. Biblical truth is under a massive attack in our day and even many so-called Bible scholars are denying the inerrancy of God's Word. Many false teachings are seeping into the church and challenging the truth of Scripture. With the massive amount of information on the web, and other worldviews dominating the culture, our young people need to be equipped to stand firm on the Word of God. Do they know how we got our Bible and do they know that it can be trusted?

169

"All Scripture is breathed out by God and profitable for teaching, for reproof, for correction, and for training in righteousness, that the man of God may be complete, equipped for every good work" (2 Timothy 3:16-17).

Since all Scripture is breathed out by God, we need to interpret it soundly and form a proper Biblical doctrine in our minds.

Going right along with this topic of the inerrancy of Scripture is the need to teach our children Biblical apologetics. They need to know how to accurately defend Biblical truth. In his book *Already Gone*, Ken Ham says, "Most church-going adults cannot adequately defend the basics of their Christian faith or basic doctrines, let alone defend the faith against the skeptical questions of this scientific age. How many can really even properly answer questions such as: Where did the Bible come from? What does it mean to have faith? What does it mean that the Bible is inspired? Aren't there other books that some say should be in the Bible? How do you know Jesus is God?—just to name a few." [17] Giving our children a good grasp of creation science that is consistent with Genesis is a good foundation for them because God's Word will be viciously attacked in most of the scientific information they will gather in the secular world. Now is the time to equip them with a foundation that they can build a right worldview upon.

We have been giving our children resources from ministries such as Answers in Genesis, the Institute for Creation Research, and Biblical Discipleship Ministries since our oldest children were very young. Learning to defend your faith can be a lot of fun for kids. A couple of years ago, my husband took our children to a cave in Texas called Natural Bridge Caverns. On the tour, the guide told them how many thousands of years it took for the stalagmites to form. Our oldest daughter raised her hand and asked the guide if she had heard about cases of stalagmites forming over Coke bottles that had been left in caves. These Coke bottle demonstrations give proof that such geological formations can happen much quicker than modern science will admit. The guide was clearly uncomfortable with the challenge from a 13-year-old and quickly changed the subject to something else. Teaching children to defend the faith not only gives them confidence in what they believe but also confidence to face secular critics even at a young age.

In this information and scientific age in which we are raising our children, we need to equip them with a Biblical metaphysics (that is, a proper view of reality). What does the Bible say is the essence or nature of man and reality? Much of the entertainment today via books, movies, etc. is feeding our young people a confused message about what constitutes reality. There is such a focus on fantasy that I fear many young people are losing sight of what is real. Also, many young people are running to these wrong metaphysical ideologies because they are looking for an escape from their own realities. It is of paramount importance that our children understand that God is the Creator and we are the created. That gives Him all the right to be Lord in our lives. Our young people can try to escape this reality but, in reality, they cannot.

"Where shall I go from your Spirit? Or where shall I flee from your presence? If I ascend to heaven, you are there! If I make my bed in Sheol, you are there! If I take the wings of the morning and dwell in the uttermost parts of the sea, even there your hand shall lead me, and your right hand shall hold me. If I say, 'Surely the darkness shall cover me, and the light about me be night,' even the darkness is not dark to you; the night is bright as the day, for darkness is as light with you" (Psalm 139:7-12).

Similarly, it is also important to make sure that our children have a good grasp on a right epistemology. Epistemology is a big word that Merriam Webster's Dictionary defines as "The study or a theory of the nature and grounds of knowledge, especially with reference to its limits and validity." Simply put, it is the study of how we know what we know. Again, are we guiding our young men and young women to understand and accept what is real and what God-given limits are in our lives? God is ultimately the author of knowledge.

"For the Lord gives wisdom; from his mouth come knowledge and understanding" (Proverbs 2:6).

Following on the tail of a proper perspective of metaphysics and epistemology, our families need to understand Biblical ethics. Webster's Dictionary from 1828 defines ethics this way:

"The doctrines of morality or social manners; the science of moral philosophy, which teaches men their duty and the reasons of it."

From a Biblical worldview, what are the duties of man and the reasons for it? When we answer this question properly we are holding to a Biblical ethic. What does God say about life and the taking of life? Here is a springboard to teach our families why abortion is against God's Word.

"For you formed my inward parts; you knitted me together in my mother's womb" (Psalm 139:13).

"Your eyes saw my unformed substance; in your book were written, every one of them, the days that were formed for me when as yet there was none of them" (Psalm 139:16).

God forms the inward parts in a mother's womb, and He has all the days of a person's life preordained. Who is man to try to end the life of a new person God is creating? Also, since abortion is the taking of life, it clearly violates one of the Ten Commandments.

"You shall not murder" (Exodus 20:13).

This is how we can take Scripture and break it down with our young people on any topic whether it be abortion, euthanasia, morality, and many more things. A discussion of what is right and what is wrong always needs to start by looking to Scripture. It should be the Christian's plumb line. Sadly, so much of culture is embracing secular humanism, relativism, a wrong metaphysics, a wrong epistemology, and no sense of morality or ethics. This is a challenge for parents in the twenty-first century. We are strongly swimming upstream to try to pattern our families on the firm foundation of God's eternal Word. The divine, inspired Scriptures do not change with the revolutions, reconstructions, advancements, modifications, permutations, and diversities of cultures. These Holy Scriptures remain the same and are to be fully obeyed by all peoples at all times.

"The sum of your word is truth, and every one of your righteous rules endures forever" (Psalm 119:160).

Teach Them Church History

Something I did not begin learning much about until my adult years is church history. You may wonder why I think this is important to teach our children. I believe it is very helpful for us to understand church history so that we can try to avoid many of the same mistakes and heresies of centuries past. A lot of false teachings that may seem new on the scene are really just old heresies that have resurfaced in modern packaging. If we have a firm grasp on the struggles of the church gone by we will have greater perspective in understanding, discerning, and evaluating issues confronting the church today. There is a lot to be learned from studying the past. Remember what Solomon said in Ecclesiastes?

"What has been is what will be, and what has been done is what will be done, and there is nothing new under the sun" (Ecclesiastes 1:9).

When we take the time to learn church history, we can see how God has moved in the past, we remember the heroes who have stood for truth in generations past, we remember our rich heritage of faith, we gain greater discernment in evaluating current trends of the day, and our view of God is magnified as we see His faithful hand in preserving the Church throughout the continuum of history. History is, after all, His story.

Teach Them Sound Doctrine

Going along with church history is the study of sound doctrine. It will benefit our children to know something of the famous church councils of the past such as the Council of Nicaea where the doctrine of the deity of Christ was affirmed and other major defining moments, such as the Protestant Reformation. Mostly they need to be rooted and grounded in sound doctrine so that they can discern false teaching. There is a lot of false teaching going on in today's evangelical circles, and we try to talk these things through with our children. We want them not to be taken captive by every wind of teaching but to be grounded in the truth.

There are many myths that circulate on blogs and websites that spread false information about the history of the Church. It is not uncommon to come across a story that misrepresents the Council of Nicaea by stating the Church never believed Jesus was God until then. That is where it is important to be familiar with early Church writings such as Ignatius of Antioch, Clement of Rome, the *Didache* and other important documents that date before the Council of Nicaea in AD 325. We also need to know what Nicaea was about, what was being debated, and what documents were produced. The Nicene Creed is still a great statement of faith to be familiar with.

> We believe in one God, the Father, the Almighty, maker of heaven and earth, of all that is, seen and unseen.

> We believe in one Lord, Jesus Christ, the only Son of God, eternally begotten of the Father, God from God, Light from Light, true God from true God, begotten, not made, of one Being with the Father. Through him all things were made.

> For us and for our salvation he came down from heaven: by the power of the Holy Spirit he became incarnate from the Virgin Mary, and was made man.

> For our sake, he was crucified under Pontius Pilate; he suffered death and was buried. On the third day, he rose again in accordance with the Scriptures; he ascended into heaven and is seated at the right hand of the Father.

He will come again in glory to judge the living and the dead, and his Kingdom will have no end.

We believe in the Holy Spirit, the Lord, the giver of life, who proceeds from the Father and the Son. With the Father and the Son he is worshiped and glorified. He has spoken through the prophets. We believe in one holy catholic and apostolic Church. We acknowledge one baptism for the forgiveness of sins. We look for the resurrection of the dead, and the life of the world to come.

Amen.

Our world is changing at an alarming rate and many false teachings are being embraced. When we can take a given issue or doctrine and look back at history to see where great men of faith have stood for thousands of years, it can help us to recognize pit falls and danger zones in our shifting society. What would men such as John Knox, Martin Luther, John Calvin, Charles Spurgeon, John Bunyan, Richard Baxter, and George Mueller have to say about some of the teachings in our brave, new world? What have been the consistent positions of the faith for thousands of years before our own radically evolving cultural landslides into cultural destruction?

"So that we may no longer be children, tossed to and fro by the waves and carried about by every wind of doctrine, by human cunning, by craftiness in deceitful schemes. Rather, speaking the truth in love, we are to grow up in every way into him who is the head, into Christ" (Ephesians 4:14-15).

There are those who say doctrine divides but love unites. I disagree with that statement. Instead I believe that sound doctrine should be a uniting agent, bonding believers in the cords of love. If you look at the verse above it is warning us against being thrown about by false teaching and urging us to speak the truth in love. Truth (sound doctrine) and love should coincide. It is not an imbalance of all truth without love nor of love and emotion without truth. In this dual relationship of truth and love there is beauty and protection.

Memorize God's Word

Imagine that one day all of our Bibles are confiscated from us by the government. I truly hope this will never be the case but that potential is there. The government can never take from us what has been hidden in our heart. This is one reason Scripture memorization is very important. Our children need to know that the Scriptures hold a most precious priority in our homes and are not just something we pull out on Sundays. They need to see us opening and cherishing the Word of God day by day.

"Your words were found, and I ate them, and your words became to me a joy and the delight of my heart, for I am called by your name, O Lord, God of hosts" (Jeremiah 15:16).

The Scripture is also another means by which we are protected from sin.

"I have stored up your word in my heart, that I might not sin against you" (Psalm 119:11).

The Honor of Suffering for Christ

We are living in an increasingly pagan culture. Even now Christians in our country are being challenged for holding to Biblical truth and refusing to compromise. I think it is important for us to prepare our children for the possibility of persecution in their lifetime. That is where I am so grateful for biographies and DVD stories about great heroes of the faith and those who have even been martyred for the faith. In 1 Peter, the apostle Peter is addressing Christians who were dispersed to various parts of the Roman Empire due to persecution. He reminds them not to be surprised at fiery trials.

"Beloved, do not be surprised at the fiery trial when it comes upon you to test you, as though something strange were happening to you. But rejoice insofar as you share Christ's sufferings, that you may also rejoice and be glad when his glory is revealed" (1 Peter 4:12-13).

"Yet if anyone suffers as a Christian, let him not be ashamed, but let him glorify God in that name" (1 Peter 4:16).

The apostles were beaten for preaching the name of Jesus, yet they rejoiced.

"And they agreed with him, and when they had called for the apostles and beaten them, they commanded that they should not speak in the name of Jesus, and let them go. So they departed from the presence of the council, rejoicing that they were counted worthy to suffer shame for His name" (Acts 5:40-41, NKJV).

Also, Jesus said that His people should expect opposition.

"If the world hates you, know that it has hated me before it hated you. If you were of the world, the world would love you as its own; but because you are not of the world, but I chose you out of the world, therefore the world hates you. Remember the word that I said to you: 'A servant is not greater than his master.' If they persecuted me, they will also persecute you. If they kept my word, they will also keep yours. But all these things they will do to you on account of my name, because they do not know him who sent me" (John 15:18-21).

The hymn writer Isaac Watts wrote about suffering for Christ in the hymn, "Am I a Soldier of the Cross?"

Am I a soldier of the cross,
A follow'r of the Lamb?
And shall I fear to own His cause,
Or blush to speak His name?

Must I be carried to the skies
On Flow'ry beds of ease,
While others fought to win the prize,
And sailed through bloody seas?

Are there no foes for me to face?
Must I not stem the flood?
Is this vile world a friend to grace,
To help me on to God?

Sure I must fight if I would reign;
Increase my courage, Lord;
I'll bear the toil, endure the pain,
Supported by Thy Word.

Thy saints in all this glorious war
Shall conquer, though they die;
They see the triumph from afar,
By faith's discerning eye.

When that illustrious day shall rise,
And All Thy armies shine
In robes of vict'ry through the skies,
The glory shall be Thine.

One way of teaching our children to be cognizant and concerned about Christian persecution is by praying with them for the persecuted church and those imprisoned for the faith. This makes them aware that it is not always easy to follow Christ and that many are making huge sacrifices to follow Him. This should both make them thankful for the freedoms we currently enjoy and also prepare their hearts should they one day have to pay a high price for following Jesus. They need to know that it is worth any cost to remain faithful to their calling. Lately, it has warmed my heart to see my young, tender Lilly Faith reminding us to pray for a Christian man imprisoned and facing persecution in another country because of his faith in Christ. It has been sweet to see her remember and remind our family to pray for this saint. When we stop what we are doing and go before the Lord in prayer, petitioning on his behalf, my children are learning the importance of making prayer a regular and integral part of their lives.

Our world and culture are in a rapid decline, and many are saying that loss of Christian liberties and freedom of speech may be taken away. It is a scary thought to think of facing persecution for one's faith, and yet I have heard astounding accounts of God supplying the measure of grace needed to walk through even torture. One thing for us to remember is that God has not given us the grace to face severe persecution or torture now, but should we be called to that in the future, that is when we will have the grace we need. The Lord does not give us tomorrow's grace today. He gives the measure of grace that is needed to us day by day. Here is one such moving testimony about the grace that was given to martyr Thomas Hauker.

Thomas Hauker: England, 1555

"Thomas," his friend lowered his voice so as not to be heard by the guard. "I have to ask you this favor. I need to know if what the others say about the grace of God is true. Tomorrow, when they burn you at the stake, if the pain is tolerable and your mind is still at peace, lift your hands above your head. Do it right before you die. Thomas, I have to know."

Thomas Hauker whispered to his friend, "I will."

The next morning, Hauker was bound to the stake and the fire was lit. The fire burned a long time, but Hauker remained motionless. His skin was burnt to a crisp and his fingers were gone. Everyone watching supposed he was dead. Suddenly, miraculously, Hauker lifted his hands, still on fire, over his head. He reached them up to the living God, and then, with great rejoicing, clapped them together three times.

The people there broke into shouts of praise and applause. Hauker's friend had his answer. [18]

Learning to Obey

Obedience to God-given parental authority is a foundational lesson God would have our children learn in their formative years. There are a lot of voices in today's Christian culture telling parents that they should quit taking obedience so seriously. Many will even make spiritual arguments focusing on the mercy of God and advocating that we should not discipline our kids because we just need to shower them with grace, grace, grace. I believe this is a wrong conclusion to come to, because the Word of God speaks clearly to children obeying their parents and to parents training their children.

"Children, obey your parents in the Lord, for this is right. Honor your father and mother (this is the first commandment with a promise), that it may go well with you and that you may live long in the land. Fathers, do not provoke your children to anger, but bring them up in the discipline and instruction of the Lord" (Ephesians 6:1-4).

"The rod and reproof give wisdom, but a child left to himself brings shame to his mother" (Proverbs 29:15).

If our children could train themselves to honor God-given authority and to grow in Christ-like character they would not need parents. God places children under parental authority as a training ground for learning to submit to all future earthly authorities and, ultimately, to the Lordship of Christ. In his book *The Duties of Parents*, J.C. Ryle puts it this way:

> Parents, do you wish to see your children happy? Take care, then, that you train them to obey when they are spoken to—to do as they are bid. Believe me, we are not made for entire independence—we are not fit for it. Even Christ's freemen have a yoke to wear—they "serve the Lord Christ" (Col. 3:24). Children cannot learn too soon that this is a world in which we are not all intended to rule, and that we are never in our right place until we know how to obey better. Teach them to obey while young, or else they will be fretting against God all their lives long, and wear themselves out with the vain idea of being independent of His control. [19]

In the context of the homeschool setting, if we do not first master obedience and respect from our children, our schooling efforts will be frustrating and greatly hindered. Although it is never too late to go back and work on respect and obedience, the best time to establish this is when our young ones are little tots. In all of our training and disciplining of our children, love should prevail. Yes, we give training and consequences but it should not be in harshness or anger. Our children need to understand that when we hold them accountable we are loving them and obeying what God has called us to do as their parents. We love them too much to let them go their own way and face greater consequences down the road.

I often see out-of-control kids and angry parents when I'm out and about. Additionally, I see teenagers who are displaying disrespect to their parents. These things are painful for me to observe. Our society has lost the expectation that children will obey and respect their parents, and the results are everywhere, as we see wide-spread anger and frustration, both in the parents and in the young people. This is what happens when a culture casts aside Biblical principles. I remember driving by a shopping center and observing a situation involving police and a young man in a parking lot. The young man had blond, shaggy, overgrown hair and was wrestling against the police officer who was trying to arrest him. His complete lack of self-control and apparent anger gripped my heart with sorrow. I do not know how old that young man was, but it is very possible that he was still in his teen years. It sobered me to think that, perhaps sixteen to eighteen years ago, he was a newborn baby who was probably very cute and lovable. Unfortunately, that young man never learned to surrender to God-given authority and obviously had no intention of submitting even to the law officer. If we do not teach our children to obey parental authority, it will be hard for them to obey the Lord or any other authority figure.

Character Training

Second Corinthians 3:18 says, "And we all, with unveiled face, beholding the glory of the Lord, are being transformed into the same image from one degree of glory to another. For this comes from the Lord who is the Spirit."

As we walk through life the goal for us and our children is to continually be transformed more and more into the image of the Lord Jesus. For that reason, character training is an ongoing process we are always trying to encourage our children in. We want them to be reflecting the beauty of Christ in increasing measure. As we set the bar high for their character, we remind them that they cannot be like Jesus in their own strength. They are sinners and this is why Jesus died—to rescue them from spiritual death, to give them new life, and to enable them to grow to be more like Christ. We will never reach perfect sanctification until we reach heaven, so our pursuit of growing in godly character needs to be an ongoing focus.

"Do not conform to the pattern of this world, but be transformed by the renewing of your mind. Then you will be able to test and approve what God's will is—his good, pleasing and perfect will" (Romans 12:2, NIV).

"For it is God who works in you, both to will and to work for his good pleasure" (Philippians 2:13).

Some claim that to teach children character traits is just creating young Pharisees. I would agree with that idea if we are not also teaching them how incapable they are of living out God's standard of righteousness. I like the way the book *Behold Your God: Rethinking God Biblically* states this. It says that "Pharisaism is a nickname for a life that attempts to be right with God by a system of rule-keeping." [20] The book gives an explanation of what sanctification is. "Sanctification is the process by which we grow in holiness." So if our children are only practicing good character in an attempt to win God's favor they will be acting as little Pharisees. If we teach them, however, that they can never earn God's favor and that we work out sanctification only by His grace in our lives, then this is not the same as Pharisaism. It is dangerous to confuse holiness, sanctification, and Pharisaism. The difference lies in the attitude or posture of the heart. Is all being done to the glory of God? Are we trusting in Christ and not our own efforts to bring forth this godly character? Now, for our little tots, there is only so much they will understand, but as we are teaching them and reminding them to obey Mommy and Daddy, we can tell them that they need Jesus to help them be kind, polite, obedient, etc.

"But put on the Lord Jesus Christ, and make no provision for the flesh, to gratify its desires" (Romans 13:14).

We know that godly character is within the will of God for all ages, including our little ones who have not yet fully trusted in Christ as Savior. It is like obedience; we do not wait until we see evidence of salvation before we teach a toddler not to touch the stove or run into the street. In the same way, we start teaching character lessons when children are little. This is part of training them "in the way they should go." We can see some of the character qualities to work on in Galatians 5 and also in 1 Corinthians 13, which is known as the love chapter.

"But the fruit of the Spirit is love, joy, peace, patience, kindness, goodness, faithfulness, gentleness, self-control; against such things there is no law" (Galatians 5:22-23).

"Love is patient and kind; love does not envy or boast; it is not arrogant or rude. It does not insist on its own way; it is not irritable or resentful; it does not rejoice at wrongdoing, but rejoices with the truth. Love bears all things, believes all things, hopes all things, endures all things" (1 Corinthians 13:4-7).

There are many other character traits that our families should focus on, such as punctuality, diligence, promptness, thoroughness, neatness, joyfulness, and many others. Teaching our children these virtues is important and should start early in their lives. When our children disobey and fail to show character, it is an opportune time to once again visit the glorious good news of the gospel. We need a great Savior to help us in our weaknesses.

The Importance of Serving

Teaching our children to serve the Lord by serving others is something my husband and I feel motivated to do but need to grow in. One way we have been trying to engage in this kind of Kingdom work is by practicing hospitality on our farm. It has been a blessing to share family worship with our guests as they have stayed with us for dinner or overnight. We want to find ways to take the light of Christ out into the darkness as well. We want to walk with our children into the darkness while they are under our protective wing and teach them how to engage the darkness with the gospel of Jesus Christ. There are so many ways a family can creatively get involved in ministering to a broken world. Below is just a small sampling of ideas to get your creative juices flowing:

Abortion/Crisis Pregnancy Ministry

While we have never gone to the front lines of an abortion clinic to plead with mamas to choose life for their babies, we did enjoy a day of getting together with friends and putting together blessing bags for mamas who choose life. These bags contained a few small baby items, handwritten notes of encouragement, and some items to pamper the mama herself. Because homeless people often wander up to people ministering at abortion clinics, we also put together bags that could be handed out to the homeless people. These bags contained snacks and toiletry items along with tracts. The children and I were blessed to be able to participate in the abortion/homeless people ministry in this way.

My husband has also taken the children to a local pregnancy help center to serve. They often need help in small ways such as cleaning, taking out trash, or stuffing envelopes. Even the youngest ones can wipe down counters or clean windows. My husband will take our children to serve for a few hours and then take them to get pizza. The children seem to rise to the challenge when they know they are helping to save lives even by these small menial tasks.

Operation Christmas Child Boxes

There is a ministry called Operation Christmas Child that operates under the bigger ministry of Samaritan's Purse. Operation Christmas Child delivers thousands of shoe-sized boxes across the world to impoverished children. Many churches and organizations participate in this ministry by filling these boxes with all sorts of small gifts to delight the hearts of needy children. According to the Samaritan's Purse website, 11,213,010 boxes were collected and delivered in 2015. It is heart touching to realize that, for many of the recipients, this will likely be the only Christmas present they will receive. The wonderful thing about sending these boxes around the world is that the children are told the good news of Jesus Christ as they receive their gift. SamaritansPurse.org states, "As shoebox gifts are distributed, local pastors or church leaders present the Gospel in a fun way designed for kids while family and friends listen in. Along with their shoebox gift, children also receive The Greatest Gift, a colorful presentation of the Gospel in their own language." Our family has participated in this ministry for several Christmases, and my children always find joy in giving in this way.

Local Christmas Giving

We have a tradition that we have observed some Christmases. We have found ways of meeting needs of others and gone around one day in December meeting practical needs. Some years we have donned Christmas hats just to make the outing extra memorable. The children and I have found joy driving around and blessing others with practical needs that we could meet.

Overseas Sponsorship

A wonderful way of sharing the love of Christ on an ongoing basis is by sponsoring a needy child around the world. Through a monthly financial donation a child can have basic physical needs met while also hearing the good news of the gospel. What an eternal investment! The children are able to write letters and keep track of how the sponsored child is doing.

Ministry to the Disabled

A few years back the children and I went on a tour of Joni and Friends' headquarters in California. While there, we learned about the many ways they minister to the practical and spiritual needs of disabled people around the world. One way is by taking wheelchairs into parts of the world where they may have never owned a wheelchair. As they deliver this life-changing chair to someone who may have been bed ridden their whole life, they also share the gospel of Jesus Christ. What an opportunity to gather the family together, write out a donation check for a wheelchair, and pray that the Lord will prepare the heart of the disabled recipient to respond to the good news being offered.

Volunteer

There are numerous ways that a family can reach out and get involved in volunteer work. You might look for a ministry you appreciate and offer to help with mail outs, clean the facilities, make phone calls, etc. Perhaps your family could hand out literature or run a booth at a conference. You could even look into volunteering for the political campaigns of leaders who uphold upright policies. Soup kitchens and food pantries are other ideas for family volunteer opportunities. Your family could do yard work for a needy neighbor or clean the church building. Just start somewhere and teach your children the joy of serving.

The Gift of Appreciation

At Christmas or anytime it is a thoughtful thing to take baked goods and thank you notes to the local servants of the community such as police, the post office, etc. Since we live on a farm, we have a lot of people come to us, such as delivery men, the guys who fills our propane tank, the bug man, etc. Anytime is a good time to offer a baked good, a word of thanks, and a gospel tract. This is an opportunity to tell them you appreciate their faithful service to the community and to your family.

I believe when our children see needs outside of their own it stirs gratitude within them for what they have and makes it easier for them to appreciate their blessings. I think if children are so sheltered that they never see the sobering needs of others and the devastating results of sin, then it is very easy for them not to realize what a great salvation they have been called to. They can easily take the blessings of Christian parents and the stability of a godly home for granted if they never smell the stench of darkness. While we would never want to throw our children into a dangerous situation, I think it is needful to walk with them at various points into poverty and brokenness. They need us to show them how to penetrate the darkness with the light of Christ. Yes, for the most part we want to protect them from the evil of the world, but at times we need to strategically take them out and show them how to get their hands dirty for the cause of Christ. The difference is that we don't let the world just come in and overtake our family. No! We make a game plan on how to take our children out under our wings and reach out to the hurting with God's love, His truth, and the hope that only Jesus gives.

You see, we do not raise godly children so that we can sit in our pristine perfect families and enjoy the blessings of the Lord. Certainly, we want our homes to be havens of rest reflecting Christ in every way, and yet there are times when we need to lead our children hand in hand to pierce the darkness with the love of Jesus. This needs to be done carefully and strategically as we discern that our children are able to handle it.

On our last family vacation, we were walking around sightseeing along Main street on Galveston Island. Our oldest walked up to some hard and slightly risqué-looking street musicians and handed them a gospel tract. They were sitting on the sidewalk, and Lauren reached down and sweetly spoke to them, handing them a tract. It was a beautiful sight to see my daughter reaching out to broken people with the light and love of Christ. Normally, I would be very hesitant about her walking up to people who looked like that, but we were all there as a family and the Lord gave me a peace about it. In that instance she was being covered by parental protection as she engaged with darkness for just a moment. We would never send her out on her own to encounter situations like that, but under the watchful eye of parents, it was a really good thing for her to see where sin can lead and for her to reach out with compassion and hope. As parents we need to give our families vision for the spiritual battle the Lord has called us to engage in. They have to know God created them to be arrows, and that our vision is to shoot them out into this world to do Kingdom work. I pray that my children will be Kingdom minded and not blinded by the mediocrity of this world. We are raising our families within the midst of a spiritual battle, and we need to train our children to live with purpose, intentionality, and vision for the Kingdom of God.

Teach Them Contentment and Gratitude

"Gratitude is a lifestyle. A hard fought, grace-infused, biblical lifestyle" [21] (Nancy Leigh DeMoss).

We live in such a narcissistic age of entitlement that we often forget that the Bible teaches us to be content. It is very status quo for even Christians to walk around whining and complaining about petty things in life. If our children learn to have an attitude of gratitude, they will be able to rise above the self-centered spirit of this age. From a prison cell the Apostle Paul wrote:

"Not that I am speaking of being in need, for I have learned in whatever situation I am to be content. I know how to be brought low, and I know how to abound. In any and every circumstance, I have learned the secret of facing plenty and hunger, abundance and need. I can do all things through him who strengthens me" (Philippians 4:11-13).

I am convicted that this lesson of contentment and gratitude is most effectively caught and not taught. As a very busy and often stretched-thin mother it is easy for me to lose my joy and focus. Far too often my children have seen me dragging through my day with less than a grateful heart. My natural resources run short, but I am encouraged to remember that God is able to make all grace abound to me. As I learn to lean more heavily upon Him, He will be strong through me and will infuse me with the joy, gratitude, and peace I need for my day.

"But he said to me, 'My grace is sufficient for you, for my power is made perfect in weakness.' Therefore I will boast all the more gladly of my weaknesses, so that the power of Christ may rest upon me. For the sake of Christ, then, I am content with weaknesses, insults, hardships, persecutions, and calamities. For when I am weak, then I am strong" (2 Corinthians 12:9-10).

If anyone has a living testimony of this kind of joy and supernatural strength, in spite of physical suffering and weakness, I think of Joni Eareckson Tada. I love how she refers to contentment as an internal quietness of heart.

"Paul was talking about an internal quietness of heart that gladly submits to God in all circumstances." [22]

Contentment and gratitude are truly fruits that only the Spirit of God can work out in our lives. By His grace let us seek to model this kind of attitude before our children so that they will learn to look at life through grateful hearts rather than develop the victim mentality that is so prevalent in society today. When our families are joyful and grateful, the lost world can see something that attracts them to the Savior.

A Culture of Hymnody in the Family

I love the great hymns of the faith; they are a deep part of my heritage, and thankfully there has never been a time in my life void of the blessing of hymns. One of the beauties of hymns is that they connect us with the saints from hundreds and thousands of years back up to the present. We benefit from the wisdom of believers throughout history and not just the ideas of our own modern culture.

Over the past several decades many praise and worship choruses have been written and are taking the place of hymns in many worship services. Some of these choruses are wonderful, and, yet, I hope that we can still preserve hymnody for future generations. Hymns often convey much deeper doctrinal truths than worship choruses. Many times a hymn will be four, five, or even more verses that recount who God is and what He has done. In contrast, some worship choruses repeat themselves over and over and often tend to be more about man and his emotions than about the magnitude and greatness of God. Conversely, some praise music is God centered and a real encouragement to the heart. Not all praise and worship music is the same. A good question to ask when listening to music is, "Is this music magnifying God or man?" Here is a quote from pastor John MacArthur on the value of the old hymns of the faith:

"Before the middle part of the 19th century or so, hymns were wonderful didactic tools, filled with Scripture and sound doctrine, a medium for teaching and admonishing one another, as we are commanded in Colossians 3:16. Most hymns were written not by teenagers with guitars, but by pastors and theologians: Charles Wesley, Augustus Toplady, Isaac Watts." [23]

In an old 1999 newsletter Elisabeth Elliot quoted singer Michael Card saying, "So many of today's worship songs are all about us: 'We do this, we do that, we worship You ...' without presenting the depth and richness of who God is, proclaiming His greatness and His might. You can read the lyrics of one of these old hymns and learn so much about God's attributes and His creation." She then goes on to say, "Everywhere I go I try to point out what a tragic loss is the disappearance of these powerful aids to spiritual stamina. A true hymn has rhyme and meter, a logical progression from the first verse to the last, and I feel like jumping up and down and "hollering" to get my message across, but I try to keep it to merely begging and imploring folks to get their hands on a good hymnbook. Where to find them? they ask. Perhaps they are moldering in the church basement. More than likely they've long since been dumped—'Young folks don't like hymns,' we're told. But of course, they don't like them—they don't know them. Alas!" [24]

Our world is shifting and changing at lightning speed and yet the hymns I grew up with are a constant that has not changed. I find it comforting that, even though so much has changed throughout my life, the hymns are friends that are still with me. I have clung to hymns in joy and in sorrow, and the truth conveyed in the hymns renews my mind and perspective. Even recently I stood at my grandmother's funeral singing "Amazing Grace" which is a hymn I have heard and sung my whole life. When I think about that particular hymn I think about it in the different contexts which I have sung it and heard it. One association is singing it to my daughter Annagrace because of her name. Another association is singing it at church, while another association is the funerals I have sung it at. As I go onward through my life's journey, the same hymn becomes more and more meaningful to my experiences. In this way the great hymns of the faith have become friends and treasures to my heart.

A familiarity and love for hymns is something my husband and I desire to pass as an endowment to our children. We want them to have the friendship of great hymns to accompany them throughout life. As we have tried to create an atmosphere of hymnody in our home it has been funny to hear some of their sweet renditions as they are learning a hymn. Sometimes they try to sing a hymn and get a word or two off which gives us a good laugh. Our Lilly Faith's first rendition of "Rock of Ages" went like this, "Rock of Ages Broccoli!" That was a bit off from the standard "Rock of ages cleft for me," but she was learning and it was cute. I also remember singing "The Gloria Patri" to Lilly Faith every night when she was a baby. It was a sweet moment with her to close out another day.

One hymn I remember singing to Abbie Joy when she was a baby is the hymn "Blessed Assurance," which is a hymn she began singing as a little girl. It has also been enlightening to see what children learn from the song service at church. One Sunday when Abbie Joy was a little girl she whispered to me during the song service, asking me what a certain word meant that we were singing in the hymn. It shocked me that she realized she did not know the meaning of that word and wanted to know what it meant. I was reminded that our little people are sponges, picking up on more than we know. One church we were members of had a hymn of the month that we would sing every Sunday. That hymn was printed in the bulletin each week and the families were encouraged to practice the hymn together at home. Then each Sunday of the month we would sing the hymn together as a congregation. It was precious to hear the little children singing out because they were really getting that particular hymn down. Currently, I am doing a hymn of the month with my children as part of our morning circle time.

One Sunday morning, Abbie Joy came into my room as we were preparing to leave for church. She asked me if I knew why she likes to go to church. I asked her why, to which she responded, "I like to sing the song at the end." And then she added, "But I don't sing loud. I just whisper." What she was referring to was when our whole church—men, women and children—would close the service by singing the "Doxology." Even the young children knew it, and it was beautiful to hear all ages singing in different parts … and always a cappella. I pray these sorts of things are making imprints on her life and will help to steer her future.

We will often end our mealtime with singing a hymn as a family. It is usually something we are all familiar with, such as the "Doxology." One thing I have noticed with our babies, since we have implemented this practice, is that when we start singing, it really grabs their attention. Sometimes they will make noises from their highchairs to try to join in. I think that utterance must make the heart of our Heavenly Father glad.

"And they said to him, 'Do you hear what these are saying?' And Jesus said to them, 'Yes; have you never read, 'Out of the mouth of infants and nursing babies you have prepared praise'?" (Matthew 21:16).

Another observation about hymn singing at the dinner table is that it seems to lift the atmosphere, even if it has been a stressful dinnertime. A hymn at the end will sometimes just ease the stress or tension a bit. There is something about singing together and putting our focus on the Lord that does a world of good for us.

I have done some hymn studies with my children to enhance the meaning of the songs we are singing. We have a few books that discuss both the hymn and the story behind how the hymn was written. Oftentimes, there are inspiring stories and testimonies behind the hymns that we know and love. When we know these background stories it can enhance the meaning of the hymns a great deal. Some of our books are written on an adult level, such as the "Then Sings My Soul" series by Robert Morgan, while others are geared towards children. One series we have enjoyed is called "Hymns for a Kid's Heart" written by Joni Eareckson Tada and Bobbie Wolgemuth (who is now home with the Lord). Recently, I purchased a book of illustrated hymns. It is a neat resource especially for visual learners. Artistic children might even enjoy trying to illustrate a hymn with their own artwork.

One thing that has happened with some of our children is that we have ended up with a special hymn or two that we have sung to a particular child. Right before Lilly Faith was born, her daddy took out his guitar and started singing "The Lily of the Valley." From time to time he sings that for her, and it is a sweet thing between him and her. As I mentioned above, I have often sung "Amazing Grace" to our Annagrace because her name has the word grace in it. I know she feels as if this is her special song. Then there have been certain songs that we have ended up singing to certain children for other reasons and it is a special memory. We will forever remember our two-year-old Nathaniel for his frequency in bolting out, "Hallelujah! Thine the glory. Hallelujah! Amen. Hallelujah! Thine the glory. Revive us again!" from the hymn "Revive Us Again."

There is one hymn that I especially remember my mother singing to me when I was a little girl, and I do not know why this hymn stands out, but it brings back sweet memories of her tucking me in at night and singing softly to me. The hymn is not even one I ever hear, but somehow this one song sticks out in my childhood memories. Here is the first verse and chorus of this hymn:

"My Father is omnipotent
And that you can't deny;
A God of might and miracles;
'Tis written in the sky.

Chorus
It took a miracle to put the stars in place;
It took a miracle to hang the world in space.
But when He saved my soul,
Cleansed and made me whole,
It took a miracle of love and grace!"

I think that the years of early childhood are a sweet juncture in time to lovingly impart Biblical truths to our young ones while we softly sing and stroke their hair and say goodnight with love and kisses. These special moments are forever etched on the hearts and minds of our children and will help guide them as they grow older.

Amongst many reasons that Matt and I desire to pass on a rich heritage of hymns to our children is that we believe the Lord will bring back the truths in those hymns to minister to them at various seasons of their lives. Joni Eareckson Tada was in a diving accident when she was seventeen that left her a quadriplegic for life. She recounts how the Lord used the hymns she learned in her childhood to help her through dark and scary days after her accident: "Spend time with me, and I'll have you singing along on a hymn—I love the words to the old hymns! When I was first injured and laying in my hospital bed in the dark, I would chase away fear by softly singing my favorites. God used the timeless words of those beautiful hymns to lift my spirits and draw me close to Him." Joni never quit singing and has gone on to use her love of hymns to minister to thousands of people for many decades. I had the blessing of hearing Joni speak at the True Woman 2012 conference in Indianapolis. At that conference she shared these powerful words: "Hymns are important to me because I have to sing. If I don't sing I might cry. Being a quadriplegic for forty-five years and dealing with chronic pain and cancer and being in my sixties with other aches and pains and issues, I choose to sing. I have to sing. I'm glad to sing because when I wake up in the morning and start singing, 'Savior, like a Shepherd lead us,' I'm already being led. I'm already setting the course of my attitude for the day. And, for me, singing is a way of praying without ceasing morning, noon, and night. I'm so grateful for the songs that God puts on my heart." I love the way she says, "I choose to sing." Sometimes I do not feel like singing, and sometimes my children do not feel like singing, but we can follow Joni's example. We can choose to sing and let the Lord lead our emotions to catch up with our obedience.

I am going to close out this section on hymns with a personal story from our family. One day, I was trying to assemble freezer meals, which is a messy and involved process, while Matt was out working in the garden. I also had dinner on the stove, and our toddler had just run into the house from outside, needing a bath. I asked my older son to give his brother a quick bath while I tried to keep all the kitchen chaos under control. Just about this time our power went out, and the sun was going down. Thankfully, dinner had cooked enough, and I was able to transfer it to the table and call everyone to gather around. We ate dinner by candle light and then lingered there and sang hymn after hymn. We had a sweet family time singing to the flicker of the candles. The amazing thing is that, just as we were wrapping up our hymn singing time, the power was restored. The Lord gave us just the right window of time to sing by candle light and then He provided the light we needed to get everyone ready for bed. Our faithful Father is good and works all things for our good and for His glory.

Chapter 16
Two Essentials You Must Not Ignore

Two of the greatest ways we can invest time in our families is through reading God's Word and praying. It is through prayer and studying the Word that we enter into a closer walk with Christ. Through the years I have felt like the Lord has been showing me that even our academics can often be taught from the context of Biblical truth. As I have prayed about various homeschool curriculum decisions, I have sensed that the Lord has been asking me to bring more and more of His Word into the flow of our day and educational experience.

Through the years I have been touched to observe my husband's dedication to praying for our whole family by name. At times he has risen extra early to get up and pray for me and for each of our children. Sometimes he has used a prayer journal where he writes down his requests for each of us. This has required a sacrifice of time and sleep on his part. Seeing his faithfulness convicts me all the more about how much I need to be praying for our family as well. Sometimes we pray together for our children and, oftentimes, we pray on our own. As our children are growing older and moving towards serious life decisions we are learning more of the meaning of "praying without ceasing" (1 Thessalonians 5:17).

As I have tried to express throughout this book, there are two sides to the coin of parenting. There is faithfulness on our part to what the Lord has called us to do. (That is the "Train up a child in the way he should go" side of the coin.) More importantly, there is the flip side of the coin which is what only God's Holy Spirit can do. We cannot save our children by good parenting and training. We must be faithful to train, but only the Lord can draw our children unto Himself. That is a God-sized job that no parent can do in his own strength. The Lord has a timetable in which He is working in their hearts. We must not put our faith in a parenting style, homeschooling, vigilant training, a pristine Christian environment, moral friends, a good church, or anything else. Part of our faithfulness will include such things as sharing the gospel in a faithful and loving way, keeping close heart connections with them, modeling an authentic Christian life before them, teaching them God's truths, and warning them of counterfeit truths. While we strive to parent faithfully, only the Lord Himself can save our children. Ultimately, we rest in the sovereign work of Christ to do the redeeming and sanctifying work in their lives. There are no guarantees on the outcome in our children's lives, so this should ignite a fire in us to faithfully pray for the Holy Spirit to grant our children both repentance and faith that they will follow Him. Beseeching the throne of grace should be a top priority in our parenting.

Pray

Not only is it vitally important to pray for our children, but I believe it is also important to pray *with* our children. We want them to live constantly in the presence of the Lord, going to Him in their joys and sorrows and when they need direction for life. Especially in the context of homeschooling we can lead our children into the presence of the Lord all through the day and night. Has something exciting happened? Why not pause and give thanks to the Lord? Have you just heard about a serious need in the life of a family member or friend? This is a good opportunity to stop whatever is going on and pray over the need as a family. Is a child dealing with fear during the night? You can lovingly stroke their hair and remind them that, "In peace I will both lie down and sleep; for you alone, O LORD, make me dwell in safety" (Psalm 4:8).

Whatever is going on in the midst of your day, it is always a good time to grab hands and lead your children into the Father's presence. This is training for life. By God's grace may they be doing the same with subsequent generations. Prayerfully, the spiritual seeds we are sowing today will bless our grandchildren to come.

The Word

We never want our children to come to see the Bible as just a quaint, antiquarian book of stories. No, we want them to know it is God's very words to them—their guidebook for life. It is the eternal, inspired, infallible Word of God.

> "The law of the Lord is perfect, reviving the soul; the testimony of the Lord is sure, making wise the simple; the precepts of the Lord are right, rejoicing the heart; the commandment of the Lord is pure, enlightening the eyes; the fear of the Lord is clean, enduring forever; the rules of the Lord are true, and righteous altogether. More to be desired are they than gold, even much fine gold; sweeter also than honey and drippings of the honeycomb. Moreover, by them is your servant warned; in keeping them there is great reward" (Psalm 19:7-11).

From Genesis to Revelation the gospel story of God's love and redemption runs through every chapter. A Bible story should not primarily be about Moses, Noah, or David. It should be about the mighty God who did great things in and through the lives of such men. This sovereign God is in control of all of history from beginning to end. He is working His eternal plan from the Fall in the garden to the glorious redemption we eagerly await. The Bible is a narrative that tells us the gospel story of Creation, Fall, Redemption, and Restoration. This is the most important thing of all for us to teach our children. This story by far trumps any math, science, or spelling lesson. The Bible gives us the tools that we need for our lives.

The prince of preachers, Charles Spurgeon, put it like this:

"This great book, the Bible, this most precious volume is the heart of God made legible; it is the gold of God's love, beaten out into gold leaf, so that therewith our thoughts might be plated, and we also might have golden, good, and holy thoughts concerning Him." [5]

As Christian families I believe that God's Word should be elevated to a place of prominence in our homes. Whenever there is question as to a decision to be made or as to what is right or wrong, the Bible should be our guide. We would do well to not just tell our children what to do but to take them straight to the source of all truth. I do not want my children to derive their code of ethics based on what Mama believes. That may work when they are young, but the day will come when they will become more independent thinkers. If I have taught them from the onset what the Bible *says* rather than what Mama thinks, then they will have a foundation that is built upon the authoritative Word of God rather than their mama's ideas. Even when I know my ideas are coming straight from Scripture, I think it is more effective for me to present it to my children by taking them directly to the source rather than just conveying truths I know. This teaches them how to go to the Word for themselves as well. May our families and our homeschools be Word-saturated environments, because loving, faithful instruction and application of prayer and the Word of God are foundational to a healthy, fruitful Christian home.

Conclusion

As homeschooling parents we have an incredible opportunity to shape the lives of our children in ways that will stay with them for life. We are afforded so much more time with our children than parents who send their children to school. This no doubt calls for much sacrifice in terms of time and energy, but it is an investment of eternal value. Now that my oldest is sixteen I realize how true it is when people say, "Don't blink; they grow up so fast." I find myself thinking of all the things I want to impart to my daughter in the years I have left. What gaps need to be filled in? What is she going to need to know to navigate through this world? What memories do I still want to create with her? What life skills can I still teach her? It brings tears to my eyes to realize how fast my Lauren has transitioned from a difficult little toddler that I could barely keep up with, into this lovely young lady who is much taller than her mama. Knowing that my time is limited with her is a sobering reality. I am so thankful for the memories we have created simply because we had more time together. She has not grown up being gone from me eight hours a day. She has been with me through moments of laughter, of stress, of painful pregnancies, of chaos with younger siblings, of trying to clean house for a last-minute showing, of hours and hours of reading good literature, of Bible studies we've done around the table, of cooking dinner together, and the list goes on. Even so, it feels like a quick flash of time and here we are inching very close to adulthood. It is bittersweet to see this growth happening. My eyes water when I think about the little blond-headed Lauren that had me pulling out my hair, and my heart swells to see the young lady God is shaping her to be. She has matured in ways I could not have imagined back when I was reeling her in from eating strangers' potato chips on the beach! She loves the Lord and His Word and blesses our family in so many ways. I share this about her, because she is my oldest, but I have a string of other children growing up close behind her. Even with all the time I have been blessed to spend with them I still feel like my babies are growing up way too fast. I am thankful that homeschooling has provided so much extra time for me to develop heart relationships with my children.

Do the Next Thing

Homeschooling is not for the faint of heart. I would say that is especially true for the large family. Yes, it is often very chaotic, and I often feel I am falling short in many ways. I believe, however, that the Lord sees my heart and is using my efforts in ways that I do not always see. I may see the ten things that are not getting done at any given moment, but I may be failing to see how much the one thing I am getting done is impacting one or several of my children for life. This journey is teaching me how to rely on the Lord when I feel in over my head. The Lord does not expect me to do everything perfectly all the time. What He asks is that I walk in obedience to what He desires me to do at any given moment. Elisabeth Elliot quoted an old Saxon poem that she has oft been remembered for. Many busy mamas have found encouragement in the words of this poem. Although we cannot do everything at once or even ever accomplish everything we would like, we can always look to the Lord and ask Him, what is our "Next Thing"?

A poem quoted by Elisabeth Elliot:

> Do the Next Thing
> "At an old English parsonage down by the sea,
> there came in the twilight a message to me.
> Its quaint Saxon legend deeply engraven
> that, as it seems to me, teaching from heaven.
> And all through the hours the quiet words ring,
> like a low inspiration, 'Do the next thing.'
> Many a questioning, many a fear,
> many a doubt hath its quieting here.
> Moment by moment, let down from heaven,
> time, opportunity, guidance are given.
> Fear not tomorrow, child of the King,
> trust that with Jesus, do the next thing.
> Do it immediately, do it with prayer,
> do it reliantly, casting all care.
> Do it with reverence, tracing His hand,
> who placed it before thee with earnest command.
> Stayed on omnipotence, safe 'neath His wing,
> leave all resultings, do the next thing.
> Looking to Jesus, ever serener,
> working or suffering be thy demeanor,
> in His dear presence, the rest of His calm,
> the light of His countenance, be thy psalm.
> Do the next thing."

I was at a True Woman Conference several years back when emcee Bob LePine asked speaker Holly Elliff, a mother of eight, how she got everything done. Her answer to him has stuck in my mind. She said, "I don't." [25] She went on to say that she has learned to walk moment by moment with the Lord and to keep asking Him what is the next thing He wants her to attend to. This was a huge testimony to me and has stuck with me as an example to be followed. I will say, however, that this is really hard for me. I want to make a plan and execute it. It is easy for me to fall into discouragement when I feel like I'm falling very short of my ideals. This is where I am painfully learning to surrender my plans and my ideals to what the Lord has for me on a given day. If I had planned a morning of productive school time and one of my children requires discipline, talking to, and discipleship, then that is the main thing that God has for my morning. Usually if this scenario happens, not only am I not accomplishing what I had intended but I am also falling behind as maybe other children are making messes and life is happening while I am dealing with that one child. This truly can deflate my bubble, but I am learning to rest in the goodness and the plans of the Lord, even in the midst of the mess and frustrations. I do not believe we need to glory in our messes, but when things are crazy we need to choose faithfulness. All the while, we can be seeking the Lord for greater wisdom and victory as our family continues to grow in Him.

Embrace Your Calling

As Christian parents home educating our children we are choosing a life of ministry to them. We have been called to a mission field that is located, not across the seas but in our own homes. We have been called to a spiritual battle that rages within the walls of our own homes. Our enemy does not want our children to follow Christ, and he is cunning and always looking for a way to throw us off track. This is not an easy calling, but it is a worthy one. We have probably sacrificed many things in order to walk this path the Lord has placed us on. We want to do our best and have a Christ-honoring outcome, all the while remembering that we can do nothing apart from "abiding in the vine."

Keep Priorities in Order

After decades of observing many homeschooling families I believe it is important to have our priorities in order. Paramount to our families should be the saving gospel of Jesus Christ. This is not just a one-time prayer we lead our children to pray. This is mentoring them to choose to seek Jesus every day, to say "Yes, Lord" to His leading, and to practice ongoing repentance of sin. It is helping them to see the dangers of following the philosophies and trends of this world's system. It is leading them to the Scriptures over and over to find answers to life's questions, and it is teaching them to "pray without ceasing." If we only train our children to look good outwardly and miss these fundamental things of the heart, we will miss the mark. Balance is key here; while we want to work very hard at training their character and helping them to carry themselves to be "salt and light," we must constantly be revisiting the posture of their hearts before the Lord. Are they bowing the knee to Christ from surrendered hearts? Are the externals of character, God-honoring dress, God-honoring friends, and God-honoring activities propelled out of hearts that want to honor Christ, or are we making a religion of moralism in our homes by letting our children trust in their good behaviors for their salvation? Are they just conforming to our parental standards or has there been an authentic new birth in their hearts? Have they been transferred from the kingdom of darkness into the Kingdom of light? I want to be careful here because so many run to the extremes of legalism or liberty. Those who are afraid of legalism run to liberty and those who are afraid of Christian liberty run to legalism. In my life and Christian experience, I have been exposed to all of the above. I see great pitfalls in both ditches, and I do not want either extreme for my family. I never want my children to feel that they are righteous before God because they were born into a Christian home, homeschool, know the right way to act, dress, speak, etc. On the other hand, I am not willing that our family throw all caution and wisdom to the wind because we fear that teaching our children to be different from the world will lead to rebellion. We must not give into a Christian, pragmatic approach to parenting that offers our children to the systems of the world just because we don't want to rock their boat and possibly cause rebellion. I surmise that many of the homeschool graduates who have jumped ship and are now partying with the world have either come from a home that was more focused on rules than the heart of the gospel or that was too permissive and did not teach them to "love not the things of the world."

"Love not the world, neither the things that are in the world. If any man love the world, the love of the Father is not in him. For all that is in the world, the lust of the flesh, and the lust of the eyes, and the pride of life, is not of the Father, but is of the world. And the world passeth away, and the lust thereof: but he that doeth the will of God abideth for ever" (1 John 2:15-17, KJV).

Those are two polar opposite styles of Christian homes, and I do not believe either strategy works well. We certainly cannot oversimplify the matter and just make a quick assertion about why a particular young person from a Christian home has turned out to be a prodigal. I'm just speaking in overarching terms that, in many cases, I believe families have fallen into one ditch or another.

Discern the Times

I believe we need to be discerning about the times we are living in. We are raising children in a post-Christian era, so teaching them to walk in godliness is going to look very countercultural. I do not believe that Christians need to adopt the ways of unbelievers in order to reach them. This philosophy will take our Christian families further and further down a path of pagan practices and annihilation. The world around us should not be our barometer but, rather, God's Word should be our guide. My encouragement to Christian families is to commit to God-honoring, Biblical standards and to teach good and right behavior, but to make it clear to their children that God's standards cannot be righteously met in our own strength. Only He can regenerate our hearts, granting us the desire to love and obey Him. His commands are not burdensome, and His ways are always best. I often think of the evangelical culture at large as being like a small boat dragging behind the big ship of secular culture by about fifteen to twenty years. The things that the lost world embraced when I was a little girl are now the things that many Christians embrace, even in our churches. This is what happens when the Church looks to the world as its standard. The Church can always look better than what is happening in the world, but as pagan culture goes deeper into darkness, the Church is often being dragged in that direction as well. I think it is past time for Christian families to stop looking to the world, to their church, or to fellow believers to measure what their standards should look like. Paul told the Corinthians that this comparison game was not wise.

"Not that we dare to classify or compare ourselves with some of those who are commending themselves. But when they measure themselves by one another and compare themselves with one another, they are without understanding" (2 Corinthians 10:12).

We are living in confusing, baffling times, where every Judeo-Christian belief is being challenged and there is much division in the church at large. This is a great time for Christian families to tune out all the loud voices screaming around us and to go with humble, teachable hearts back to the Bible to get a vision for how God wants us to look, live, and behave. All of our family standards should be rooted in God's eternal truth, not cultural norms or the philosophies of man. The safest route for all believing families is to dive deep into the Scriptures and to see first what God says about relationship with Himself and, secondly, about the fruits of righteousness that should spring forth when we are walking with Him. What if we had only the Bible and no other influences such as podcasts, media, Facebook, blogs, etc.? If we based our lives only on what we read in the Scriptures how might things look differently in our families? In what ways have we allowed the opinions of man as seen on Facebook and social media to alter our perception of Biblical truth? Are we spending more time reading man's thoughts online than we are studying God's inspired words in the Bible? The Lord has revealed Himself through His Holy Word, which is living and active and able to guide our paths.

"For the word of God is living and active, sharper than any two-edged sword, piercing to the division of soul and of spirit, of joints and of marrow, and discerning the thoughts and intentions of the heart" (Hebrews 4:12).

Persevere

In conclusion, parenting is hard work, and homeschooling is even harder work. If we wish to attain anything of value in life we must be willing to put in the effort necessary. We must be willing to obey the Lord's calling and stay faithful when the going gets hard.

"Those who sow in tears shall reap with shouts of joy! He who goes out weeping, bearing the seed for sowing, shall come home with shouts of joy, bringing his sheaves with him" (Psalm 126:5-6).

However, we are not called to do this ministry in our own strength. We are told in the book of John that it is the work of the Father flowing through us that is able to grant us the ability to do His will.

"Abide in me, and I in you. As the branch cannot bear fruit by itself, unless it abides in the vine, neither can you, unless you abide in me" (John 15:4).

We are also encouraged in 2 Peter that we are granted the power to do His will.

"His divine power has granted to us all things that pertain to life and godliness, through the knowledge of him who called us to his own glory and excellence" (2 Peter 1:3).

Homeschooling is no guarantee that our children will know and love Christ, but it is a powerful instrument that we can use to prayerfully seek to lead them in that direction. If we had guarantees, it would not be a walk of faith, and we might be tempted to believe that we can do this feat in our own strength. As in every area of life, our Lord calls us to rely on *His* strength, not our own. Through this book I have bared my heart, and I want to leave you with the reminder that it is God who works in us for His divine purposes. Keep seeking Him as a family, stay focused on the gospel every day, be in the Word with your children daily, have a prayerful home, work at character training, cooperate with the Lord in areas of growth, in sanctification, and, in every way, seek to honor the Lord Jesus as a family. We are His ambassadors to a lost world. Let's reflect His glory in ways that are refreshing, different, enticing, and offer real hope. Let's not be apathetic and watch our families plunge into the abyss of sinful living, playing the card of cheap grace. God's grace is amazing, it is sweet, and it should propel us to holiness. Be encouraged that your sacrifices are making a difference. Your children will remember the things you taught them; your voice will go with them and will not be easily forgotten. By God's grace, will you join me in taking the parental responsibility of discipling our children in the ways of the Lord seriously? May we give our all to this endeavor to the glory of God.

I leave you with a quote from Charles Spurgeon, a man my father loved to read as I was growing up. Remember that, when you spend your days teaching your children the ways of the Lord, you are the voice that they will long remember, even once they spread their wings and fly.

> The voices of childhood echo throughout life. The first learned is generally the last forgotten – C.H. Spurgeon. [5]

References

[1] K. Ham, "Why Build an Evangelical Ark," in *Teach Them Diligently*, Nashville, 2015.

[2] A. Grant, M. W. Smith and W. Kirkpatrick, Composers, *Place In This World. Copyright © 1990 Universal Music - Brentwood Benson Songs (BMI) (adm. at CapitolCMGPublishing.com) /Sony/ATV Cross Keys (ASCAP) / Sony Atv () / Age To Age Music (ASCAP) All rights reserved. Used by permission.*

[3] W. Y. Fullerton, "Charles Haddon Spurgeon A Biography," Delmarva Publications, Inc., Harrington, 2014.

[4] K. Ham, B. Beemer and T. Hillard, Already Gone: Why your kids will quit church and what you can do to stop it, Green Forest, AR: Master Books, 2009, p. 24.

[5] J. Snyder, Behold your God, Tupelo, MS: Media Gratiae, 2013. Multiple quotes from the public domain are taken out of this book.

[6] B. D. Ray, "National Home Education Research Institute," EMWD, 30 January 2015. [Online]. Available: https://www.nheri.org/research/gen2-survey-a-spiritual-and-educational-survey-on-christian-millennials.html. [Accessed 11 July 2017].

[7] B. Ray, "Gen2 Survey," Generations with Vision, Elisabeth, 2015.

[8] M. Peace and K. Keller, Modesty: More Than a Change of Clothes, Phillipsburg, NJ: P&R Publishing Company, 2015, p. 17.

[9] J. MacArthur, "gty.org," Grace to You, 8 August 1971. [Online]. Available: https://www.gty.org/library/sermons-library/1207/what-in-the-world-is-the-church-to-be-part-1. [Accessed 11 July 2017].

[10] L. Beachy, Our Amish Values: Who We Are and What We Believe, Eugene, Oregon: Harvest House Publishers, 2015.

[11] L. DeShazo, Composer, *Ancient Words. Copyright © 2001 Integrity's Hosanna! Music (ASCAP) (adm. at CapitolCMGPublishing.com) All rights reserved. Used by permission.*

[12] W. Bradford, Of Plymouth Plantation, New York, New York: Random House, Inc., 1981.

[13] A. Dunagan, "Mission-Minded Families," Kajabi, 13 July 2017. [Online]. Available: https://www.missionmindedfamilies.org/blog/about-us. [Accessed 13 July 2017].

[14] J. Cotton, The New England Primer, Aledo, TX: WallBuilders, Inc., 1991.

[15] T. J. Nettles, Teaching Truth, Training Hearts: The Study of Catechisms in Baptist Life, New York: Calvary Press, 1998.

[16] S. Brown, Early Piety: A Call to the Rising Generation, Wake Forest, NC: The National Center for Family Integrated Churches, 2016, p. 29.

[17] M. Henry, Matthew Henry Concise Commentary on the Whole Bible, Nashville: Thomas Nelson, Inc., 1997.

[18] K. Ham and B. Beemer, Already Gone: Why your kids will quit church and what you can do to stop it, Green Forest, AR: Master Books, 2015, p. 48.

[19] The Voice of the Martyrs, Jesus Freaks, Tulsa, Oklahoma: Albury Publishing, 1999, p. 144.

[20] J. C. Ryle, Duties of Parents, Codex Spiritualis Publication, 2012, p. 42.

[21] J. Snyder, Behold Your God, Tupelo, MS: Media Gratiae, 2013, p. 104.

[22] N. L. DeMoss, Choosing Gratitute: Your Journey Back to Joy, Chicago, IL: Moody Publishers, 2009, p. 29.

[23] J. Eareckson Tada and S. Estes, When God Weeps: Why Our Sufferings Matter to teh Almighty, Grand Rapids, Michigan: Zondervan, 1997, p. 171.

[24] J. MacArthur, "gty.org," Grace To You, 16 June 2009. [Online]. Available: https://www.gty.org/library/Articles/A261/Style-or-Substance. [Accessed 12 July 2017].

[25] E. Elliot, "Elisabeth Elliot," 1 May/June 1999. [Online]. Available: http://www.elisabethelliot.org/newsletters/1999-05-06.pdf. [Accessed 12 July 2017].

[26] H. Elliff, "True Woman," in *Revive Our Hearts*, Indianapolis, 2012.

Made in the USA
Columbia, SC
27 August 2017